THE INEVITABLE BANDSTAND

THE MEXICAN EXPERIENCE
William H. Beezley, series editor

The Inevitable Bandstand

The State Band of Oaxaca and the Politics of Sound

CHARLES V. HEATH

UNIVERSITY OF NEBRASKA PRESS
Lincoln and London

© 2015 by the Board of Regents of
the University of Nebraska

All rights reserved
Manufactured in the United
States of America

Library of Congress
Cataloging-in-Publication Data
Heath, Charles V., 1960–, author.
The inevitable bandstand: the state band of Oaxaca
and the politics of sound / Charles V. Heath.
pages   cm—(The Mexican experience)
Includes bibliographical references and index.
ISBN 978-0-8032-6967-5 (cloth: alk. paper)
ISBN 978-0-8032-8419-7 (pbk.: alk. paper)
ISBN 978-0-8032-8420-3 (epub)
ISBN 978-0-8032-8421-0 (mobi)
ISBN 978-0-8032-8422-7 (pdf)
1. Banda del Estado de Oaxaca—History.
2. Oaxaca (Mexico: State)—History—19th century.
3. Oaxaca (Mexico: State)—History—20th century.
4. Music—Political aspects—Mexico—Oaxaca
(State)—History—19th century.
5. Music—Political aspects—Mexico—Oaxaca
(State)—History—20th century.
I. Title.   II. Series: Mexican experience.
ML1315.7.O28H43   2015
784.06′07274—dc23   2014047951

Set in Minion by Westchester
Publishing Services.

Para la maestra rural y la Banda

CONTENTS

List of Illustrations   ix

Acknowledgments   xi

Introduction   1

1. Closing the Colonial Past   12

2. Nineteenth-Century Invasions and Influences   23

3. Inception, Institutionalization, and Venue   34

4. The BME during the Porfiriato and the Mexican Revolution   56

5. *Mestizaje*, Musical Pedagogy, and the Socialist State   80

6. Municipal Control to Innes's Reign   96

7. From Political Proselytizer to Economic Engine   118

Conclusion: Gauging the Political Tool   136

Appendix 1. BME Directors   147

Appendix 2. Oaxaca Military and National Guard Units, 1846 and 1848   149

Appendix 3. BME Dependencies   151

Appendix 4. Extraordinary Performances, 1966 (Partial) 153

Notes 157

Glossary of Song and Dance Forms 195

Bibliography 197

Index 209

ILLUSTRATIONS

MAPS

1. Seven regions of Oaxaca   6
2. Indigenous languages and ethnic groups of Oaxaca   7
3. The Oaxaca Zócalo   52

FIGURES

1. Teatro Macedonio Alcalá   2
2. "Canción Mixteca" sheet music cover   4
3. Observance of a saint's feast day   8
4. Spanish Army of the Americas organizational chart   15
5. Carlos Paris, *Batalla de Tampico, Tamaulipas*   26
6. Benito Juárez   28
7. The present-day Oaxaca kiosk   54
8. Porfirio Díaz   57
9. The BME at the end of the nineteenth century   63
10. "Himno Socialista Regional" sheet music cover   92
11. "Himno Socialista Regional" sheet music cover, reverse   94

12. Invoice for the purchase of various musical instruments   98
13. The BME, ca. 1947   104
14. Director Diego Innes with Bulmaro Yescas Vázquez   114
15. The BME in 1951   115
16. Maestro Eliseo Martínez García   138

ACKNOWLEDGMENTS

I cannot pretend that I am the sole author of the following pages. In writing this book, I have transcribed, transmitted, and taken out of context the work of numerous historians and chroniclers, most of whom I will never meet. This investigation took me far from the fields of my training and expertise; the vast and rich secondary literature I depended upon deserves more recognition than simple citations in the bibliography. I am indebted to all these strangers. Particular thanks go to my intellectual guides and mentors during my doctoral studies at Tulane University who read messy drafts of the present work and offered invaluable criticism and insight. They are Dr. Colin MacLachlan, Dr. Susan Schroeder, and Dr. Bruce Raeburn. All mistakes are my own.

Several institutions have generously supported this project. I offer special thanks to the staff of the Archivo General del Poder Ejecutivo Del Estado De Oaxaca, especially Gregorio Manuel García Ríos and Luz Stella Camargo, and the staff of the Archivo Histórico del Municipio de Oaxaca. I also wish to thank the personnel at the Archivo Histórico de la Secretaría de la Defensa Nacional in Mexico City. Also of great assistance were personnel of the Latin American Library at Tulane University and the Nettie Lee Benson Latin American Collection of the University of Texas at Austin. Generous gifts from the Friends of the Department of

History at Sam Houston State University also helped make this work possible.

Professors, colleagues, and friends have read, helped, and encouraged me to complete this project. They include Francie Chassen López, Bill Beezley, Mark Brill, Sergio Pellicer Navarette, and Brian Domitrovic. I also wish to thank Bridget Barry and her colleagues at the University of Nebraska Press. The wonderful maps and drawings were done by Erin Greb of Erin Greb Cartography. A close friend and personal editor read every word below a half dozen times: Leah Goodwin, I could not have done this without you. I know that I have left out innumerable others.

Most of all, I thank the Banda de Música del Estado de Oaxaca (BME). Maestro Eliseo Martínez García opened his office and archives to me, allowed me to travel with the band, and even let me raise the baton to conduct the band during my time with his organization. His administrator, Héctor Cortés Reyes, will remain a friend forever and was indispensable to me, as was the band's entire staff. I appreciate the warm welcome and personal histories that each musician provided me during my trips to Oaxaca. Without the BME, this work would not exist.

Finally, I thank my family for their unflagging support during my time at Tulane University and Sam Houston State University.

The title of this work is from a scene that takes place in the desolate Mexican village of La Candelaria in Graham Greene's novel *The Power and the Glory*: "'Mula. Mula,' the priest said, urging the mule on, past the inevitable bandstand and a statue in florid taste of a woman in a toga waving a wreath: part of the pedestal had been broken off and lay in the middle of the road—the mule went round it." Since then, I have encountered similar phrases in the works of literary masters as diverse as Cormac McCarthy and Saul Bellow. The phrase is as ubiquitous as the bandstand itself and speaks to what I believe to be the importance of the bandstand in Mexican history.

Greene's phrase was perfect, except for one thing: there was no music in the scene he described. This book seeks to fill that lacuna.

Introduction

> But of Oaxaca I shall say no more, but conclude that it is of so temperate an air, so abounding in fruits, and all provision requisite for man's life ... that no place I so much desired to live in whilst I was in those parts as in Oaxaca.
>
> Thomas Gage, *The English-American*

According to the announcer who introduced the evening's performance, the night of 16 October 2005 was a "historic" one for the Banda de Música del Estado de Oaxaca (Music Band of the State of Oaxaca, BME).[1] For the first time in its 137-year history, the BME would be accompanying a world-renowned, classically trained baritone. The audience filled the beautifully restored Teatro Macedonio Alcalá, a late nineteenth-century theater built during that period's Liberal state-building architectural project, influenced by a distinct gaze toward *belle époque* France. (See fig. 1.) The musicians took the stage in their vaguely bureaucratic-looking uniforms—blue suits, white shirts, and blue ties—and bowed deferentially as their director, Eliseo Martínez García, dressed in a tuxedo, ascended the podium. The program began with the overture from Gioachino Rossini's opera *La gazza ladra* (*The Thieving Magpie*).

The performance acquired a distinctly Oaxacan flavor when Carlos Sánchez, a native of the Mexican state of Querétaro,

FIG. 1. Teatro Macedonio Alcalá. Oaxaca de Juárez, Oaxaca, Mexico. Photograph by Ulises Estrada. Licensed under Creative Commons, 2014.

performed the "Canción Mixteca" ("Mixteca Song"), a deeply nostalgic ballad eulogizing the state's northern Mixteca region. (See fig. 2.) Notwithstanding the song's regional sentiments, Oaxacans from throughout the state have made it their own. Its lyrics speak to the powerful sentiment of *patria chica*, a quasi-patriotic allegiance to one's region or hometown:

> How far I am from the place
> Where I was born;
> Immense nostalgia

Invades my thoughts
And seeing me lost and sad
like a leaf in the wind
I wish to cry, I wish to cry
from grief.²

The audience was rapt: some sang along under their breath; others shed a few tears. An extended standing ovation, whistles, and shouts of "Bravo, bravissimo" followed the song. Sánchez himself seemed moved by the audience's reaction. The BME acquitted itself beautifully, accompanying the baritone as he continued with a Spanish pop song, a waltz, and Bizet's "Toreador Song" from the opera *Carmen*. Sánchez's performance concluded with "Granada" by the famed Mexican composer Agustín Lara.

Following intermission, the BME performed selections from Tchaikovsky's ballet *The Nutcracker* and closed the performance with the Russian composer's *1812 Overture*. The *1812 Overture*, one of the world's most recognizable works of musical nationalism (the composition includes a theme from a Tsarist anthem), celebrates the Russian victory over Napoleon's forces. The triumphant coda, which is both bellicose and celebratory, includes cannon fire and bell ringing, which the theater's crew resoundingly replicated. The casual music lover in attendance that evening was likely unaware of the totality of events and influences that had resulted in such an eclectic program, while those Oaxacans who were familiar with their own history knew that the Banda de Música del Estado de Oaxaca was merely fulfilling a more than century-old charter.

That conclusion, however, belies complexities that merit further investigation and raises the question, "How did the BME arrive at this point?" The theater's modern acoustics and architectural design recall the state's modernizing project. The BME's instrumental makeup reveals influences from abroad that include musical instruments both predating and derived from the Industrial Revolution. The band's repertoire draws on Eurocentric, national, and regional music and compositions. The songs' themes range from bombastic

FIG. 2. "Canción Mixteca" sheet music cover. Archivo General del Ejecutivo Poder del Estado de Oaxaca.

nationalism to sentimental regional nostalgia. Even the BME's uniforms allude to a state-sponsored civil project and are worthy of consideration. The BME, a civil organ nearly as old as the modern state of Oaxaca itself, provides a lens through which to examine broader questions about the histories of Mexico and Oaxaca, and its distinctly hybrid musical tradition permits a glimpse into the forces at work in the consolidation of a modern political state.[3]

Music performed by a state band is a political tool. The present work examines the BME's role as a part of the array of popular political culture that the state government of Oaxaca employs in an attempt to bring unity and order to its domain. Over the course of its 146-year history, the BME has performed each of these functions. Its music has a variety of functions: it may provide order and cadence to military maneuvers; it may create a spiritual sense of community, as it does when it accompanies a religious function; it may be used to teach political culture or proselytize for a civic religion; and often it simply entertains. Originally a National Guard band, the BME once accompanied military forces as they trained and fought. The BME performs at saints' feast days and at national festivals, propagating beliefs both sacred and secular. The state government has also, at times, asked the BME to educate its once largely illiterate population in the ways of liberal democracy. Finally, in order to provide respite from life's burdens, the government has also asked the BME to perform at strictly diversionary functions such as *serenatas* (serenades) and *dominicales* (Sunday matinees).

The state government of Oaxaca has conceived all of these roles for the BME in order to unify, educate, and entertain the diverse and fragmented elements within the state of Oaxaca. The BME's history therefore mirrors the historical trajectory of both Oaxaca and the nation of Mexico, from the mystical pre-Hispanic era to the military-spiritual Spanish colony, from a militarized and fractured young nation subject to foreign threats and influence to a consolidated post-Revolutionary quasi-socialist state, and from a predominantly Catholic entity to an ostensibly secular one.

Oaxaca: An Accidental State

The isolated pockets found among the mountain ranges of Oaxaca contain one of the most culturally diverse regions in the world. (See map 1.) Oaxaca is home to sixteen indigenous language and

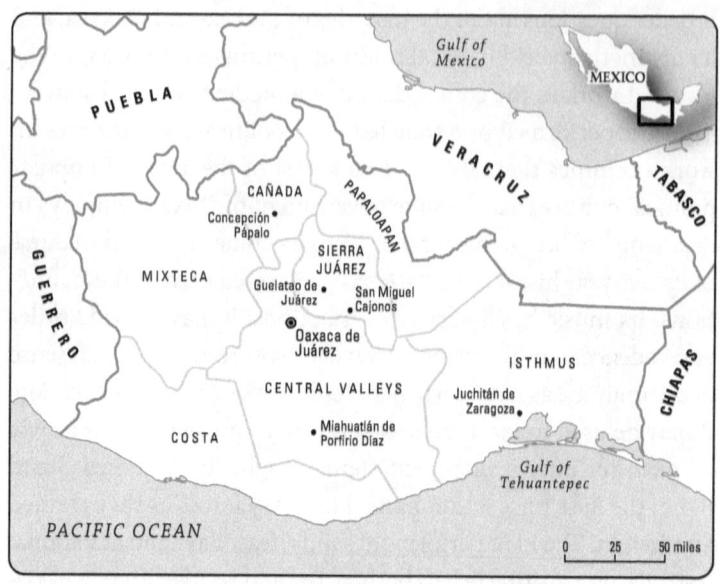

MAP 1. Seven regions of Oaxaca. Erin Greb Cartography.

ethnic groups that are as diverse as the geography surrounding them.[4] (See map 2.) The predominant groups are the Zapotecs and Mixtecs, Mesoamerican peoples with rich histories that long predate the Spanish invasion.[5] Among these groups, even greater diversity inheres. For example, the Zapotec language consists of at least sixteen identifiable and mutually unintelligible dialects; a *Serrano* (highlander) Zapotec is therefore unable to communicate with an Isthmus Zapotec in his ancestral language.

The arrival of the Spaniards gave rise to a rich and complex hybrid culture.[6] However, music almost immediately served if not to unify the participants of the encounter, then at least to join them in ritual. (See fig. 3.) The region's diversity, when coupled with extractive Spanish colonial economic projects, further aggravated the uneasy and unequal social situation and resulted in eruptive rebellions. Furthermore, the overlaid Spanish administrative jurisdictions, loosely based upon preexisting indigenous ones, created

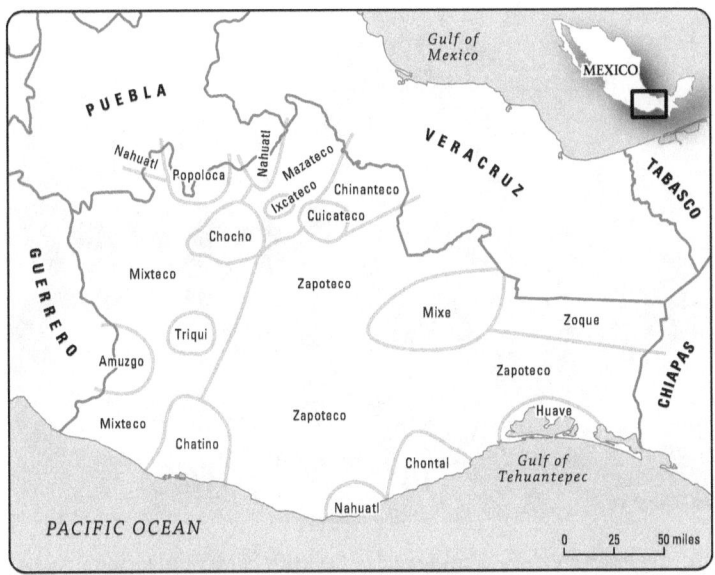

MAP 2. Indigenous languages and ethnic groups of Oaxaca. Erin Greb Cartography.

in Oaxaca "the most complicated [geographical] jurisdiction" in Nueva España (New Spain); it contained several noncontiguous segments, including the broad, mountain-ringed valley of Oaxaca, and extended to the northern continental divide in the Papaloapan region, and as far south as the Pacific Ocean.[7] After the Spanish conquistador Hernán Cortés received the valley of Oaxaca as his own marquisate, a confusing chain of events followed, resulting in a "patchwork of small jurisdictions and outlying subject villages" that prevailed through the colonial period.[8]

The establishment of the Catholic Church in Oaxaca further complicated the pattern with new civil and ecclesiastical jurisdictions.[9] This colonial heritage persists today, and the multiplicity of municipalities simultaneously works for and against political unity in the state. While governmental power in Mexico theoretically resides at the municipal level, a vertically integrated system put in place by one particular political party in fact controls the

FIG. 3. Observance of a saint's feast day. Courtesy of Mexican Pictorial Manuscript Collection, the Latin American Library, Tulane University.

diffusion of power to the municipal level.[10] The result is an "accidental state," a complex mosaic of countless tesserae that the modern state must somehow unify.[11]

Civil Religion, Nationalism, and Political Culture

Civil religion is the idea of a transcendent universal religion of the nation.[12] Where other institutions such as religion and the economy embody their social associations in churches and businesses respectively, civil religion claims no identifiable social group short of the entire nation itself. The shared common characteristics expressed through civil-religious beliefs, symbols, and rituals imbue all civil life with a religious dimension.[13] Political leaders may attach social and political meaning to events such as commemorations, national holidays, and public festivals; and they may manipulate national heroes and events in an attempt to instill sentiments of patriotism, loyalty, and unity.[14] In Mexico, the government and intellectuals alike advocated that the components of civil religion be promoted in order to forge unity within the diverse nation and inspire loyalty to the government. Music accompanied most civil-religious manifestations in Mexico.

Civil religion furthers the idea of national identity. In the nineteenth century, nationalism, the principal ideology of new modern nation-states, arose from Romantic notions of sentiment and identity. Nationalism, unlike liberalism or communism, does not reflect any formal doctrine; instead, it assumes varied forms—such as attitudes, texts, practices, and images—that are included in a broad range of phenomena, including music.[15]

At the time of the Spanish invasion of Mexico, music fulfilled multiple purposes for both conqueror and native. For each group, music could be bellicose, violent, and noisy when used to signal attacks. Music could provide order amid the chaos of battle or provoke disorder among the opponent. For both the Spanish and the native Mesoamericans, military conquest included a strong sacred component, and religious music, both incantatory and proselytizing, offered spiritual reward and release from temporal chaos. Military and sacred music also propagated each group's imperial aspirations. Finally, music for both peoples could be celebratory and entertaining, providing respite from quotidian hardship and labor. The same musicians often fulfilled these multiple musical functions: military, sacred, and diversionary. They were familiar with the various musical forms and passed easily between the different realms of musical production.

New musical practices and forms arose as the two cultures mixed. The BME reflects the military, spiritual, and diversionary heritage of the musical forms present at the Spanish invasion, as well as the hybrid musical forms that have arisen across nearly five centuries.

Organization of This Book

Chapter 1 examines military and ecclesiastical musical practices in colonial Oaxaca, as well as musical practices during the transitional period to Mexican independence, which was achieved in

1821. Military musicians performed liminal roles, passing back and forth between functions that were military and civilian, sacred and secular. With independence came the inception of Mexican civil religion and patriotic festivals.

Chapter 2 examines the Oaxacan role in responding to the political chaos that characterized the half-century following independence. Out of the ignominies of multiple foreign invasions (beginning in the present work with the U.S. invasion of Mexico in 1846), as well as civil war and the French Intervention of 1860, the first heroes of Oaxaca's civil pantheon arose, inspiring celebratory songs for the growing nationalist repertoire. The foreign invasions also introduced new and unforeseen influences to the already hybrid Mexican band form.

Chapter 3 begins with the founding of the BME in 1868 and follows the band as it became institutionalized within the War Department, added a professional director, and grew increasingly involved in the propagation of Mexican civil religion. The chapter also examines the reconfiguration of the plaza in Oaxaca and its adaptation as a site of musical production, including the addition of the BME's most important venue, the kiosk.

Chapter 4 recounts the band's history during Porfirio Díaz's thirty-four-year presidency (a period known as the Porfiriato, 1876–1910) and the Mexican Revolution (1910–1917). The gradual civilianization of a once–National Guard band began during the period; during that time, the BME became an increasingly important tool for successive governors. The chapter also examines the band's increased visibility not only throughout the state of Oaxaca but also nationally. The period also included the beginning of the tenure of its longest-reigning director.

Chapter 5 examines the new pedagogical role of the BME within the post-Revolutionary era of roughly 1917 to 1929. The chapter examines the effects upon the BME of the new "socialist" ideology that prevailed in Mexico and the government's project to valorize indigenous and mestizo cultures.

Chapter 6 recounts the passing of the band to municipal control in 1937 and the proliferation of municipal bands created to fill performance requirements for the expanding civil-religious calendar to which the Revolution had contributed. After ten years, the band reverted to state control, and another long-term director arrived to leave his mark on the organization.

Chapter 7 examines the BME's transformation into a state-sponsored cultural organization responsible for assisting in the marketing of Oaxaca as a tourist destination during the second half of the twentieth century. It also explores the BME's role in Oaxaca's biggest annual music and dance performance, the Guelaguetza, and attempts to detail the quotidian and mundane aspects of life within the BME.

The Conclusion rounds out the present work by examining the last military and ecclesiastical vestiges of the BME and summarizing the effectiveness of music as a political tool in the hands of the state of Oaxaca.

Since its creation in the nineteenth century, the "accidental" state of Oaxaca has presented its government with a difficult task: how to bring political unity to one of the world's most diverse regions. Oaxaca is, geographically and demographically speaking, an accidental state that requires a unifying force to cobble it together and make it politically viable. One result of its diversity is the violent nature of Oaxaca's trajectory toward a consolidated modern state. Music can bring forth order from the "noise" of violence. Noise, according to Jacques Attali, is violence, or the disruption or disaggregation of any social process, and music holds the power to sublimate violence to a created order, especially through political integration.[16] Music can also provide social cohesion amid dizzying diversity. The BME has been charged with that task for more than a century, but the question remains: how effective is music as a political tool?

1 Closing the Colonial Past

> To close the colonial past... to substitute the Catholic religion with atheistic paganism... [and] the centralist viceroy with republican federalism.
> Antonio Caso, *México (Apuntamientos de Cultura Patria)*

Settling Oaxaca

In 1456 the Aztecs began their incursions into the territory that comprises the modern-day state of Oaxaca but never completely subjugated the region. They established an encampment in an acacia forest and felled the trees to construct the village of Huaxyacac (from the Nahuatl for "the nose of the acacia tree"), from which the name *Oaxaca* is derived. The Zapotecs and Mixtecs, tribes native to the region, allied to impede the Aztec advances; ultimately, a marriage between Zapotec and Aztec royalty brought forth the kingdom of Tehuantepec.[1] To preserve a tenuous peace, however, the Zapotecs accepted a tributary role in the Aztec empire.

In 1521, along with some four hundred Aztecs, Spanish troops under Gonzalo de Sandoval and Francisco de Orozco founded Villa Segura de Frontera, the first colonial settlement in Oaxaca. Before long about five hundred Spanish families arrived, some directly from Spain. Extraction of resources and tribute began immediately, and the prime plots of land were divided among the conquistadors.[2]

In 1527 a royal decree changed the village's name to Nueva Antequera. When the village was divided in 1526, Juan Peláez de Berrio, the first mayor of La Villa, placed the central plaza of Oaxaca (Plaza de Armas) at a point equidistant from the two rivers that cross the Central Valley, the Atoyac and the Jalatlaco.[3] A subsequent royal decree on 25 March 1532 changed the name of the village to Oaxaca.

The village of Oaxaca grew fitfully as the result of a series of events that included disputes among the Spanish landholders and natural disasters such as earthquakes and floods. The Spanish yoke weighed heavily on Oaxaca's indigenous people. Repression was severe: they were forced to labor in mines, fell victim to disease, and were uprooted and resettled as the Spanish population grew. During the colonial period, Dominican missionaries may have softened the brutality and deprivation for the indigenous peoples, whom they found predisposed to "civilized" life and whose vigor and vitality impressed them.[4] Church construction, one of the hallmarks of Spanish settlement, began in earnest.

The Late Colonial Period

In 1786 the Spanish Bourbon regime converted Oaxaca to an intendancy. The intendancy of Oaxaca assumed the approximate territory and shape of the present-day state. Oaxaca was a "multiple reality," integrated differently from any other part of New Spain.[5] In the Mixteca Alta, for example, distribution channels connected indigenous communities with the market system and the colonial mercantilist structure. In the densely populated Central Valley, indigenous populations remained relatively consolidated and controlled the majority of agricultural production and trade between indigenous and nonindigenous communities, preventing the solid formation of *latifundios* (landed estates) that took place, for example, in the north of New Spain. Finally, in the less populated regions of Oaxaca, cattlemen and commercial agriculturalists competed with the indigenous communities for land. In those subregions, indigenous communities often suffered disintegration, fragmentation, and impoverishment.[6]

Bourbon Military Reform

The Bourbons inherited a fragile and fractured colonial defense system from the Hapsburgs. New Spain was relatively peaceful, although disputes and factional rivalries between colonial landholders, as well as occasional indigenous and Afro-Mexican uprisings, did require intervention. Spanish troops in the Americas endured poor pay, which was often late, and some probably had to resort to a second occupation to support themselves and their families. Some trafficked in goods from Spain, both legally and illegally, while others dedicated themselves to outright banditry, robbery, extortion, and rustling.[7] As members of the Spanish Army of the Americas (see fig. 4), military musicians likely found itinerant forms of employment performing at fiestas or within the church.

During the sixteenth and seventeenth centuries, soldiers had been a rare sight in Oaxaca.[8] However, foreign threats resulted in the establishment in September 1784 of the Provincial Battalion of Oaxaca, a white infantry regiment consisting of 423 "well-disciplined men."[9] Companies in other regions of Oaxaca proliferated. For example, in the Mixteca region, the Southern Division was created to protect the Pacific coast. In Oaxaca Spaniards became officers while Indians were excluded from service, so that the weight of service necessarily fell on mestizos.[10] To risk one's life for the caprice of a European king made the idea of military service unappealing; to be called up likely meant hardships and possibly a cruel and thankless death.[11]

During the late colonial period, the Oaxaca militia was most visible at its musters and exercises in the small plaza known as the Llano de Guadalupe (Plain of Guadalupe), while firing honors at funerals, and while participating in coronation celebrations for the Spanish Crown. The militia musicians performed martial,

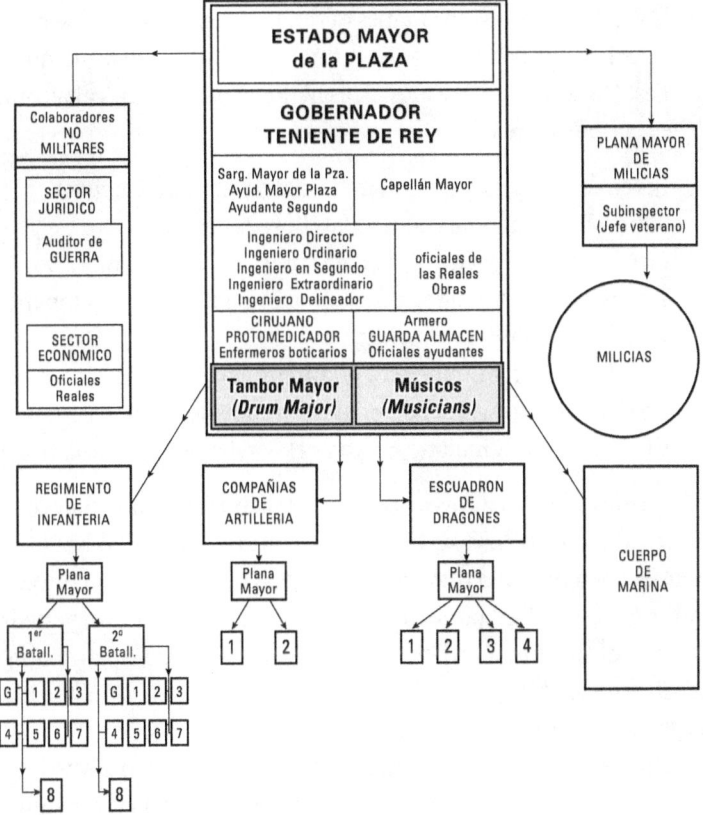

FIG. 4. Spanish Army of the Americas organizational chart. Based upon Juan Marchena Fernández, *Ejército y milicias en el mundo colonial Americano* (Madrid: Editorial Mapfre, 1992). Erin Greb Cartography.

spiritual, and celebratory functions. With the February 1794 coronation of Carlos IV, in an event presaging countless others to follow, the city of Oaxaca "was illuminated, fireworks were set off, coins and trinkets were flung at the townspeople, and the fiestas ended with three days of dances at the town hall."[12] (In order to ensure flawless military comportment within society, the Bourbons even taught their officers to dance.[13])

Marriage contracts and death certificates in Oaxaca's ecclesiastical archives reveal the names of militia musicians.[14] These men, assigned to various provincial militia battalions, constituted the earliest Oaxacan military musicians in the colonial historical record. They included the following individuals:

> Lorenzo Morales, español, músico del Batallón (ca. 1765)
> Simón Rosalino, músico del Batallón (ca. 1765)
> José Barragán Machuca, soldado músico del Batallón (1777)
> Tomás Manuel Castillo, miliciano músico de la sexta compañía del Batallón Provincial (1781)
> Domingo Barrera, morisco, pífano miliciano (1781)
> José María Flores, español, pífano segundo de las milicias (1784)
> Vicente Aguirre, mulatto, pífano del Batallón de Veracruz (1785)

These musicians' racial castes, as well as their inclusion in the ecclesiastical archive,[15] evoke the liminal nature of colonial life (and musical practice): did these musicians pass back and forth between military and sacred performances? Unfortunately nothing else is known of these men, whose biographies are crucial to providing a better understanding of military musical production in New Spain shortly before Mexican independence.

On the eve of the insurgent rebellion that became the Mexican War of Independence (1810–1821) the population of Oaxaca numbered approximately 419,000 inhabitants,[16] comprising groups quite diverse in their ethnicity, language, and socioeconomic status. The vast majority of Oaxacans dedicated themselves to pursuits such as agriculture and domestic artisanal production.

Religious, Political, and Musical Transition

The Bourbons sought to diminish the power and presence of the Catholic Church. Reformers saw the endless feast days, lifecycle events, and religious celebrations, especially among the indigenous, as an obstacle to economic development. Sacred musical production forged a link between colonizer and colonized, however, and the heart of musical production in New Spain was the church.

Religious music entered a period of decline during the mid-eighteenth century, gradually ceding its preeminence to "profane" music.[17] The Catholic Church initially permitted "loud" instruments like drums, bass, and cornet within the church, but reforms attempted to remove such instruments from the church's liturgy and interior. Popular music eventually usurped sacred music as the most important musical product of the late colonial period. The eighteenth century saw the introduction in New Spain of musical genres from Europe that included chamber music, Italian lyrical music, and even performances of symphonies composed by Joseph Haydn and Wolfgang Amadeus Mozart.[18] The advent of new performance venues such as theaters, opera houses, and parks accompanied the introduction of these novel musical forms in New Spain. The late colonial period thus brought to its inhabitants both new sounds and new ways of listening.

With the role of military musical corps instituted within the military hierarchy, the increased military presence in New Spain brought a corresponding increase in the number of musicians. They performed at imperial celebrations, saint's-day processions, and even bullfights. No concrete evidence emerges from the historiography of New Spain's musical traditions to distinguish specifically the roles of church musicians from those of military musicians. On the contrary, the musicians are often seen alternating between both institutions, passing back and forth between them. A new type of musical group, however—a formally structured civil wind band—would emerge from independent Mexico's military. While such bands were created in response to new political realities, they still owed much to their colonial-era roots.

Army and Nation Ascendant

The military now rivaled the church as the political leader of the colony and brought its ideological derivatives—patriotism, loyalty, unity, heroism, and a dawning sense of the nation—leaving its boot print on all of society: "Where the Hapsburgs used priests, the Bourbons employed soldiers."[19] As will be shown below, during the nineteenth century, especially in large cities, the sounds of religious celebrations competed with state-sponsored patriotic festivals. Military band performance came to share a space that had formerly belonged exclusively to Christian festivities.

After independence, the Mexican military was responsible not only for the chaos that characterized the first few decades of the new Mexican republic,[20] but also for perpetuating traditions of military musical performance after independence. The bellicose character of the decade-long struggle for independence had ramifications for musical production: while music still held identifiable vestiges of its pre-Hispanic and colonial roots, the triumphant state now installed itself in the soundscape and created new musical forms for its political repertoire.

Rubén M. Campos writes, "The *bandas de música* are the sonorous joy of our people," then follows with the question, "But when did popular life emerge?"[21] In his analysis of Mexican band traditions, Campos does not rigidly define the bands that arose during the colonial period. Instead, he writes of "city bands," "village bands," and "rural bands," attesting to their ubiquity. According to Campos, the violent political changes and upheaval that took place in early nineteenth-century Mexico led to the disintegration of all "civil bands" of the colonial tradition. Mexican military bands, designed to serve the new political purposes of the nascent nation and its regions, replaced their colonial predecessors.[22]

The new nation required a strong military to overcome its problems and remain viable. Mexico's leaders immediately created legislation aimed at organizing the army so that it could protect the nation's sovereignty. As it had in the colonial period, the military played an important role in political, social, and military life throughout nineteenth-century Mexico. The Mexican armed forces followed the models of the Spanish army and the provincial militias.

The enormous Mexican army consumed the majority of the nation's annual budget; each new president or governor saw in the military budget a voracious corporation whose fiscal demands subjugated the public's needs. The leaders considered reducing the military's size, but the precarious nature of Mexico's newly found independence and political system mandated a strong army to counter threats and provide stability. A similar problem (which persists to the present day) confronted the state in regard to funding military bands. As we will see later in this study, when military music was cut from the budget, the state almost invariably reinstated it once reminded of the importance of bands in the public realm.

Civilian traditions celebrating Mexican independence developed almost immediately, with military bands providing the musical accompaniment. The first recorded celebration of Mexican Independence Day (16 September) took place in the village of Huichapan (in the present-day state of Hidalgo) in 1812, only two years after Father Hidalgo's Grito de Dolores, the mythic pronouncement for revolt. One year later in Oaxaca, on 16 September 1813, the newspaper *Correo del Sur* published an article entitled "One American's Rapture of Patriotic Enthusiasm on the Happy Anniversary of 16 September 1810."[23] The Mexican people celebrated their victories not only with civic celebrations that included military bands, parades, and speeches by the nation's heroes and saviors, but also with Catholic masses in honor of the fallen.

After independence a mix of professional forces and regional militias was responsible for Mexican defense. In 1823 the national government formed the Milicia Activa (Active Militia), whose objective was to function as a "disciplined intermediary between military and domestic life" and to help the professional military "in emergency."[24] The formation of the Active Militia indirectly conferred the role of cultural mediators upon its musicians. In the same year the Milicia Cívica (Civic Militia) was formed to defend the *pueblo* (people or village) and to provide occasional escorts where no permanent army was available.[25] In Oaxaca in 1828, Article 43 of the "Regulations for the Civic Militia" decreed that in the infantry "the Plana Mayor [military unit] will consist of a colonel, a lieutenant colonel, a first assistant, a second assistant, a sub-assistant, a drum major, a chief cornet, eight sappers, and twelve individuals to drum for the military band."[26]

Mexican militias served in provincial capitals, in city plazas, and at outposts that the government deemed strategically significant in the interior and on the coasts. A decree of 5 May 1823 created the national artillery militia, establishing companies of between thirty and forty artillerymen, pickets of between twenty and twenty-five men, and a drummer and fifer in each company.[27] Further ordinances and decrees established the positions and salaries of military musicians depending on the branch in which they served—infantry, cavalry, or artillery—and standardized the *toques militares* (musical orders or signals) the musicians in the different divisions practiced.

Military musicians performed at public events that featured a multiplicity of characteristics. For example, while visiting Mexico City in April 1840, Madame Frances Erskine Calderón de la Barca described a Good Friday procession that included a military band whose music was forced to compete with informal street musicians. The long citation merits inclusion for its description of the diverse elements within the separate but converging civil and religious celebrations:

> The music began with a crash that wakened me out of an agreeable slumber into which I had gradually fallen; and such discordance of instruments and voices, such confusion worse confounded, such inharmonious harmony, never before deafened mortal ears. The very spheres seemed out of tune, and rolling and crashing over each other. I could have cried *Miserere!* with the loudest; and in the midst of all the undrilled band was a music-master, with violin-stick uplifted, rushing desperately from one to the other, in vain endeavouring to keep time, and frightened at the clamor he himself had been instrumental in raising, like Phaeton instructed with his unmanageable coursers.

The noise was so great as to be really alarming; and the heat was severe in proportion. The calm face of the Virgin seemed to look reproachfully down. We were thankful when, at the conclusion of this stormy appeal for mercy, we were able to make our way into the fresh air and soft moonlight, through the confusion and squeezing at the doors, where it was rumoured that a soldier had killed a baby with his bayonet. A bad place for little babies—decidedly. Outside, in the square, it was cool and agreeable. A military band was playing airs from *Norma*, and the womankind were sitting on the stones of the railing, or wandering about and finishing their day's work by a quiet flirtation *au clair de la lune*.[28]

Was the "inharmonious harmony" Calderón described merely a combination of sounds unfamiliar to her Western ears? Were they the live sounds of the process of cultural hybridization at work? The answer may be yes to both questions, for when Calderón heard the military band playing "airs from *Norma*," she recognized something familiar and therefore comforting; she finds order amidst a disorder so pervasive that even a baby may have suffered violence. The "airs from *Norma*" comfort the woman so greatly that the scene transforms to the pastoral; even the weather seems to change!

Toward a Mexican Civil Religion

A civil religious celebration (where the state has replaced the church as the object of veneration) contains elements of religious theatricality, but the consolidation of a Mexican civil religion was still ongoing when Calderón put pen to paper. In the first half of the nineteenth century in Mexico, two musical spheres, the military and the sacred, still competed for space in Mexico's streets. However, the imposition on the nation of liberal ideology, with anticlericalism at its forefront, was less than two decades away, and while theatricality with recognizably religious attributes remained part of the civil religion, sacred music would no longer be performed. As the term suggests, "civil religion" is a "religion," and the Mexican variant would rely on symbols, words, and rituals that drew not only on civism but also on those ideals found long established and readily available in Catholicism.[29]

A true cradle of Mexican liberalism, Oaxaca quickly developed its own civil religion. It found its martyrs and saviors in the ranks of military heroes, its symbols in classical civism, its rhetoric in ancient texts and pragmatic, eloquent prose. This book now turns its focus to Oaxaca during the epoch of foreign invasions and civil war, the crucibles in which Mexican and Oaxacan civil religion were forged.

2 Nineteenth-Century Invasions and Influences

> Without music, the state could not exist.
>
> Molière, *Le Bourgeois gentilhomme*

Mexico suffered a long list of ignominies during its first fifty years of independence: the bloody decade-long war that culminated in a failed first Mexican Empire; the Spanish invasion of 1829; the secession of Texas; the war with the United States in 1846 and the resulting loss of half of the new nation's territory; the civil war of the Reform; the taking of the port of Veracruz by European forces in 1861; the French Intervention; and numerous barracks revolts, indigenous uprisings, and epidemics. The Mexican populace grew accustomed to having troops in its midst, not to mention the sounds of the accompanying military music. With the bands that accompanied the invading forces came unanticipated influences on musical performance, organization, repertoires, and programs. These foreign influences added to the process of musical hybridization and nourished a budding new role for the Mexican wind band.

Oaxaca during the War with the United States

War with the United States of America obliged the Mexican government, for the first time in its brief history, to mandate obligatory universal military service. Federal law decreed, on 11 September 1846, that all Mexican males between the ages of sixteen and fifty must enlist or face the loss of their civil rights. Local militias were reorganized as the Guardia Nacional (National Guard), and included with the troops a drum major, cornetists, and eighteen musicians.[1]

In 1846 the state of Oaxaca confronted the U.S. invasion of Mexico with patriotic fervor and military expansion.[2] On 9 August 1846, the plaza garrison of Oaxaca rose in support of the Plan de la Ciudadela (Citadel Plan) to protect their state against the foreign invasion.[3] On 11 August 1846 the legislative junta of Oaxaca established the state's National Guard with its first decree.[4] The National Guard battalion comprised eight companies, each including a drummer and fifer among its troops. Following the Bourbon schematic, the Plana Mayor included among the staff and specialists a drum major and a chief of cornets. Pay ranged from a high of MXN $100 per month for the colonel to $9 per month for the soldiers, with musicians earning $10 per month.[5] The junta simultaneously created the identically structured Tehuantepec Battalion on the Isthmus. Within a year the Oaxaca National Guard had been mobilized against the invading American forces.[6]

Twenty years before he gained national prominence at the Battle of Puebla, sixteen-year-old Porfirio Díaz sat in a logic class in which his professor spoke of the need for the young men of Oaxaca to enlist and serve their country against the invaders from the north.[7] From his seat in the Instituto de Ciencias y Artes (Institute of Sciences and Arts, ICA), young Díaz would have heard the strains of the military musicians accompanying exercises in the nearby Plaza de Armas.

So began a lifelong and mercurial relationship between the future general and his home state's National Guard. Stirred by his professor's call to service, Díaz enlisted along with some classmates. When the governor of Oaxaca, Joaquín Guergué, reprovingly asked the schoolboys, "What in the devil have you all done?," they replied that it was a "spontaneous inspiration of our duty given the national situation."[8] In his memoirs, Díaz wrote, "I never saw any active duty in our battalion besides providing military exercises for holiday celebrations, some guard duty, and some patrol duties when the active troops had been called away."[9]

Military bands accompanied United States forces during the invasion and occupation of Mexico (1846–1848). In the United States, during the interim between the War of 1812 and the Mexican War, military bands had proliferated in part-time militia regiments—more so than in the federal army. Rival regiments' bands competed for honors against one another, and qualified American citizens could fulfill their military service by performing in a unit's band.[10] Any glamour associated with playing military music, however, dissipated quickly during wartime. In the heat of battle, musicians on either side often had to drop their instruments to fulfill such horrible battlefield duties as stretcher bearing and assisting in amputations. Figure 5 features the image of a Mexican drummer assisting a fallen comrade in the foreground of Carlos Paris's painting *Batalla de Tampico, Tamaulipas.*

General Antonio de León, First in the Oaxacan Pantheon

In 1847 Santa Anna ordered Oaxacan general Antonio de León (1794–1847), a native of Huajuapan in the Mixteca, to raise troops and join the battle outside of Mexico City. León raised various National Guard battalions and in April, along with the Batallón Activo de Oaxaca (Active Battalion of Oaxaca), marched to join Santa Anna's forces. In the crucial battle of Molino del Rey, a defensive position along the Chapultepec River, Mexican forces for a short while succeeded in delaying the U.S. advance on Mexico City. But the American general, Winfield Scott, believing that Molino del Rey held a considerable artillery force, put the site to

FIG. 5. Carlos Paris, *Batalla de Tampico, Tamaulipas*. Licensed under Creative Commons, 2014.

siege. Casualties on both sides were great; General de León died in battle on 8 September 1847.[11] León, "moving serene and unmindful, passing in the midst of a shower of balls, and without flinching one step from his post, received a severe wound and fell, terminating his career in a glorious manner and leaving a grateful reminiscence to Mexicans."[12]

In December 1847 the seventh Constitutional Congress of Oaxaca declared General de León "Benemérito del Estado" ("Meritorious of the State") and decorated all combatants from the Oaxaca National Guard. The *escudo de distinción* (shield of distinction) was two inches in diameter, made of either gold or silver, and inscribed with the battle's date and the phrase "They fought for Independence with valor." Memorial celebrations were held in the Cathedral of Oaxaca, as well as in all the state's parishes. Congress decreed that a speaker be hired to "excite the faithfulness and patriotism of the citizens."[13] Over a century later, performances by the BME still celebrated the anniversary of the Battle of Molina del Rey. In 1912 Oaxacan composer José López Alavés would write "The

Hymn to the Meritorious General Antonio de León,"[14] a song that remains in the BME's repertoire to this day.[15] León entered Oaxaca's pantheon of heroes even before Benito Juárez and Porfirio Díaz, and local conductors still raise their batons to play this anthem each year, lest Oaxacans forget.

Civil War and Foreign Intervention: Oaxacans at the Forefront

During the civil war of the Reform (1855–1860), Mexican president Benito Juárez, Oaxacan-born and a full-blooded Serrano Zapotec, led the Liberal challenge to Conservative hegemony. (See fig. 6.) After the war, the victorious Liberal government faced a desperate economic situation that forced Juárez to suspend payment of the external debt, provoking Mexico's creditor nations—England, France, and Spain—to intervene in Mexico in order to recover their loans. After a series of negotiations, Juárez reached an accord with England and Spain in which their forces would retire from the port of Veracruz, which they occupied between December 1861 and January 1862. But the French military remained in Mexico, and the Mexican Conservative Party proposed that the French impose a monarchy on Mexico. France accepted the offer, and Napoleon III, Emperor of France, installed the Austrian Hapsburg archduke Maximilian in Mexico.

Along with another Oaxacan, General Ignacio de Mejía, Díaz led the most important (if only symbolically so) battle in Mexican history, the Battle of Puebla, on 5 May 1862. In their first attempt to take Mexico City in 1862, French imperial forces met unexpected resistance at Puebla. An ill-advised attack on the hilltop fortifications led to the death of almost 500 foreign soldiers. Cinco de mayo (5 May) is hallowed in Mexican history not because it was a decisive date in the struggle against the Interventionists but because it signified Mexican bravery in the face of overwhelming odds. One year later, the French returned to Puebla and laid siege to it for two months, ultimately forcing the city to surrender.[16]

FIG. 6. Benito Juárez. Courtesy of Library of Congress.

French forces sought to combat Díaz in his home state. For three years, he led the Army of the East and achieved a series of victories that cemented his fame as a fighting general. Díaz counted upon a mobilized and impassioned populace to counter the French in Oaxaca.[17] On 17 March 1864 a passionately worded circular issued by the military-led state government in Oaxaca invoked the heroes of Mexican independence and the "sacred duty" of Oaxaca's citizenry to confront the Interventionists. The people needed to exhibit "valor," perhaps even "sacrifice" themselves for liberty and reform. The circular equated Juárez with the heroes of the French Revolution, and its prose verged on the biblical with its metaphors of betrayal and sacrifice, even suggesting such Old Testament themes as retribution. At the same time, however, the language was secular and nationalist and invoked the Mexican state as the "highest power."[18]

New Musical Influences and Practices

During the War of the Reform, military bands performed at the *fiestas patrias* (national festivities) in Oaxaca. In September 1859 governor Miguel Castro published official programs for commemorating Mexican Independence Day, to be celebrated over two days, 15 and 16 September.[19] The complete program included bell ringing, speeches by political dignitaries, a musical *serenata*, fireworks, military exercises, and a parade led by military musicians.[20] *Fiestas patrias* also continued during the Intervention. In 1863 Maximilian decreed the observance of Mexican Independence Day, the feast day of the Virgin of Guadalupe, and even his own birthday.[21] Priorities and contingencies in Oaxaca that year, however, influenced then-governor Porfirio Díaz to suppress military bands temporarily, arguing that they cost the treasury more than $800 per month, a sum better used to arm and sustain more soldiers. "It is not the time for entertainment," he said, "and soldiers to fight the enemy are needed more than musicians: arms that lift a rifle or lance and not a bugle or clarinet [are] what the Fatherland demands until seeing itself freed from the foreign invader."[22] The ban was brief, for the following year the garrison band in Oaxaca was again active, offering a serenade in the Alameda to celebrate the first "glorious anniversary of Cinco de Mayo 1862."[23] In 1866 military musicians entertained the people of Oaxaca during the celebration of Empress Carlota's birthday.[24]

In the nineteenth century, the serenata gained importance for the military bands in Mexico, the public having been accustomed to the strains of military bands since the colonial period. The serenata has roots as early as the sixteenth century and is therefore another near-medieval European custom brought to the New World. The root of the word is *serena*, a troubadouresque composition, which in medieval Castile was usually performed at night.[25] Today in Oaxaca, the serenata remains one of the BME's most visible (and audible) types of performances.[26] The serenata usually takes place in the city plaza, a park, or a public garden, as part of a reconception of public space that had begun in Europe with the French Revolution.[27] Nineteenth-century public policy in Mexico sought to introduce nature into the urban setting. City dwellers could now enjoy pastoral charms in their midst, as the streets, and especially the city plazas, were no longer solely filled with markets, shops, and ambulant vendors. Ornate, salubrious gardens transformed the colonial plaza.

Wind bands had taken part in the public ceremonies of Europe and its colonies (both current and former) since the French Revolution, and both military and civilian musicians performed with artistic effects in mind. Bands achieved such levels of proficiency and popularity that they exercised great influence on behalf of the state while simultaneously raising the taste and critical judgment of the public.[28] In some cases, wind ensembles became the representatives of the "official music" of the state. Wind bands in Mexico became a fixture at the most important official acts and assemblies, but the serenata may be viewed as "unofficial" given its nod to the popular. However, the serenata's unofficial status should not obscure the fact that the state was still (though subtly) using these musical performances to apply music as a tool for its own purposes.[29] When Díaz decided in 1863 to suspend military music (a rational choice based upon economic concerns), at first he may not have understood the (nonrational) importance of music to his soldiers and the public alike; once realizing his mistake, however, he quite rationally decided to reinstate it. Besides the functional aspect of military music, which retained an important role in the upkeep of military forces, Díaz must also have recognized its diversionary utility.

Emma Cosio-Villegas provides a poetical description of a Sunday afternoon in the Alameda in Mexico City, where the strolling public enjoyed the harmonies of Verdi and Donizetti offered by alternating civil bands, either the Gendarmes Band or the Zapadores Band.[30] An acoustic "box" (perhaps a kiosk?) where the military band was situated was located in the densest part of the forest, "as if the trees had drawn near the band in order to better hear." The passage includes a program that was eclectic yet foundational, already standardized, and soon to be universally adopted:

1. March, *Tristán* by Sehaki
2. "Convivialidad," redowa, by Romero
3. "Alzira," chorus and cavatina, by Verdi
4. "Aroldo," polka, by Albert
5. Overture, *Haydée*, by Auber
6. "Ababel," waltz, by Godfrey
7. "Somnambula," cavatina, by Bellini
8. "No te hago caso, No me da la gana, ¿que siempre te vas a España?" *Danzas*, by Salvatierra[31]

The passage not only places musical performance in the pastoral Alameda, a refuge within the urban chaos available to any and all, regardless of social status, who might happen on it, but also includes a relatively early example of the era's musical programs for bands similar to the BME. It is no surprise that a march begins the program, given Mexico's militaristic traditions, but the appearance of Italian operatic overtures and assorted dances requires a brief explanatory digression.

The fact that Italian singers debuted the Mexican national anthem is indicative of the fact that opera eclipsed all other forms of music in nineteenth-century Mexico.[32] The 1840s and 1850s saw numerous visits of European singing companies that performed Italian operas in whole or in part, in either Italian or Spanish. Opera reached the Mexican interior, for example, when several Verdi operas, with Jaime Nunó Roca (who composed the music of the Mexican national anthem) as orchestral director, premiered in Puebla in 1864. Guy P. C. Thomson argues that the taste for opera in Mexico was not reserved for the elite and that its popular diffusion in the country was spurred by several factors: its absorption into church liturgy, the template it provided for national anthems, and its privileged place within the stock repertoire of wind bands.[33]

The French Intervention had long-lasting effects on Mexican music in general and military music in particular. The emperor's flag united a polyglot conglomeration of troops from around the world: Frenchmen, Austrians, Belgians, Hungarians, Liberal and Conservative Mexicans, blond Teutons, Slavs, even Confederate forces from the United States.[34] Included among the Imperial forces were some bands of excellent quality that performed the latest in compositions and arrangements. The French Foreign Legion, for example, sent at least three bands containing approximately forty musicians each to Mexico.[35] Rafael Antonio Ruíz Torres has painstakingly reconstructed the performance history of the French and Austrian bands in Mexico City; he writes that the serenatas permitted the foreign soldiers to ingratiate themselves with the Mexican people, thereby softening the soldiers' image as invaders.[36]

In December 1867 Félix Díaz, brother of Porfirio and governor of Oaxaca (1867–1871), dissolved the National Guard, believing that the restoration of the Mexican republic rendered the National Guard in Oaxaca an "apparatus of war, now without use."[37] Oaxaca had been an armed camp during the War of the Reform and the French Intervention, and Díaz probably recognized the threat that a standing army within his midst posed, because a moderate-radical split among Oaxacan Liberals meant that retribution was the order of the day. But the soldiers were needed at home on their farms to secure the harvest. Staff, critical support personnel, and the "military music," however, remained in commission. Musical accompaniment at patriotic festivals was still funded: the state grasped the importance of the musical tool.

Foreign invasions and occupation had long-lasting effects on Mexican military bands. The invaders introduced new technologies, instrumentations, arrangements, and repertoires. The crucible of war with foreign powers brought the wind-band revolution into the heart of Mexico at the same time that Mexico's liberal republic was finally restored. Persistence in the face of adversity added heroic men and acts to Mexico's civil-religious pantheon. The open-air, which had become popular during the French Intervention, perfectly suited the propagation of liberal ideals and the celebration of both nation and national heroes. If only the state could fashion a tool to send forth the sound waves!

Shortly after the expulsion of the French, the state of Oaxaca did just that. A musical-political tool, in the form of the BME, was now forged and awaiting its purpose. The state lifted and began to wield it.

3 Inception, Institutionalization, and Venue

> Like a landscape, a soundscape is simultaneously a physical environment and a way of perceiving that environment; it is both a world and a culture constructed to make sense of that world. The physical aspects of a soundscape consist not only of the sounds themselves, the waves of acoustical energy permeating the atmosphere in which people live, but also the material objects that create, and sometimes destroy, those sounds. A soundscape's cultural aspects incorporate scientific and aesthetic ways of listening, a listener's relationship to their environment, and the social circumstances that dictate who gets to hear what. A soundscape, like a landscape, ultimately has more to do with civilization than with nature, and as such, it is constantly under construction and always undergoing change.
>
> Emily Thompson, *The Soundscape of Modernity*

The year 1868 was a watershed for military music in Oaxaca. First, the incorporation of a military band director forever altered the mission and scope of military music.[1] Second, a *junta patriótica* (patriotic council) was seated to coordinate public festivals to observe the expanding civil-religious pantheon and calendar.² Third, a municipal commission was installed to oversee the care of the Alameda (the body was responsible for planting trees and flowers in the Alameda, its care and cleaning, and its decoration and ornamentation for public festivities). The ordinances also called for strict maintenance of public order and sobriety in the Alameda.³ The position of director and the location of the BME's most important performance site set the BME on its trajectory toward becoming not only a long-time state corporate body, but also one of the most visible (and audible) government organs of Oaxaca.

The First Directors and the *Fiestas Patrias*

The first directors of Oaxaca's BME served in the Guerrero and Zaragoza battalions of Oaxaca's National Guard. Pablo Vásquez of Zaragoza served from January to June 1868, and Bernardino Alcalá of Guerrero served from January to October 1868.⁴ From July 1868 until 1875 an Austrian military officer, Francisco Sakar, directed the bands of both battalions. Little is known of Sakar except that he had remained in Oaxaca after the fall of Maximilian. Musicians from both battalions served in what was then known simply as *la música militar* (the military music). The majority of Sakar's sixty-three musicians were also European.⁵

Establishing a permanent director for the BME meant creating a more institutionalized role for the band within the state; doing so required technical and administrative reform. In an 1853 series of articles entitled "Reform of Military Orchestras," Mexico City journalist Vicente María Riesgo had called for the reform and reorganization of Mexican military orchestras.⁶ Taking as a model "the new organization of the musical bands of European armies," Riesgo elaborated his reform project. Aiming to wrest control of military bands from commanders and officers who considered their regiments their personal fiefdoms, Riesgo recommended that a director lead all military bands. In order to elevate the status of Mexican military music, each director was to serve as a band's sole authority, thereby avoiding "the abuse that some music directors are accustomed to practice."[7] The director would be responsible for ensuring minimal levels of musicianship, examining and classifying the musicians, and overseeing composition and instrumentation.

Riesgo's articles suggest the influence of a positivist ideology, containing as they do a hint of utopian socialism in their rigidly constructed hierarchies and technocracies, as well as a promise of social perfection through scientific and economic development. In Oaxaca, less than two decades later, a document appeared in the *Colleción de Leyes, Decretos, y Circulares* calling for "the scientific and administrative reform" of the National Guard, indicating the possible penetration of positivist ideology into the state government's War Branch. Decree Number Nine cited a similar reform within the federal army.[8]

Perhaps due to prevailing Liberal trends to diminish (or eliminate) the importance of the indigenous contribution to Mexican history, neither Riesgo nor the Oaxacan archival records make any reference to the existence of indigenous traits within Mexican military bands. Given the Eurocentric and positivist ideologies that seem to inform Riesgo's reforms, and given the prevalence of the ideology of scientific racism in the mid-nineteenth century, probably the last thing Riesgo wanted to hear from a military band was any indigenous influence.

The state exercised control over that most primordial of Mexican events, the fiesta, and placed the BME at the center of the scheduled fiestas. On 4 February 1868 the state published a program for a civil festival. Governor Félix Díaz charged the Oaxaca Junta Patriótica with organizing a civic festival to commemorate the Mexican Constitution of 1857. Federal law mandated Constitution Day as a national holiday, but due to the upheaval since its adoption (and the fact that the day's celebration had never truly been enforced) Oaxacans only began to celebrate their federal constitution in 1868. The Junta Patriótica published a festival format still recognizable today:

Considering that the aforementioned day is declared by law as a national holiday for the anniversary of the fundamental Charter of 1857; considering that this festival must be celebrated with the most enthusiasm possible, not only to comply with the law but also to demonstrate to the foreign enemy and to the insignificant minority who fought against this Codex that this celebration is the frank and explicit expression of the great majority of the Nation, that by which it wishes to be governed, as has been in the fight that just ended, spilling torrents of blood, [the Junta Patriótica] issues the following program subject to the Governor's approval:

Article 1. At midnight on 4 February, this program will be solemnly published, customary artillery salutes will be fired, and all public buildings will display the flag.

Article 2. At sunrise, at noon, and at 6:00 a.m. on 5 February, a twenty-one-gun salute will remind the people of the Constitution's anniversary; the musicians of the Garrison Corps, on sounding the *diana*,[9] will parade through the streets of this City, departing from the Plaza de Armas. The flag will remain raised.

Article 3. At 10:00 a.m. the Patriotic Council will convene in the State Government Palace with the authorities, employees, and other citizens who wish to join. The President of the Council will take the flag, and the committee will accompany him on the customary procession, escorted by the Garrison Corps, ending in the Alameda, where an elegant shrine will be prepared in which to place the Flag of the Republic. In the same spot, the named orator will give his speech. Having concluded the act, the committee will accompany the Governor to the State Palace and then disperse.

Article 4. Immediately following, the Garrison Corps will parade in front of the Palace, forming a column of honor.

Article 5. At 3:00 p.m., the same corps will execute maneuvers, formation, and artillery exercises at the mausoleum field.

Article 6. The Alameda and public buildings will be adorned and illuminated, placing in the shrine a framed copy of the Constitution. A guard of grenadiers will do the Ordinance Honors. In the evening there will be a serenade in the Alameda, cheers at 11:00 p.m., and then the musicians will leave from the Alameda and parade the streets.

Article 7. At 9:00 p.m., bright fireworks will be set off in the plaza, and all public buildings will be illuminated.

Article 8. All citizens are invited on the day of the fifth to adorn and illuminate their houses. The same invitation is extended to the city's businesses, which are permitted to close except for those offering necessities.

Article 9. All citizens are free to demonstrate the joy that their patriotism dictates.[10]

Another program blending the civil and martial took place on 2 April 1868, in honor of Díaz's assault on Puebla the previous year. The decree described the battle as the principal event in the expulsion of the foreign invaders and the fall of the Empire. The decree also referred to the patriotic fervor that had gripped Mexico after the defeat of the French. The program for the patriotic festival further demonstrates the state's project of standardizing patriotic celebrations, as well as the role of military music within them:

Article 1. At sunrise on the expressed day of 2 April, the musicians of the Garrison Corps, meeting in the Plaza de Armas, will sound the diana and then parade through the main streets of the city. At the same time, the flag will be raised in all public buildings and the Artillery will fire a twenty-one-gun salute in the Plaza. The salute will be repeated at noon and at 6:00 p.m.

Article 2. At 7:00 p.m., the Alameda and Government Palace will be illuminated, and the military musicians will perform in the Plaza de Armas until midnight.

Article 3. At the conclusion of the serenade, the musicians will parade through the streets. The townspeople are free to express their joy following the dictates of their patriotism.[11]

Finally, the program for Cinco de Mayo 1868, whose wealth of civil religious imagery made it essential to the construction of civil religion in Oaxaca, appears in its entirety below:

Article 1. At dawn on 5 May, the flag is to be raised in all forts and public buildings, and will be saluted by the strong Zaragoza [battalion] and the musicians and military bands that will be opportunely situated in the Plaza de Armas. They will play dianas, parading through the city streets to remind the people of one of the most brilliant glories of the Fatherland.

Article 2. At 9:00 a.m., united in the Government Palace, all public employees, the Town Council, the Patriotic Council, and all other citizens who wish to participate in the grand splendor of this act will parade, presided over by the Constitutional Governor, who will carry the flag and be escorted by the garrison through the streets decorated with bunting and flowers until their arrival at the Alameda, which the commission will have prepared to resemble a shrine in which will be placed a portrait of the immortal hero Ignacio Zaragoza.[12]

Article 3. The designated speaker will pronounce a speech alluding to the day's solemnity.

Article 4. Directly following, the Constitutional Governor of the State will proceed to distribute the medals decreed by the State Legislature on 11 February to those corresponding individuals. This act will take place in the presence of the Garrison Corps, and the recipients will be saluted by the same military. Having concluded this act, the tribune is dismissed.

Article 5. At the conclusion of that act, the Committee will go to the Government Palace, and the Garrison, in column formation, will sound the Ordinances.

Article 6. At noon and at 6:00 p.m. a battery will repeat the salvo in the Plaza de Armas.

Article 7. From 4:00 p.m. the military musicians will situate themselves in the Paseo de Guadalupe, where a balloon festooned with garlands and allegorical emblems will ascend in tribute to the citizens who have contributed to the good of the Fatherland.

Article 8. That evening the Alameda will be perfectly illuminated and the military musicians will play there. The four portals that surround the Plaza de Armas, the Cathedral atrium, and all public buildings will also be illuminated. All inhabitants are invited to clean, decorate, and illuminate the streets and their house fronts that day and night.

Article 9. At 10:00 p.m. colorful fireworks will be lit, and afterwards the citizens are free to demonstrate their joy following the dictates of their patriotism.[13]

The programs contain all the elements of civil religion. They are communal and solemn, but punctuated with joy and music. Speeches, emblems, and banners are their liturgy, relics, and standards. Where religion commands adherence to its rituals and tenets, however, the liberal Oaxacan state merely encouraged its citizens (albeit by official decree) to demonstrate their joy "following the dictates of their patriotism."[14]

The Cult of Juárez

Porfirio Díaz retired from military life after the defeat of the French in 1867, but when Juárez decided to run for a fourth term as president in 1871, Díaz and Sebastián Lerdo ran against him. No clear winner emerged, and the Congress, where Juárez supporters held the majority, awarded Juárez the presidency. Lerdo accepted the results, but Díaz did not; on 8 November 1871, he declared the rebellious Plan de la Noria. The revolt failed, Juárez died shortly thereafter, and Lerdo assumed the presidency. Díaz temporarily returned to private life.

The Juárez cult arose only days after his death, with a state decree dated 29 July 1872 mandating a memorial celebration and providing its program.[15] Garrison troops, with their respective musical contingents, accompanied state officials and public employees to the gravesite at the Panteón de San Miguel in Oaxaca City. Drummers led the funeral procession, and the musicians played with their mutes in place. The soldiers of the fifth battalion led the march, their arms at funeral position. Three twenty-one-gun salutes were fired at the plaza of the ex-convent of Santo Domingo, each salute preceding a different stage of the procession. At the conclusion of the ceremonies at the cemetery, which included a graveside eulogy, members of the procession returned "to their respective barracks, their arms at their shoulders or third position and the band playing their respective calls without mutes."[16] Decree Four of 10 October 1872 institutionalized the Juárez cult in his home state.[17] It required the placement of Juárez's portrait in all public buildings, state and municipal. The portrait included the caption "Benito Juárez, Citizen of the Mexican Republic and Meritorious of America." The state government purchased the San Pablo Guelatao home where Juárez had been born and ordered the construction of a "modest monument" in honor of his birthplace. The decree also mandated the construction of two primary schools, one each for boys and girls, and ordered that a Juárez biography be used as their reading primer. The secretary of public education in Oaxaca was charged with producing and distributing a complete biography of Juárez nationwide. Congress changed the name of the state's capital city to "Oaxaca de Juárez" and awarded pensions and tax exemptions to Juárez's descendents. A statue was to be made of "bronze over a marble or granite pedestal, inscribed with memorial phrases of the hero's most glorious acts." On the anniversary of Juárez's death, 18 July, flags were to fly at half-staff, and the state congress was required to fund the decree in perpetuity.[18]

Institutionalization

In 1875, a *padrón* (census) was compiled in the capital. The data collected demonstrated a city in transition. Those inhabitants who paid the *capitación* (head tax) were grouped by occupation, and the results were compared to the 1842 census list. The comparison revealed the city's gradual transformation through indicators including newly created categories for inhabitants dedicated to the fine arts, such as sculptors, lithographers, and "philharmonics." The segment of the population identified as "musicians" had increased considerably, from twenty-nine in 1842 to seventy in 1875, not including eighteen others identified as "philharmonics."[19]

On 4 January 1875, Governor José Esperón (1874–1876) approved the budget for the formation of a band from the First Battalion of the Oaxaca National Guard and assigned it to the Plana Mayor.[20] The budget clearly differentiated this military musical band from the various drum-and-bugle corps that continued to exist within their respective companies. Earlier that year, a budgetary line item under the Ramo de Guerra (War Branch) had earmarked $6,336 for "haberes de treinta y nueve músicos" (assets for thirty-nine musicians) but had not specified a separate line item for a director's salary.[21]

The fact that the BME was assembled from an existing National Guard battalion suggests a possible reorganization of the Guard, but the archives offer no explanation for why such a restructuring might have taken place at that time. Such a move might have kept the band active while the rest of the Guard was deactivated. It is clear, however, that Esperón instituted a sweeping economic plan for the state of Oaxaca: mining programs were expanded; commerce and administration careers were offered at the ICA; the state pawn shop was reopened; primary schools were ordered established in all villages with populations of 100 or more inhabitants; commercial expositions that focused on the state's agricultural production were initiated; a public register was created to oversee property ownership; and the construction of the Mexico City–Veracruz railroad was approved, though the railroad was never built.[22] Such commercial expansion could benefit from the fanfare that state-sponsored music could provide. The creation of a separate military musical entity was the first step in the BME's eventual demilitarization. The economic and educatory programs that Esperón initiated foretold the transformation of the BME into an organization responsible for both formal and informal didactics, located in a new soundscape in which tourist dollars would lubricate the state machine.[23]

Previously referred to only as "the military music," the 1876 state budget specifically directed funds to the "músicos de la banda militar" (musicians of the military band). That year's budget for the band was $6,244—2 percent of the War Branch's total budget of $298,558.53 and 0.8 percent of the total state budget of $740,635.15.[24]

It should be noted that military participation in civic festivals was not without its dangers. On Constitution Day in Oaxaca in 1876, the artillery was arranged for the traditional twenty-one-gun cannon salute. During the salvos, one of the artillery pieces exploded, killing an unfortunate attendee who happened to be passing in front of the guns.[25]

The BME during the Porfiriato

In 1876, another member of the Alcalá family, Bernabé, became director of the BME and directed the band until his death on 9 February 1880. On that day, the members of the BME draped themselves in black crepe in honor of their respected director.[26] That same year Porfirio Díaz emerged again, this time brandishing his Plan de Tuxtepec charging President Lerdo with violating the "Supreme Law of No Reelection of the President of the Republic."[27] This time Díaz's revolt triumphed: he took Mexico City in November 1876. He submitted to Congress a no-reelection amendment to the Constitution and successfully ran for president, assuming office on 5 May 1877. With the exception of a brief interregnum from 1880–1884, Díaz remained in office for the next thirty-four years, continually disregarding the very rule that had carried him to the office.

In 1877 Oaxaca celebrated the fifteenth anniversary of Cinco de Mayo (and its native son's first day as president) with a solemn program. At 10:00 a.m. the Patriotic Council, civil functionaries, and public employees gathered at the Government Palace. From there they proceeded, along with students from city schools and the Artisan's Society, with the customary march through the city streets. They arrived at a "national altar"[28] and deposited a crown of olive branches. The BME sounded the diana. That night the city's public buildings were illuminated, and at 10:00 p.m. the band accompanied a fireworks display. As usual, the governor encouraged his citizens to display their patriotic enthusiasm "without passing the limits of morality and decency."[29]

Following Bernabé Alcalá's death in 1880, José Domingo Castro served as provisional director of the BME until 19 April 1880, when yet another member of the Alcalá family, José, became director.[30] José Alcalá, son of Macedonio, was also a composer and a renowned violinist: he had played first violin in various Italian opera performances in Oaxaca.[31]

Díaz's revolts during the second half of the 1870s caused much political violence and upheaval in his native state. On 17 February 1876 Colonel Francisco Meixueiro (1876–1879, 1880–1881) replaced General Fidencio Hernández (who served for only two weeks in January 1876) as governor of Oaxaca. The BME performed at Meixueiro's inauguration.[32] Meixueiro, who had led the Oaxacan Serrano forces that supported Porfirio Díaz's Plan of Tuxtepec, dedicated his energies to military activities in the Sierras in anticipation of a possible federal attack from Mexico City. He took office amid political factionalism and violence.[33]

On 1 January 1881 Meixueiro decreed that new uniforms be designed for the National Guard, modeling them on those of the Mexican Army. The uniforms consisted of a

> dark blue frock coat with half-lapel and two rows of seven buttons each. The coat will have a pocket flap with crimson piping in the coattail pleat, and a generous and straight neckline with embroidered *granadas* (pomegranates).[34] The length of the coat will be twenty-five centimeters below the waistline with two pouches over the skirt. The trousers will also be dark blue, of medium width with double stripes and crimson piping measuring three centimeters. The kepi will be dark blue, carrying in the center an insignia of two cannons and a granada. The visor

will be of black patent leather lined with black sheepskin and trimmed in black. The sleeve of the kepi will be of four pieces with black chinstrap. The necktie will be of black thread around a straight-necked shirt with white buckskin gloves; strong boots. The belts will be of black patent leather and adjusted with a square buckle carrying in the center an embossed shield of the Mexican eagle, with gold fittings; and the braiding and tassels of crimson silk. Band members will carry two groups of four yellow wool ribbons on their sleeves, joined at an angle, and with small tufts at the extreme. The ribbons are separated by four millimeters. The groups will be placed one between the elbow and shoulder, and the other six centimeters lower. Band sergeants' ribbons will be of silk.[35]

The BME had forty-four musicians when Meixueiro presented his *Memorias Administrativas* (*Administrative Memories*) in September 1881.[36] In his review of the War Branch, the governor expressed pleasure at the relative public peace during the preceding year and praised the National Guard's loyalty and integrity, describing it as a "privileged class" forged in crisis.

Meanwhile, Díaz's "no reelection" stance (now federal law) meant that he had to step down from the presidency in 1880.[37] In 1881 he entered and won the governor's race in Oaxaca. It was the third time he had served as the state's governor. Díaz encountered a state in the throes of extreme economic depression and a bankrupt treasury. On 12 December 1881, in his first act as governor, Díaz deactivated the National Guard.[38] Four months later Díaz eliminated both the state and Oaxaca city police, transferring their service to the National Guard battalion, Auxiliares de Oaxaca (Auxiliaries of Oaxaca) and placing them at the service of the Federation.[39] The act preceded Díaz's eventual centralization of security forces during his presidency. Although the Guard remained deactivated, Díaz fully funded the military, including the BME, and included $20,000 in the budget for 1883 to "establish the National Guard when the Executive believes it necessary."[40]

It is not surprising that a shrewd general like Díaz would deactivate those forces most likely to threaten his governorship. Juárez himself had also held the liberal belief that many of Mexico's problems, such as frequent changes of government, stemmed from military interference in civilian affairs.[41] A depressed economy provided a plausible reason for deactivating the National Guard. Furthermore, the economic world of the 1880s was quite different from that of 1847, when the National Guard had been created. In 1847 economic and political power had resided largely at the state or regional level, but Díaz now led a state in which national economic concerns and might overshadowed those of the individual states. The men of the Guard were also needed to contribute to the economy. All arms, munitions, uniforms, and supplies were ordered returned to the quartermaster's inventory for safekeeping. Some officers were put on half pay and assigned to the barracks; other officer positions were eliminated. According to the budget for 1882–1883, the only remaining National Guard forces were one artillery brigade and the Auxiliares. The BME, however, received funding and continued to perform.[42] Had Díaz recognized the importance of music and its role in maintaining an occupied and happy populace? Or did he find in the BME an institution sufficiently malleable and functionally flexible (and very likely popular) to bolster his power in peacetime without directly threatening the population or his grip on power?

The rhetoric that accompanied the deactivation of the Guard provides insight into the prevailing political sentiments of the times. The speeches given on the day that Díaz took power praised the Guard while simultaneously criticizing the political instability that had made the Guard a necessary evil. On 1 December 1881, President of the State Legislature Francisco Bermúdez said that the permanent presence of the National Guard in Oaxaca was "improper, and [did] not befit a people that only desire[d] to live the life of Liberty."[43] Bermúdez asserted that the Guard was necessary only when "the imperious necessities and exceptional circumstances of the Fatherland so demanded, [but] to condemn a free man to live always with arms is the greatest sarcasm that one could impart to a people presumed to abide by democratic institutions."[44] In his ensuing farewell speech, Governor Meixueiro praised the National Guard's service, saying that the Guard had performed with loyalty and patriotism and had helped restore and maintain public order "where the bastard interests of audacious individuals had sought to alter it."[45]

Might these speeches now be read as cynical, or at least ironic, since power was being handed over from one general to another? Is this cynicism pathological? Given the state's belligerent recent past, it may have been difficult to uphold the liberal ideal that disfavored a standing army in the midst of a democracy. And where did the BME fit in, now that it was being separated from its roots? Clearly a distinction was being made between the Guard and its band, perhaps with the realization that the band could provide at least the veneer of a civilian government. The ruling class, mostly from the ranks of the military, tried hard to treat their fellow Oaxacans as citizens, but in reality they treated them more like simple inhabitants. Whether state-sponsored music could provide unity or whether it simply glossed over political, cultural, and economic inequality was a conundrum with which the government still grappled.

The Kiosk: An Acoustic Temple of Modernity

As both president of Mexico and governor of Oaxaca, Díaz, together with his administrators, made development and modernization their priorities. Curiously overlooked in most analyses of "Porfirian development," however, is the widespread construction of bandstands, or *quioscos* (kiosks) as they are called in Mexico. The Oaxacan plaza and kiosk are indispensable parts of the BME's history and mission. From the kiosk, the BME has "educated" the Oaxacan populace by exalting patriotic values and entertained them by diffusing to the people the masterworks of music, all within the confines of the plaza, where the environment reconciles nature with culture and stimulates human interaction.

If, through its 146-year history, the BME has performed in the plaza or kiosk an average of three times a week, and if as few as one hundred people have attended each of those performances, the BME has performed for more than two million people in their plaza performances alone! In order to understand the importance of this venue, we must first examine the history of the plaza in Mexico.

For thousands of years before the arrival of the Spanish, the people of Mesoamerica had gathered in outdoor public spaces that served as sites for ritual, commerce, and the performance of music.[46] Shortly after invading Mexico in the sixteenth century, the Spanish organized "villages of evangelization," or Indian communities, to attend to the religious needs of the newest converts to Catholicism. These communities were grouped around a vast space that served as a plaza mayor and a marketplace at the same time, usually on the analogous former pre-Hispanic site.[47] The square was the heart of the town and the center of community life: "Here one found the fountain and the gibbet. It was surrounded by public buildings: the church, the schools (usually placed near the church), and the town hall. . . . These buildings were usually constructed of good stone."[48] One of the final acts when formalizing the founding of these new communities was "a great Indian military parade."[49]

The plazas of Mexico's cities are located in the city center from which its principal streets radiate. The same is usually the case in Mexican pueblos, not just out of imitation or influence but also out of the logical principle of function. The plaza's New World plan reflects both Mediterranean and Mesoamerican influences, and the fusion of the two consolidates the necessary urban criteria of a clear, enclosed area of public access.

After the Spanish invasion, the Mediterranean tradition of the plaza mayor was extensively adopted in the colonies as a principle element of urban design. The buildings that demarcated the plaza, the distribution of gardens and trees, and decorative elements both symbolic and practical denoted the activities that would take place there.⁵⁰ The traditional grid pattern of the colonial Spanish American city placed the main plaza at the center of the political, religious, and social life of its inhabitants. The Spaniards knew what they were doing: constructing churches, arcades with market stalls, and government buildings on sites already dense with cultural meaning created a potent spatial hybridity.⁵¹

Humanity's social nature is made evident in the plaza, which provides a communal space in which to encounter, interact, and participate in social activities with fellow citizens. Here are concentrated the local inhabitants, street amusements, celebrations and civil acts, commercial transactions (when marketplaces are included), popular demonstrations and religious festivals, and annual fairs that not only stimulate recreation but also increase interactions with neighboring locales.⁵² Through the years, municipal governments have remodeled and rebuilt these sites as a part of urban-renewal projects, and users of these spaces have responded in various ways. The plaza remains, however, one of the truly democratic forums for public celebration (and dissent) in civil society.⁵³ This is certainly true in Oaxaca, as political protesters frequently occupy the Zócalo⁵⁴ to demonstrate. Yet the massive influx of foreign capital, the burgeoning tourist trade, and rampant Mexican consumerism have combined to restructure urban life even in the plaza. In Oaxaca, though, social activists have limited the intrusion onto the plaza of foreign corporations such as McDonald's, and the tradition of BME performances continues.⁵⁵

The most characteristic element of the plaza, kiosks are found throughout the republic, with the single exception of the Yucatán peninsula.⁵⁶ The word "kiosk" comes from the Turkish *kiuchk* (lookout), a structure that, after its adoption in Spain, maintained its "eastern" style and began to function as a small, ornate edifice within both private and public gardens.⁵⁷ In seventeenth-century England, kiosks, often in the form of stylized pagodas, became popular when the wealthy sought to replicate stylized Chinese gardens in their own gardens. In pre-Revolutionary France, pleasure gardens often featured kiosks, many of prefabricated design and available for purchase from a number of catalogs. With the French Revolution came a reinterpretation of public space; in the spirit of a democratizing society, the "new order" appropriated musical performance for itself. Soon kiosks became sites of musical performance.

It was around the kiosk, during the performance of music (often military), that citizens demonstrated their patriotism and love of music, and the kiosk became one of the great nineteenth-century monuments to republicanism in France and the United States.[58] Mass marketing of prefabricated kiosks through catalogs did not diminish the people's sentimental attachment to the structures, nor did the expanding global diffusion of the kiosk render it banal. Late in the nineteenth century, the kiosk morphed into the great pavilions of the world's expositions and fairs. Kiosks provide a venue for the social necessities of music: to entertain, to educate, and to unite.

By the end of the nineteenth century, the kiosk was a familiar sight in the plazas of Mexico's state capitals. But its presence was not limited to state capitals: kiosks arose in smaller cities and even in some pueblos. Kiosks came to occupy the central and preferred site within the public plaza. Given its central position in the plaza and the naturally occurring surrounding public, the kiosk became a "stage" for spectacle and entertainment, as it had previously in Europe and the United States. Its functions were multiple. Depending on the municipality's resources, a wide variety of entertainments took place: singers, speeches, orchestras, and bands transformed the kiosk from a simple architectural construction to a political platform, a tribunal, a salon, or a conservatory. When unoccupied by a special activity, the kiosk became a site of recreation, a place to meet for conversation, or simply a source of shade on a sunny afternoon. Thus, the kiosk became for the modern Mexican city an "indispensable part of the urban landscape."[59]

Aurality is an often-overlooked aspect of modern life. The experience of modernity is one of profound temporal and spatial displacements, of accelerated and diversified shocks, of new modes of society and experience—and it is decisively shaped by technological media.[60] In spite of the fact that modern cultures are more immersed in sound than ever before and that life in modern culture places a significant emphasis on listening to things and listening differently, modernity has been looked at and read but seldom "heard."[61] In Mexico the state used the kiosk as a widespread and prominent site of political proselytization via music, amplifying its power. In late-nineteenth-century Mexico, the kiosk became the secular liberal state's acoustic temple of modernity.[62]

Plaza and Kiosk in Oaxaca

In 1526 Charles V of Spain, initiated the distribution of *solares* (plots) to the conquistadors and other persons desiring to live in the village of Antequera. In 1529 the city center was located not at the geometric center of the city but equidistant from the village's most important physical features, the rivers Atoyac and Jalatlaco and the Cerro de Fortín. This deviation from the cardinal points in selecting Oaxaca's city center provided the most sunlight possible during the daytime hours.[63] The city developed as did other Spanish cities, with the civil government, the church, the vendors and businessmen, and the people taking up their places around the plaza.

In 1739 colonial officials placed a fountain surrounded by four marble obelisks in the plaza. Water flowed from an aqueduct north of the city center and was collected in the plaza in a veined-marble basin surrounded by four obelisks in the shape of "pyramids," with lamps on top. A pomegranate-shaped spigot of bronze filled the basin.[64] When water began to flow on 28 October 1739, the church held a celebratory procession for the entire population that left from the cathedral, and it is likely, though not verifiable, that a group of militia musicians led the procession.[65]

From 1824 to 1826 the State Congress of Oaxaca funded a project to illuminate, clean, and guard the city. The plan suggested "beautifying" the plaza by planting fig and ash trees to provide shade for the public.[66] The plan took years to implement, however, and the plaza remained a market more than anything else. On

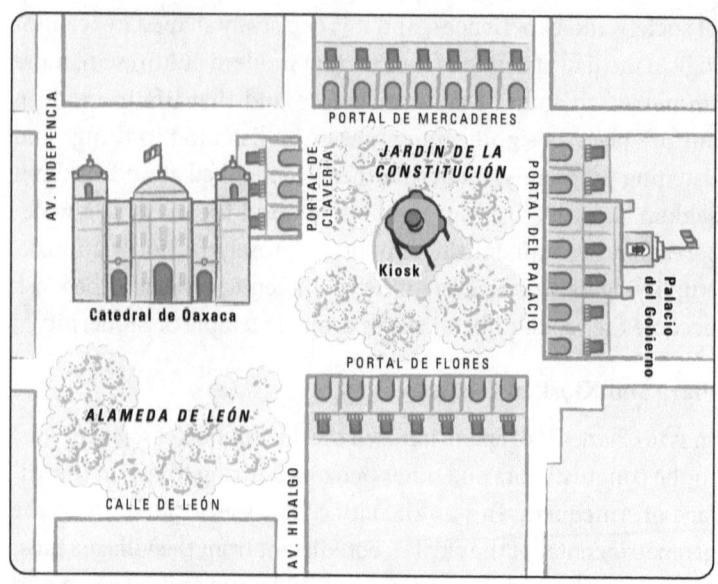

MAP 3. The Oaxaca Zócalo. Erin Greb Cartography.

6 February 1857 Juárez expanded the size of the plaza's market and again called for the planting of trees, the placement of benches, and lighting, but the trees were not planted until 1868![67] A description from 1875 reflects the organization of the current plaza: a rectangular space delimited by benches, trees, and lighting (see map 3). In 1868 Governor Félix Díaz convened a commission for the conservation and maintenance of the Plaza de Armas and Alameda. Trees were planted, the pavement was repaired, the old fountain was refurbished, and stone benches and lamp fixtures were placed around the perimeter.[68] The Plaza de Armas, a former site of military maneuvers, had been effectively converted into an urban garden.

Until 1881 the Plaza de Armas in Oaxaca remained the same, but the Porfirian preoccupation with self-image made public spaces a priority. The addition of a kiosk transformed the BME's mission at the same time that it transformed public life in the Oaxacan plaza. That year Governor Meixueiro ordered another renovation of the Plaza de Armas: the water basin was removed, and a kiosk took its place; fountains were placed in each corner; the pavement was modified to better serve new modes of transportation, and iron benches replaced the stone ones. Only the trees were saved.[69] Years later, during the tenure of governor Martín González, the kiosk was replaced with a new, more elegant, and taller kiosk.[70] The kiosk provided the venue for the always-important democratic open-air performances, and the open-ended and eclectic repertoires of military bands provided social classes other than the higher urban class with an idea of musical refinement and progress. (See fig. 7.)

Governor Mariano Jiménez (who served for five months in 1882 while Díaz attended to other public works) memorialized the remodeling of the Plaza in his *Memorias Administrativas* from 1882:

> And finally, in the Plaza de Armas, situated in front of the State Government Palace, previously deserted and abandoned, a picturesque garden has been planted, and in whose center a svelte kiosk was raised that stands out like a *figura aérea* [aerial figure] where the military musicians, today so outstanding, are protected by the acoustic box, and give magnificent serenades that present their harmonious sounds. Thanks to the initiative of General Francisco Meixueiro, we have this improvement that was generously protected and has been moved forward by the meritorious caudillo of the Republican troops, General Díaz, and we are grateful to present it, now concluded, to the service of the public, . . . which seems to have been well accepted by our society and looked upon with general applause.[71]

Although Jiménez credited Meixueiro with initiating the project that included the remodeling of the plaza and the construction of the kiosk, Meixueiro's 1881 report on public improvement only listed paving and cobblestoning of the streets around the Plaza and the

FIG. 7. The present-day Oaxaca kiosk. Courtesy of Adam T. Beauchamp.

Palacio Municipal. Had Meixueiro also noted the importance of the BME in the daily lives of his citizens? Or had the governor noticed an increase in public acclaim that might be considered politically useful?

The present-day form of the BME began to emerge after the French Intervention in 1868 with the creation of the position of director, which was first filled by a series of military band directors. Although still wracked by economic problems, the state government, no longer plagued by foreign invasion if not completely free of domestic civil disturbances, could focus some of its resources toward a state band and its performance site in the city's central plaza. Two important institutions were now in place: a director to bring order and progress to the organization and a stage from which the ideals of the consolidating liberal state could be musically diffused. We now examine Oaxaca during the continuing presidential terms of Porfirio Díaz, who until the Revolution, at least for a portion of the population, remained a hero worthy of inclusion in the state pantheon.

4 The BME during the Porfiriato and the Mexican Revolution

> The State must teach scholarship, industry, and patriotism.
>
> Porfirio Díaz, quoted in Mrs. Alec Tweedie, *Porfirio Diaz, Seven Times President of Mexico*

During the presidency of Porfirio Díaz (served 1876–1910; see fig. 8), the federal and state governments in Mexico began to use modern communication and transportation technologies, including musical performance, to their political advantage. The Oaxacan governors' words and actions revealed their awareness of the BME's growing importance as a tool of the state—they understood its function as a catalyst for political and cultural development.

The BME and the Governors

In 1882 Díaz raised the BME's budget to $6,500, and the following year he named José María Velasco as the band's director. Velasco remained in the position until 1892, and during his nine-year tenure increased the band's visibility and notoriety, most notably by infusing the band's repertoire with European music and adopting the works of various Mexican composers.[1] Subsequent governors also raised the band's budget. For example, in 1884 Governor Jiménez (serving his second term from 1883 to 1884) raised it to $8,000, and

FIG. 8. Porfirio Díaz. Courtesy of Library of Congress.

in 1893 Governor Gregorio Chávez (served 1890–1894) raised it to $9,000.²

In 1885 Governor Luis Mier y Terán (serving his second term from 1886 to 1887) quartered an artillery battalion, including musicians, in the ex-convent of Santo Domingo, as the only active detail of the still-dissolved National Guard. The battalion served only to guard the barracks in Santo Domingo and other local fortifications, or as escorts accompanying convoys when necessary. In his *Memorias Administrativas*, Mier y Terán wrote:

> In said Artillery Battalion, the band or the military music,[3] composed of its thirty-two members, will provide their services until further orders, remaining under the immediate orders of a director; said individuals, following special stipulations of their contract, pertain also to the National Guard and are subject to the Ordinance and other dispositions of the War Branch. The government celebrated with the Band a contract advantageous for the treasury and for the term of two years . . . the annual budget for the Band is $7,100, including the lighting for the evening serenades.[4]

Mier y Terán applied $900 remaining from the budgeted $8,000 to organize a third National Guard band in the state, "as had been done in Tehuantepec."[5]

The governor then took the opportunity to describe the previous day's Independence Day festivities. The state celebrated newly inaugurated public works and material improvements as part of the festivities, including a new night school, a monument to General Vicente Guerrero in Cuilapan, a new operating room in the General Hospital, and printing and shoemaking workshops in the Escuela de Artes y Oficios (School of Arts and Trades). In addition, the state distributed clothing to patients in the General Hospital, and a complete workshop was given in usufruct to poor artisans specially selected by the Society of Artisans.[6]

The following year, Governor Albino Zertuche (served 1888–1890) paved the four streets that give forth from the central plaza with *cantera*, a stone of volcanic tuff indigenous to Oaxaca. In his *Memorias Administrativas*, Zertuche decreed that state-sanctioned "official acts and festivities" were required by law to be accompanied by music and noted that the quality of the music "mark[ed] the people's culture."[7] The governor awarded the BME a new contract and pay raise, with the aim of increasing its size and improving the players' instruments and competency. He also detailed for the first time in the available historical record the composition and instrumentation of what he referred to as the "música militar del estado" (state military music),[8] including the director, José María Velasco, a roll of forty musicians, and a list of their instruments:

5 clarinets
6 saxophones
4 *pistónes*
4 bass horns
1 trombone
3 baritone horns
2 bugles
2 trumpets
4 alto horns
1 *requinto*
1 *octavina*
Percussion: bass drum, snare drum, cymbals, *gira*[9]

In July 1892 Second Lieutenant Gabriel Garzón of the Oaxaca National Guard replaced Velasco as director of the BME and remained director until April 1897.[10] Garzón is the only nineteenth-century BME director with a personnel file in the Archivo Histórico de la Secretaría de la Defensa Nacional in Mexico City. Born in Oaxaca in 1861 to a military family, he entered military service as a volunteer in the 23rd Infantry Battalion in Veracruz in 1887. Classified as a *soldado músico* (soldier musician), Garzón received a salary, uniform, and medical assistance for himself and his dependents. Within a year, Garzón made sergeant first class, and five months later he was commissioned as a second lieutenant.[11]

Garzón's personnel file contains no mention of service in Oaxaca, although it does contain records of his later service as music director in Puebla and Veracruz, as well as in Monterrey from 1903 until his death in 1906. Although reports depict Garzón as an unexceptional soldier, his musical aptitude, ability to instruct his musicians, and technique as director were lauded. For example, in Veracruz in 1902 a superior wrote that Garzón had "good primary instruction and [was] well instructed in his profession" and that "he [had] been musical director in different corps."

Garzón was decorated for his service in the Yucatán campaigns of 1901–1902 for combat "against the rebel Mayan Indians." Late in his life, problems with alcohol plagued the director. He served time in the brig for fighting with a gendarme, whom Garzón beat rather severely, and later he served house arrest for unknown reasons. An inventory made after his death showed that among the personal articles returned to Adela Cossa de Garzón, his wife of fifteen years, was Garzón's "pistón en su estuche y sordina" (trumpet in its case and mute).

During his tenure as director, Garzón led the BME at some of its most famous performances, including the inauguration of the Ferrocarril Mexicano del Sur (Mexican Southern Railroad) on 12 November 1892, and the commemoration of a statue of Benito Juárez in the Paseo del Llano de Guadalupe (today known as Paseo Juárez or "El llano") on 15 September 1894. At the latter performance, the BME participated in many of the musical selections offered to the public that day, including the "Marcha fúnebre Benito Juárez" ("Benito Juárez Funeral March").[12]

The funeral march, an example of a nonmilitary type of march music, is traceable in the Western musical tradition to at least 1694, when the English composer Henry Purcell wrote funeral music for Queen Mary of England. The genre expanded the usual march form, deviating from the military version, and may include the muffled drums of a funeral cortege, fugal development, and an expressive coda. The funeral march also has military origins through the appearance of the "march with trio" and its later incorporation into larger forms. Changes in nineteenth-century aesthetics and the rise of militarism and nationalism greatly increased the genre's richness of meaning.[13]

Accompanying funeral processions is an important historical band function. In his nineteenth-century manual for French military music, Georges Kastner wrote, "Certain instruments, such as the brass; certain techniques of orchestration, such as muffled drums; and the addition of the tam-tam on which one strikes at an interval an isolated blow, all contribute to the proper character" of the funeral march.[14] However, after the burial a definite change in tone may occur, from muted to expressive, and from solemn to joyous, as it did in the BME's accompaniment of Juárez's funeral described in the previous chapter.

Wind bands performed funeral music because of the need for high volume in the outdoor settings of funeral processions and burials. European composers such as Meyerbeer, Wagner, Dvořák, Mozart, Beethoven, and Donizetti all composed in the form, and all are represented in the BME's archive of arrangements and sheet music.[15] Trumpets and fanfares, and by extension the entire brass section, "are a means of expressing [both] the terror and deliverance of death."[16]

Juárez's funeral illuminates the "repertoire of religious theatricality" used to sanctify the secular.[17] It included music, eulogies, and patriotic panegyrics to display Mexico's material progress and to define social relations between government and governed, just as in colonial times.[18]

The Tenure of Germán Canseco, 1897–1916 and 1924–1928

Germán Canseco was born in Ejutla de Crespo, south of Oaxaca City, in 1867.[19] He began his musical studies with Bartolo Medina, the church organist and musical director in Ejutla. After moving to Oaxaca City, Canseco was a member of the First Auxiliary Army Battalion and also played flute in the BME when it was still known as the Banda de Música Militar. In 1891, Canseco moved to Mexico City and enrolled in the Conservatorio Nacional de Música de México.[20] There he joined the Banda Militar del Batallón de Zapadores (Sappers Battalion Military Band), with which he played at the Columbian Exposition in Chicago in 1893. That band also gave concerts in other American cities and received honors in St. Louis and Washington. In 1897, after returning to Oaxaca, Canseco was named director of the BME. During his tenure, he expanded the number of musicians in the band and bestowed on it an extensive repertoire and archive that he had brought with him from his travels in Germany.[21]

Canseco brought national and international experience to the position. "His arms made art," wrote Guillermo Rosas Solaegui,[22] who also praised Canseco for his work ethic, perseverance in the face of health problems, and instillation of rigid discipline in the BME. The musicians rehearsed in the ex-convent of Santo Domingo, still being used as an army barracks, from 9:00 a.m. until 2:00 p.m. every day except Sundays and national holidays. New members were obligated to practice for an additional two hours, from 6:00 a.m. until 8:00 a.m. After a lunch break, the musicians returned for section rehearsals. All breaks and rehearsals were expressly defined in the band's regulations, and Canseco awaited the musicians at the door five minutes before each rehearsal.[23]

Serenatas were held in the Jardín de la Constitución every Tuesday and Thursday evening from 8:00 until 11:00. For the dominicales, the band often descended from the kiosk to perform under the shade of nearby laurel trees, playing from 11:00 a.m. until 2:00 p.m. Customary twenty-minute intermissions allowed the band members to visit with their families and friends or just to sit and relax. Canseco tapped his baton on his music stand three times to signal the musicians to ascend the bandstand for the second half of the performance. Military bands from the Tenth Regiment and the Eighth Battalion performed on Monday, Wednesday, and Friday evenings. In total, music sounded in the plaza six times a week.

Oaxacans of all social strata met at the plaza for the evening serenades, arriving punctually in their finest attire. On Sunday mornings when the BME played outside the kiosk on the plaza

FIG. 9. The BME at the end of the nineteenth century. Courtesy of Archivo de la Banda de Música del Estado de Oaxaca.

grounds, seats were rented to the public for 10 centavos, and canopies were positioned to protect the musicians from the strong Oaxacan sun. Adolescents circled the plaza, seeking respite from parental supervision and casting longing looks at one another. The police made sure that no other noises or sounds interfered with the performance, especially those of children playing and yelling.[24] At the time, the plaza was still relatively free of the sounds of automobile traffic, radios and loudspeakers, and protests that today force the BME to compete with the din of a modern city.

Under Canseco, the band members were issued three formal uniforms: *gala* (formal), *media-gala* (semi-formal), and *concierto* (concert). They also received three other uniforms: two each of *dril con gorra* (drill with cap) for daily performances and one of *lino de blanco* (white linen) with gold buttons and a red-trimmed *kepi* for summer performances. (See fig. 9.) The director's uniform included four gold braids as insignia; the subdirector's, three; the *músico mayor*'s (chief musician's), two; and the soloists', one. The musicians were only permitted to wear the uniforms during official performances.[25]

From 1883 to 1893, the BME budget averaged approximately $8,000 per year, with the highest allocation being $9,100 in 1893. The 1901 budget of $6,499.45 included the director's salary, pay for forty military musicians, and lighting for the serenatas. This amount represented 7.7 percent of the War Branch budget and 0.7 percent of the entire state budget.[26]

In 1902 the director received a salary of six pesos per day; the subdirector, three pesos per day; the músico mayor, two pesos and fifty centavos; and soloists, one peso and twenty-five centavos. Other musicians received a daily salary of thirty-seven centavos.[27]

Instrumentation and Repertoire under Canseco

The 1902 *Memorias Administrativas* of Governor Miguel Bolaños Cacho (first term, January–June 1902) include inventories for the BME's instruments and sheet music.[28] Document No. 28 is a "manifest of the instruments that the State Music has, which were purchased in 1900 from the [music] house of Gautrot, Ainé & Cia. [and also from] the notions store of Don Tereso Villasante." The list included:

1 ebony piccolo of six keys with case and swab (D-flat)
2 ebony flutes "*Tulón*," of twelve keys with cases and swabs (C-natural)
1 Boehm ebony oboe with case, swab, and four reeds (C-natural)
1 Boehm oboe with case, swab, and four reeds (C-natural)
1 ebony *requinto* of fifteen keys and two rings, with swab and six reeds (E-flat)
2 ebony Boehm clarinets, model "Excelsior," with cases, swabs, and six reeds each (B-flat)
6 ebony clarinets of fifteen keys and two rings, with cases, swabs, and six reeds each (B-flat)

1 soprano saxophone with four reeds (B-flat)
1 alto saxophone with four reeds (E-flat)
1 tenor saxophone with four reeds (B-flat)
1 baritone saxophone with four reeds (E-flat)
1 *pistón* for soloist, engraved, of three tones with wooden, leather-lined case (B-flat)
2 pistones "Eco," of three tones, with mutes and cases (B-flat)
1 contralto bugle, model "Excelsior" (B-flat)
2 trumpets, "Excelsior," superior class (F and E-flat)
1 [French?] horn, "Excelsior," of five tones (E-flat)
3 alto saxophone horns, "Excelsior" (E-flat)
3 trombones, "Excelsior" (E-flat)
1 bass trombone of four valves, "Excelsior," superior class (C and B-flat)
2 tenor baritones, "Excelsior" (C and B-flat)
1 small bass of four valves, "Excelsior" (B-flat)
2 contrabasses, "Excelsior," of four valves (F and E-flat)
2 contrabasses, "Excelsior," of four valves (C and B-flat)
1 set of large and fine timbales with two tripods and two drumsticks[29]
1 fine brass snare drum, with carrying case of patent leather and two drumsticks
1 fine brass bass drum with carrying case of patent leather and two drumsticks
1 pair of large cymbals, Turkish, superior class
2 pairs of ebony castanets
1 pair of fine large tambourines

Document No. 29 detailed the BME's sheet-music inventory:

5 *zarzuelas*
27 overtures
47 fantasies
59 marches and *pasos dobles*[30]
34 waltzes
9 *mazurkas*

2 *schottisches*[31]
21 diverse pieces
13 diverse pieces for piano[32]

Also purchased by the government from an unidentified vendor in 1902 were the following:

Liszt's *Second Hungarian Rhapsody*
Strauss's "Treasure Waltz"
Waldteufel's "Skater's Waltz"
Roig's fandango "Echoes of the Soul"

Among the composers that appear in the 1902 sheet-music inventory are John Philip Sousa, Mozart, Johann Strauss, Beethoven, Wagner, and Verdi. Mexican airs and Spanish dances compete with mazurkas and schottisches. Airs from the Isthmus are listed alongside works by Mexican composers like Juventino Rosas (1868–1894). The sheet music and instrument inventories reveal powerful transnational forces at work upon the BME and other Porfirian-era wind bands. The former contain themes from European antiquity and modernity, of heroic military exploits, of national memories, and of sometimes hidden, sometimes conspicuously highlighted, indigenous histories. The latter, meanwhile, are examples of the transition from handcrafted, artisanal instruments to mechanically and industrially manufactured consumer products, revealing Janissary influences and the hand of New World and Iberian percussion traditions, as well as those of Western Europe. Both sheet music and instruments speak to the increased global penetration of Mexico.

Sheet music and thousands of musical manuscripts had been imported, distributed, copied, and even printed in Mexico since the early colonial period, and Mexico's musical heritage was strongly influenced by Renaissance and Baroque European music. The diffusion of European musical works greatly influenced band repertoires in Mexico. Sheet music shipped easily around the world, providing standardized notation, but the interpretation of the works remained the prerogative of individual arrangers or conductors. Music merchants sold arrangements of classical European works for bands, as well as versions for piano that could then be arranged for band instrument sections.

German music publishers, including Wagner y Levien, which was founded in 1851, dominated the Mexican market and included in their catalogs works by Mexican composers. Almost all sheet music sold in Mexico during the nineteenth century came from Germany.[33] Wagner y Levien used catalogs to sell musical instruments and sheet music. Their first catalog, published in 1886, included "instruments for military bands and for orchestra," along with "accessories for all instruments and instrumentation manuals."[34] The catalog also included method books and *solfeggio*.[35] An 1897 catalog shows that the price for most sheet music was 25 centavos.[36] In 1912 the firm announced the opening of branches in Puebla, Guadalajara, and Monterrey. Wagner y Levien invoices appear in various Oaxacan archives.[37] The publication of salon music such as waltzes, polkas, danzas, *habaneras*, and *canciones* was a major part of Wagner y Levien's business. Between 1870 and 1900, Wagner y Levien catalogs featured more than one hundred of these song styles by Mexican composers. Most sheet music was for piano, which provided the basis for band arrangements.[38]

The appearance of compositions by Juventino Rosas in the 1902 inventory, as well as the preponderance of waltzes and other waltz-derived dance forms, suggests that we should take a moment to explore the history of the waltz in Mexico, the better to understand the form's importance in the Mexican band repertoire. The waltz, a dance in triple meter, became the most popular ballroom dance of the nineteenth century both in Europe and the Americas. While the origins of the waltz are obscure, it probably derives its name from German or Latin roots meaning "to turn" or "to rotate." The waltz's gliding and whirling movements, so different from those of the stately minuet, were probably what made the former so popular, but the close embrace of the dancing couple alarmed a conservative society concerned with females' purported licentiousness. Eighteenth-century accounts of the waltz's popularity are easily found, but by the early nineteenth century its popularity was on the wane in England and France. A century of popularity is, however, a long life for any musical form, and the waltz continued to be popular in dance halls, where dance bands picked it up. Nineteenth-century Austrian composers, particularly Johann Strauss Jr., gave new life to the waltz.[39]

After a ship from Lima arrived in San Salvador (the capital of present day El Salvador) in 1810, the ship's master became embroiled in a latter-day Inquisition when authorities in Mexico City received complaints that he had introduced a "sinful, obscene, and dishonest French dance called the waltz."[40] The complainant, a native of the Canary Islands in the service of the Royal Hacienda, asserted that "the cursed seed was sown in souls both innocent and malicious [and that] the introduction of the song-and-dance form was a contagion that could only be eliminated with the tribunal's efforts."[41] But Mexican musicologist Gabriel Saldívar believes that the waltz was introduced some time before this complaint and that the complainant's judgment was exaggerated. Saldívar considers the waltz the "most innocent" of dances.[42] Aesthetic judgments aside, there is no disputing that the waltz became one of Mexico's most popular imported dance forms. Mexican composers such as Juventino Rosas made it their own, composing some of the world's most memorable waltzes.

In the 1890s Rosas's waltz became a standard for bands in New Orleans. Jazz historian Jack Stewart chronicles the song's publishing history in the United States and believes that while it may have been part of the Mexican Eighth Cavalry Band's repertoire during the New Orleans Cotton Centennial in 1884, it was probably introduced to New Orleans audiences afterward, when Rosas appeared in the city as part of another Mexican band. This latter appearance corresponds with historian and musicologist Helmut Bremmer's assertion that Rosas did in fact return to New Orleans with his own band, the Orquesta Típica Mexicana. According to Stewart, several Mexican bands visited and resided in New Orleans over a thirty-five-year period after the Centennial. The Junius Hart Music Company of 1001 Canal Street, New Orleans, published "Sobre las olas" in 1889, almost simultaneously with the Mexican version. The Junius Hart Music Company also published an extensive series of Mexican musical transcriptions, including sixty-three transcriptions for piano from the Eighth Cavalry Band's repertoire.[43]

Rosas was a full-blooded Otomi Indian who, after leaving his family's wandering string band, traveled with an opera company, as well as with a Mexican Eighth Regiment Cavalry band on its tour of the United States. Rosas received no tangible remuneration for the song's publication in 1891 and died in Cuba an indigent itinerant musician. American audiences would recognize "Sobre las olas" as a staple on carousels everywhere. Mario Lanza sang the English-language version, renamed "The Loveliest Night of the Year," in the 1951 film *The Great Caruso.*

The waltz's popularity flourished during both the French Intervention and the Porfiriato. During the latter period, Mexican composers, including some Oaxacans, cultivated the song form. The BME music archives contain more than 150 waltzes by composers from around the world, including many by Mexican and Oaxacan composers. Rarely does a serenata or dominical fail to include a waltz. The waltz in Mexico, despite colonial concerns that its risqué nature would lead to inappropriate behavior between the sexes, actually diverges from that historically Western conception and is often used for formal, ceremonial, and even somber occasions. For example, at modern *quinceañeras*[44] on the Isthmus of Tehuantepec in Oaxaca, the waltz is at once celebratory and solemn when played to introduce the teenage girl being fêted.

The BME before the Revolution

During his terms as governor of Oaxaca (1902–1911), Emilio Pimentel, himself a pianist and composer, supported the BME as generously as the government's economic situation permitted. Francie Chassen-López notes Pimentel's inauguration as the historical moment in which the guard changed in Oaxaca, from Díaz's loyal military comrades to civilian technocrats. The change may have propelled the BME further along its trajectory toward civilian status.[45]

In 1906 Pimentel established a contract with Canseco, authorized an increase in the number of musicians to thirty-eight, imported new instruments from Germany, raised musicians' salaries, and added to the sheet-music inventory. The careful reader will also note that "increasing" the number of musicians to thirty-eight appears actually to have been a diminution. The BME is an organically composed group that even today, with band size mandated by law, fluctuates in size. Iturribarría writes that eighty-six musicians played for the BME during Pimentel's tenure; I was unable to corroborate that number.[46]

A landmark in Oaxaca's civil religious calendar took place on 21 March 1906, when the state celebrated the centennial of Benito Juárez's birth. A monument and statue were placed on Cerro de Fortín (Fortín Hill), overlooking Oaxaca City. The program celebrating the centennial of Juárez's birth was a sensory feast: cannons were fired, bells rang, and the BME performed along with the National Guard's various *bandas de guerra* (drum and bugle corps). The *rurales* (President Díaz's own rural constabulary), the BME, and a vast number of the city's inhabitants followed the governor's contingent in what the periodicals described as a nearly sacred procession.[47]

Upon arriving at the foot of the Cerro de Fortín, the BME intoned the "Zaragoza March." The committee ascended the precipitous stairway to the summit, where the monument and statue were covered in a great Mexican flag; floral bouquets and garlands surrounded the statue's base. "Patriotic fervor" and "solemnity" characterized the Oaxacan people's demeanor that day, and the BME performed during a special program:

"Gran fantasia" from *El Cid*, by Massenet
Reading and dedication of the new statue

Mexican national anthem, performed by the BME at the moment of unveiling

A chorus of one hundred school children singing "Himno a Juárez" ("Juárez Hymn") by Cipriano Pérez Serna

Speech

March from *Tannhäuser*, by Wagner

Refrain of the national anthem, performed by the BME and children's chorus

The band's day did not end there, however; the festivities continued later at the newly renovated ICA. At the ICA's Patio of Honor, the BME performed the overtures from *Tannhäuser* and Rossini's *William Tell*, along with "Sobre las olas."[48]

Pimentel's *Memorias Administrativas*, presented to Congress in 1907, used the complete name "Banda de Música del Estado" for the first time, although the BME remained part of the National Guard. Constabularies increasingly replaced the military's role in civilian life; the delineation in functions was evidenced by the change in name of the "War Branch" to the "War and Public Security Branch." That year Pimentel also wrote:

> In the period of time that this memoir comprises, nothing extraordinary has occurred that would affect the National Guard, and it only seems appropriate to mention that in virtue of the fact that the contract for services that the Banda de Música del Estado has celebrated, it had to be awarded a new one in which the number of personnel is raised and their salaries increased, so that the costs of the cited band are a quantity of $15,479.90 annually, a sum that is not exaggerated given the progress that day to day this institution achieves in the services with which it is charged.[49]

Referring for the first time to the merits of Canseco's direction and the likely positive disposition, discipline, and advancements that the band had made during his tenure, Pimentel continued the tradition of governors' reporting on the BME in their annual administrative memories.⁵⁰

Traveling Band

The BME's presence throughout the state of Oaxaca increased under Pimentel. In 1907 the band accompanied President Díaz to Tehuantepec for the inauguration of the Tehuantepec National Railroad, marking the culmination of a centuries-old vision to link the Pacific and Atlantic Oceans. The project converted the Isthmus into a nexus of Mexican national development and international trade and economics, but, like other developmental plans for the state of Oaxaca conceived during the Porfiriato, it failed as an economic panacea: the Isthmus was almost immediately supplanted by the Panama Canal. In the national imagination, however, the Tehuantepec railroad loomed large, and its dedication required a soundtrack worthy of international attention. In January 1907 President Díaz, Governor Pimentel, members of the Oaxacan congress, students from the ICA, affiliates of the Escuela Normal Superior (a degree-granting teacher-training school), and the thirty-eight members of the band took a three-day train trip to Tehuantepec for the railroad's inauguration. The band provided special musical selections for the occasion, playing "a brilliant role" in the festivities.⁵¹

Francisco I. Madero visited Oaxaca during his presidential campaign as candidate of the Antireelectionist Party. After his arrival on 4 December 1909 he attended a meeting in a movie theater. His supporters had hoped to meet at the Juárez monument on Fortín Hill the following day, but when they showed up, the police refused them access, citing failure to obtain the correct permission.⁵² While campaigning, Madero employed civil-religious and patriotic trappings, including the presence of bands at his whistle stops. Historian Alan Knight writes that, even absent a "revolution" at some campaign stops, "at least [the rallies] could be done with style: a band was assembled, a national flag procured from the municipal palace, and [the supporters] marched through the streets to the sound of patriotic music, 'thus provoking unlimited enthusiasm . . .

with deafening hurrahs going up.'" The next day surely featured more bells, bands, and delirious enthusiasm.⁵³

According to Rosas Solaegui, in 1912 the BME received an opportunity to perform in the United States when an American millionaire, identified in the archives only as "Mr. Brill," entered into contract negotiations with Oaxacan governor Benito Juárez to provide the band with transport to Los Angeles, among other U.S. cities. Intending to use the BME as a tool to foster better relations between the two nations, Brill also offered the band members two months' pay while they traveled. On the day that the contract was to be signed, however, Brill suffered a heart attack and died. Dreams of the foreign tour died with the millionaire.⁵⁴

The BME played in the Alameda Central in Mexico City in 1913, alternating musical selections with the Banda de la República (Band of the Republic) and the Mexico City Banda de la Policía (Police Band), whose conductor was the renowned Velino M. Preza. A large crowd that had taken note of the ample publicity in local newspapers leading up to the performance attended the event. According to unidentified witnesses, Preza attempted to convince some of the Oaxacan musicians to defect to his band, an act that caused Canseco no small degree of displeasure. Subdirector Juan Luís (last name unknown), an excellent oboist, did, however, leave the BME for the Banda de la República, possibly defecting for the sake of greater financial reward, to advance his professional career, or simply to perform for a larger, more cosmopolitan audience.⁵⁵ During that same visit to Mexico City, the BME played in the Salon Rojo (Red Hall), an elegant cinema and dining hall, again to much popular and critical acclaim. At the conclusion of the performance, the audience showered the BME with gold coins.⁵⁶

But can reviewers of a state musical corporation criticize it without repercussions? As shown below, acclaim was not the only response the BME ever received: when faced with problems that led to a deterioration of its musicians' skills, it was roundly criticized in the hope that it could recapture its prestige. Preza's attempts to coax musicians away from the BME also belied any "friendly" competition between the bands, and real competition might have generated supportive, rather than critical, reviews.

The BME during the Revolution

A program for Independence Day 1914 appears in the Revolution-era archives. The BME performed the overture to *Ruy Blas*, a composition by Felix Mendelssohn written for a Victor Hugo drama, as well as a fantasia based upon the 1877 opera *Le Timbre d'argent* by Camille Saint-Saëns. The program called for the BME to play the "Dia de bodas" ("Wedding Day") march, attributed in the program to composer Edvard Grieg, perhaps referring to that composer's lyric piece for piano entitled "Wedding Day at Troldhaugen." The program ended with the Mexican national anthem.[57] The eclectic musical program demonstrates Canseco's familiarity with international music and composers, as well as the continual hybrid nature of the BME's repertoire.

The BME played a three-hour serenata on 15 September. Following the performance, the BME joined with other "military bands" and paraded through the city's "profusely illuminated" streets. Early the next morning, the bands paraded again. When the parade paused at a statue of Juárez, a program took place, featuring a prose reading, a speech, a poetry reading by a third grader, and the laying of flowers.[58]

That afternoon, a young woman dressed to represent "América" sang the national anthem at the Government Palace. From 4:00 p.m. to 6:00 p.m., a sports exhibition was held featuring baseball, boxing, jiu-jitsu, soccer, and a game of capture-the-flag.[59] The BME accompanied the entire event with unspecified selections. At 9:00 p.m. at the "Porfirio Díaz" market in the city center, the city prefecture held a *baile popular* (popular dance). Fittingly, the BME held center stage from 8:00 p.m. until midnight with another serenata. During an intermission at 10:00 p.m., a fireworks display was launched from the cathedral atrium. The day's program also included the unveiling of new public works, including street improvements.[60]

Disagreements between the state of Oaxaca and those loyal to Mexican president General Venustiano Carranza led a power base of Oaxacan locals to decree the state sovereign and free of federal control, and those in power ended relations with Carranza's Constitutionalist regime on 3 June 1915.⁶¹ The sovereignty movement caused serious economic problems for the state; as a result, in March 1916 Constitutionalist forces occupied the capital city of Oaxaca and began to reorganize the state's government. Sovereignty forces, led by Félix Díaz, were put down, as were other forces in Oaxaca loyal to such revolutionary leaders as Emiliano Zapata and General Francisco (Pancho) Villa. The fight continued until 1919. Finally, in 1920, in agreement with the Plan de Agua Prieta, Oaxaca was reincorporated into the Constitutionalist order.

In 1916, General Jesús Agustín Castro, governor and military commander of the State of Oaxaca, utilized the "extraordinary faculties" granted him by the legislature to increase the size of the BME—to which he now referred as "La Música Constitucionalista del Estado" (The Constitutionalist Music of the State)—to eighty members, but the increase did not last long.⁶² While the band remained at eighty strong for fiscal year 1917, in 1920, the next year for which figures are available, the size of the band had shrunk to forty-nine musicians plus the director.⁶³

The year 1916 was also the first time in which the BME budget was included in the Ramo de Gobernación (Government Branch) budget rather than the War Branch. Extensive review of official governmental documents has failed to uncover any explanation for the shift. One wonders if the "Armed Revolution" and the Oaxacan sovereignty movement had forever altered the military role of the BME. Government officials may have realized that sequestering the BME within a civilian dependency would make it less likely to become a tool in the hands of opposition forces. The records do indicate the continued presence of bandas de guerra, drum majors, and similar military musical corps within the War Branch. For the first time in the historical record, however, the BME was, fiscally at least, separated from its military roots.⁶⁴

In 1921 governor Manuel García Vigil reorganized his Department of State in an effort to streamline the "great variety of sections," which included elections, internal relations, public health, and many others.⁶⁵ The proliferation of departments had greatly complicated the Department of State's duties. The urban and rural police forces, General Police Command, Inspector's Branches, Commissary, and the BME were placed under the Department of Police and Public Security. The director of the BME now answered to the Inspector General of the Police, and at times the BME would even be referred to as the Banda de la Policía (Police Band).⁶⁶

During this period, the director of the BME was directly subordinate to the Inspector General of the Police. The BME remained within the Executive Branch, Police and Security section, until 1937, when for unknown reasons it was handed off again, this time to the municipality of Oaxaca, where it remained until 1947. The municipal period is discussed below.

The chain of command for this period therefore meant that the governor sent requests for BME performances to the inspector general, who in turn sent the request to the director. For example, when interim governor Genaro V. Vásquez saw the need to find an appropriate rehearsal site for the BME in the former Convent of San José, he sent the orders to the Inspector General of the Police, Leopold G. Neri. The ex-convent already served as a military barracks, and using the site for the band would save the government the cost of renting a private rehearsal hall.⁶⁷ In December 1926, after maintenance activities had taken place (including repairing the floors and door, whitewashing the walls, and installing electrical connections), the BME began to practice at San José.⁶⁸

Germán Canseco served as the BME's director until 31 August 1915, when he stepped down for health reasons. Daniel Baltazar accepted the directorship and remained there until 1924, when Canseco returned to the BME. In 1920 Canseco had suffered life-threatening injuries when he fell from a train in Mexico City, fracturing his skull and shattering the bones in his right foot. He underwent a delicate operation to repair his skull and remove bone splinters from his foot.⁶⁹ Although the prognosis was not good, Canseco recovered and returned to direct the band in 1924, remaining until his retirement in 1929.

The Artist as Laborer in the Socialist State I

By 1920, local newspaper reports regularly covered the BME's activities. On 12 February 1921 it was reported that the BME's personnel had received a pay raise, freeing the "modest" musicians from the mundane preoccupation of eking out an existence so that they could further their artistic aims.⁷⁰ With the new salaries ostensibly liberating the musicians from such non-artistic concerns as "work," the BME was able to dedicate more time to twice-daily rehearsals, scheduled from 9:00 a.m. until 1:00 p.m. and beginning again at 4:00 p.m. The reporter expressed hope that the BME would now be able to return to the "enviable heights they [had] attained in previous times" and that they would "conquer new laurels."⁷¹

The conflict between "artist" and "laborer" seems to have intensified after the Revolution (the role of the BME's art in the new socialist state is discussed below); in fact, the state still wrestles with the difficulty of separating the artistic from the mundane when musicians are both artists and civil-service employees. A federal project scheduled for 1921 reorganized all military bands at the state level in order to improve their conditions and benefit the musicians. In states where no band existed, one was created. Supporters hoped that the federal project would lead to "the perfection of the art of music."⁷²

A New Decade and Madero's Entry into the Pantheon

An anonymous 1920 article in *El Mercurio* alluded to a loss of prestige suffered under Baltazar's direction of the BME. A rift between Governor Jesús Acevedo and Baltazar led to a demonstration of support by the musicians for their director, and the unidentified reporter attributed the rumors about Baltazar's tenuous position to "some individual of low prestige who enjoyed the insinuation of intrigue within the band." Baltazar allegedly treated his charges harshly, but some musicians sought to give the lie to the reports of intrigue by stressing their "great appreciation" for Baltazar and his affable demeanor. The governor intervened, perhaps realizing the BME's popularity, stating that "no such accusations about Baltazar existed" and that the director enjoyed the governor's complete confidence. The episode at once demonstrated solidarity and the potential for factionalism within the BME.[73]

In February 1921 Baltazar enriched the band's repertoire when he acquired some "modern pieces" meant for performance at the following Sunday's matinee.[74] The report did not identify the new pieces, but published programs from the time contain performances of 1920s-style pieces such as foxtrots, a recently imported North American dance form.[75] Earlier, *El Mercurio* had reported that the BME was to debut a new one-step entitled "El ósculo" ("The Kiss").[76] Programs from the same period also reflect the inclusion of other "Latin" selections such as danzones and the paso doble; over the years, such pieces have become some of the BME's most popular selections.[77] For example, the program for Sunday, 23 January 1921, included a paso doble, a waltz, assorted other dances, a one-step, a march, and selections from Wagner's *Lohengrin* and *The Ring*.[78] Governor Vásquez wrote a slim tome on Oaxacan popular music in which he describes indigenous musicians as "making fun of the wicked generation of the 'Fox' and of the 'Jazz Band.'" For Vásquez, the Indians' music had "the soft aroma of the mountains, healthy and chaste."[79] As a "socialist" governor, did Vásquez regard jazz as bourgeois or decadent? As a nationalist, did he regard it as "Yankee"? The continual expansion of the BME's repertoire speaks to the worldwide popularity of new forms such as jazz, and Vásquez's response alludes to the conflict he faced in trying to mediate the popular cultural repertoire.[80]

Newspaper reports also permit a glimpse of the BME's "religious" performance schedule. In January 1921 the BME was matched against a military band in a competition. Subsequently, it performed for two days during Oaxaca's Carnival celebration and shared duties with another band on Lenten Fridays.[81] So great was public demand for holiday music during Lenten Fridays that the city's chief of operations ordered the military Banda del Estado Mayor to play along with the BME in the Paseo Juárez "to better animate these pleasant mornings."[82] These performances attest to the imperfect separation between—and, in fact, the inseparable nature of—church and state, more than half a century after the Reform, and perhaps witness even more keenly to Catholicism's indelible marking on Mexican culture.

On 22 February 1921 the BME provided music for the commemoration of the eighth anniversary of the assassination of Francisco Madero.[83] The program began with a sunrise flag-raising ceremony, followed by a public procession through the streets. At 10:00 a.m. the BME accompanied a wreath-laying ceremony. The ceremony took place at the bust and obelisk of "The Apostle"[84] on the street bearing his name, the Calzada Madero. The BME's performances of Schubert's *Unfinished Symphony* and Louis Gottschalk's *The Last Hope, a Religious Meditation* punctuated the day's speeches, readings, and recitations. The program ended with a schoolchildren's-choir rendition of the "Himno a Madero" ("Madero Hymn"), by Juan Canseco. One cannot fail to notice the religious metaphors, both musical and symbolic; the incantatory element; the sense of martyrdom; and even the sentimental aspect of this civic celebration.[85]

The BME did not march during the Revolution, at least not on any battlefield, but the post-Revolution era offered the band a new role: that of pedagogue.

5 *Mestizaje*, Musical Pedagogy, and the Socialist State

> Making noise seems to come to us from our Spanish heritage. Our Indian ancestors were not noisy. They made noise when it was imperative to do so: they beat their drums and blew their conches and flutes to convoke the religious ceremonies; they howled on throwing themselves into combat, but their normal life was quite silent. On the other hand, the Spaniard makes a racket by nature. The noise seems to please him.
>
> Alfonso Vásquez Mellado, *La Ciudad de los Palacios*

The Mexican Constitution of 1917 was the single most important document to arise from the Mexican Revolution, and it indirectly altered the BME's trajectory. The statutes within the Constitution of 1917 manifested an eclectic mix of "nationalism, secularism, anticlericalism, and social consciousness."[1] The constitution's emphasis on education transformed the BME, at least for a time, into an official didactic tool that through its music would disperse a new nationalistic cultural education. While the BME had been informally contributing to an educatory process insofar as its music reflected liberal republican ideologies assimilated from democracies around the world, before the Constitution of 1917, no "curriculum" in patriotism or nationalism had ever been formally instituted. The importance of the educatory project is evident in both the BME's own didactic functions and the proliferation of municipal bands that occurred during the 1920s, ostensibly to aid in the project. To understand these events, we must first examine the history of education in Mexico and the didactic role music played in the formation of Mexican citizens.

Education, Music, and Festivals

Article III of the Constitution of 1917 mandated free and compulsory secular primary public education for all Mexicans. The first great debates at the Constitutional Convention held in Querétaro sought to remove education from the Catholic Church's domain in order to provide "rational" rather than "religious" education.[2] The shadow of former Secretary of Public Education Justo Sierra (1848–1912) loomed large in the debates.

As a student in Mexico City at the time of the French Intervention, Sierra responded with patriotic fervor to the invasion of his country and became a lifelong militant liberal. From 1905 to 1911, he served as the Secretary of Public Education under Díaz, but Sierra never made a secret of his liberal sympathies and his distaste for the politics of the Porfiriato.

At the Constitutional Convention, Sierra's ideological supporters saw primary education as the formative seed of the new Mexican citizen, who, when educated, would advance the nation; no longer would the church be the nation's main educatory institution. Sierra's description of his vision of national education rang with the tones of the civic religion: the transformation of the Mexican population, the love of work and the march to school, the elevation of the national language, the primordial elements of the soul of a nation, the religion of patriotism, the cult of civic duty—all of these were integral to the way in which the state should create schools (and vice versa). When Article III of the Constitution of 1917 was passed, shouts filled the chamber: "¡La patria se ha salvado!" ("The country has been saved!").[3]

Sierra realized music's importance as a didactic tool in forming Mexican citizens, creating a civic religion, inculcating nationalism, and teaching Mexican history. Schools, he believed, should be responsible for teaching social morality and the duties of the Mexican citizen, and festivals featuring music provided another popular venue for such instruction. While Mexicans were already accustomed to the centrality of festivals in public life, the new (secular) state should "underline [the festivals'] content with constant secular sermons."[4] Even school festivals, which included band and other musical performances, should be educational, seeking always to prepare "the complete man, in the Mexican of tomorrow."[5]

In an article entitled "Las fiestas de la República" ("Festivals of the Republic") published in *El Federalista* in Mexico City in 1875, Sierra envisioned the government as "the educator of the people," arguing that up to that time this mission had failed. To that pedagogical end, Sierra asked, "Is there a more powerful educational element than festivals?" He thus proposed a calendar of festivals honoring the Constitution of 1857 and another honoring the Reform, as well as the patriotic days of 5 May and 16 September. Sierra suggested that the traditional celebrations for the Day of the Dead (2 November) instead honor those whose "blood and thought consecrated the nation."[6] Sierra invoked the celebrations of the ancient Greeks, who sang hymns to their common fatherland and celebrated their heroes and historic anniversaries. Festivals similar to the classical models in Sierra's Mexico need not be official but popular, Sierra noted, and the organizational committees responsible could spend less on them than they were already spending for the "monotonous pyrotechnics"[7] that currently marked such days.

Sierra need not have looked to ancient Greece for precedent. Mesoamerican cultures and the Catholic Church had long used music as a didactic tool in Mexico. Reflecting on the Mexican Independence Day celebrations in 1870, the writer and politician Ignacio Manuel Altamirano lamented the lack of patriotic songs in Mexico and lauded their virtues: "Popular songs are necessary, indispensable for a republican people. But wait! They mean the same to all the world's peoples that know the value of glorious traditions and of patriotism, [those things] that have given origin to poetry, have formed the epic, have been victorious many times. I give you 'La Marseillaise.' Popular songs educate the people, liberate them from harmful worries, free the spirit, and invigorate the ideas of liberty."[8] Furthermore, Altamirano exhorted "popular" Mexican poets and songwriters to produce such songs and not songs geared solely to mass popularity: "It makes one sad, the fabulous number of insignificant dances, monotonous waltzes, ridiculous polkas, Hail Marys, Eucharistic hymns, [and] tearful romances that our artists compose every day and that fail to enrich the art of Mexican music."[9]

Altamirano's criticism of the popular overlooked the potential educational benefits of employing popular music as a didactic tool in order to reach a broader audience. The repertoire of twentieth-century bands would have to incorporate the popular with the patriotic to expand the bands' audiences. Altamirano recognized that civic functions, especially popular and patriotic festivals, must be held not at "elite" sites like the Teatro Nacional (National Theater) but in venues that allowed access to the masses.[10] But the ideology of Sierra, who had viewed the languages of Mexico's indigenous population as barriers to the creation of a modern state and thought the indigenous peoples' tithes to the Catholic Church paid for inordinate quantities of bell ringing and candles, would have to be reconciled within fiestas planned around national heroes and music that glorified not only the state but also its diverse regions.

By the 1930s federally mandated lesson plans for primary schools in rural and industrial-agricultural regions included music and song. The first goal was the memorization of "national patriotic and regional songs," including the Mexican national anthem, the "Hymn to the Flag," and the "Hymn to Hidalgo." Contests were held to select regional songs to be sung in unison at local festivals. The state preferred songs with binary rhythms and martial tempos, and the children were to learn to sing them in unison.[11] Furthermore, songs were used to teach socialist ideology.

The curriculum included songs such as "La Marseillaise," "The International," the "Triumphal March," and the "Peasant March," as well as the "Song to Zapata."

Further broadening the hybrid repertoire were regional song types that included *jarabes, sones, chilenas, jaranas,* and *huapangos*.[12] Schools were to organize song-writing contests and prepare programs for festivals for the school's surrounding communities.[13] Some schools even included the formation of musical bands or *orquestas típicas* (typical orchestras) in the curriculum.[14] For those groups the state provided recommendations for instrumentation, band size, repertoire, and rehearsals. Festivals were encouraged, as was the cultivation of a relationship between school bands and the various cultural brigades at work in the region, as well as with other local bands.[15]

That regional music was now deployed within musical programs reflects the social and economic changes that Oaxaca experienced in the first decades of the twentieth century. Once isolated rural regions now communicated with the capital through select repertoires of song and dance forms. Furthermore, regional music became commercialized in the wake of the revolution as Mexico's population boomed and widespread migration from rural areas to cities took place. New forms of electronic media like the radio and phonograph disseminated commercialized regional music, and in Oaxaca the government canonized the musical practices.

Given the political sea change of the Revolution, education, like the utopian vision for the Mexican state, would be "socialist."[16] However, the framers of Article III were incapable of defining clearly just what comprised "socialist education." No mention was made of any cultural propagation within the "socialist" educatory project, but when Article III was amended in 1946, the concept of Mexican culture flowed from state education as part of the original Constitution's nationalist project:

> The education imparted by the Federal State shall be designed to develop harmoniously all the faculties of the human being

and shall foster in him at the same time a love of country and a consciousness of international solidarity, in independence and justice. . . . It shall be democratic, considering democracy not only as a legal structure and a political regimen, but as a system of life founded on a constant economic, social, and *cultural betterment of the people*. . . . It shall be national insofar as— without hostility or exclusiveness—it shall achieve the understanding of our problems, the utilization of our resources, the defense of our political independence, the assurance of our economic independence, and *the continuity and growth of our culture*.[17]

The BME and a Musical Magna Carta

Although the preceding educational mission statement was not appended to the Constitution until three decades later, efforts at state-sponsored cultural education began to appear soon after its promulgation in 1917. Almost immediately, the BME's mission included didactic, nationalistic performances such as patriotic festivals, cultural missions, and special "Cultural Days," all of which included music, poetry, and speech and composition contests. Classical and provincial composers elaborated a repertoire of national music for the Secretaría de Educación Pública (Secretary of Public Education; SEP). The SEP published Ruben Campos's foundational *El folklore y la música mexicana* (*Folklore and Mexican Music*) in 1928; the "work of cultural rescue and creation . . . became a repertoire to be disseminated through the schools."[18]

As early as August 1918, the state of Oaxaca asked the BME to assist in the state's musical educatory project when the Secretaría de Gobernación (Secretary of the Interior) in Oaxaca directed BME director Daniel Baltazar to provide the Departamento Universitario y de Bellas Artes (Department of Universities and Fine Arts) with information on the following topics: the "history and organization of all educative musical establishments in Oaxaca; administrative details of those establishments; student admissions and enrollments; examinations; study plans; whether courses are paid or free; whether or not grades are awarded; and whether or not internships are offered."[19]

The following month, Baltazar submitted a brief history of the BME to the governor. In the document, Baltazar described the origins of the BME and the various criteria for service in the band, wrote of the band's advancements and acclaim, and (in a fascinating turn of phrase that speaks to the important indigenous contribution to Oaxacan music) even asserted that since "prehistoric times" bands had been at the vanguard of Oaxaca's history.[20] That Baltazar responded only regarding the BME may indicate that he was already aware of the band's important educational role—or, conversely, his ignorance regarding broader musical pedagogy in Oaxaca.

Vasconcelos and the Value of Cultural *Mestizaje*

José Vasconcelos was born in Oaxaca in 1881; shortly thereafter, his family moved to Piedras Negras in the northern state of Coahuila. Vasconcelos participated in the Revolution as a dedicated Maderista, and in 1921 President Álvaro Obregón named him Secretary of Public Education. His nephew Eduardo eventually became the governor of Oaxaca. Vasconcelos was preoccupied with pre-Hispanic culture and its place in the modern Mexican state, and his efforts as Secretary of Public Education consequently shaped the Mexican cultural educatory project.

In his memoir *Ulises Criollo*, Vasconcelos evocatively recalls his boyhood memories of the role of music and its pervasive connection to the state during the Porfiriato. At the age of nine, he heard a military band performing at a dance in Piedras Negras, and at the inauguration of a customs house, Vasconcelos heard a band play "Sobre las olas" and the march "Zacatecas." He described, with more than a little sarcasm, the customs officials as metaphorical, publicly venerated, secular holy figures and saw a life-size portrait of Porfirio Díaz as a part of a civic altar dedicated to "the religion of the Fatherland."[21] Later that day, Vasconcelos witnessed what he described as a French-style, fin-de-siècle dance.[22] Ideologically,

Vasconcelos sought not the repetition of European customs but instead the glorification of Mexican (read assimilationist) culture, perhaps due to the bewildering influences he had witnessed on the border as a boy. But Vasconcelos found clarity when he attended a celebration for the Coronation of the Virgin, and "all that was the nation of Mexico, so mysterious and complex, became linked together, if but for a moment, in the plaza surrounded by barracks, the government palace, and the church."[23]

The importance of music in Mexican life influenced Vasconcelos's extensive educational plans, which included curricula supporting physical, moral, and aesthetic well-being as well as cognitive development. Basic education even included the formation of children's bandas de guerra.[24] As rector of the Universidad Nacional de Mexico (National University of Mexico), Vasconcelos stimulated a public musical renaissance in Mexico that included popular outdoor concerts in Mexico City and regional music festivals.[25] On 12 October 1921, Vasconcelos was put in charge of the new SEP, which Vasconcelos himself had proposed be created and from which he organized rural educational missions based on Franciscan models. Within the SEP was the newly created Departamento de Cultura Indígena (Department of Indigenous Culture); its teachers were called "missionary maestros."[26] The objective of the direct and simple interchanges between maestro and indigenous pupil was "to lift the simple and ignorant spirit of [the indigenous], to infuse them with enthusiasm and faith in their future and in the future of the Fatherland."[27] The project was not unlike the colonial evangelization project, but in this case the "instruction of civics and patriotism" replaced Christian doctrine.[28]

Vasconcelos was also in charge of the construction of new buildings for the SEP, including its ministry building and the Normal School in Mexico City. The architecture he envisioned for the SEP, like his ideology for education (and Mexico in general), was based on a cultural syncretism, a passion for the neoclassical, and "a desire to bestow upon the Revolution a beautiful veil that would hide the barbarity of war."[29] Vasconcelos saw in the Revolution the possibility of a new social sensibility toward art, and he oversaw Mexican participation at the world's fairs, where Mexican art and architecture occupied central exhibits. At Rio de Janeiro in 1922, a contingent of seventy-five military musicians performed at the Mexican Pavilion.[30]

With the publication of *La raza cósmica, misión de la raza iberoamericana* (*The Cosmic Race, Mission of the Iberoamerican Race*) in 1925, Vasconcelos articulated an ideology seeking to unify the peoples of Latin America and provide resistance against North American imperialism. According to the theory, from the Amazon River basin a synthesis of all Latin American races would emerge. From the best qualities of the four extant races in Latin America, a new, mestizo fifth race would emerge that would take preeminence over the Anglo race in the future.[31]

The Porfirian-era military wind bands were based on European military models; their instruments were manufactured abroad and exported to Mexico. These ensembles' repertoires included the works of composers from around the world. By presenting these bands at world's fairs, the Porfirian administration hoped to cultivate foreign interest in Mexico as a safe place to invest by projecting a modern, cultured image. However, during Vasconcelos's tenure, these bands' repertoires were altered to reflect a new "socialist," "cosmic" Latin American mestizaje reality.

The Vasconcelista project directly affected the BME's mission. A century earlier, Mexican Creoles, while tracing their "national" roots to the Aztec kings, had ignored the blood of the more common Indians that coursed through their veins. The Revolutionary educatory project sought to rectify such avoidance, and indigenous subjects and regions would come to the forefront of Mexican (state-sponsored) musical production, altering whatever standardized repertoire or program had previously existed. With the Mexican Revolution, popular influence manifested itself in Mexican fine arts; as a consequence, music oriented definitely to nationalism, with overtones of a triumphant indigenism, prevailed over the paladins of Europeanism and took its place in the SEP. Vasconcelos armed himself with ideologies as disparate as Creole patriotism and Porfirian positivism in order to found his own ideology on nationalist grounds that were as deep and fertile as possible. The role of the state band, which was already "scientifically organized," would within the socialist state be transformed into that of a "missionizing" cultural educator and mediator.

The BME and the Post-Revolutionary Education Project

In the early 1920s, Oaxaca's SEP deputy Reyes San Germán identified more than two million indigenous Oaxacans as completely deprived of primary education, receiving no instruction at all.[32] The Oaxaca delegation of the SEP asked for two hundred mission teachers, two thousand residents, and two thousand monitors.[33] Two years later, the implementation of an indigenous education policy had failed, and the cultural assimilation project itself still needed to be affirmed.[34] The state's ideology of an emerging mestizo culture suffered from the shortcomings of an incipient educational program. In November 1926, interim governor Genaro V. Vásquez decreed that in order "to elevate the intellectual and moral level of the people, and especially of the working class," the SEP should create various Centros de Cultura Popular (Popular Culture Centers) that would provide music lessons and musical materials for the formation of all types of musical groups, with the particular aim of propagating regional and revolutionary music. The centers would be modeled after existing examples in Mexico City and would be open to the public six evenings per week. Children could be enrolled in classes given by music professors "known for their competence and honor."[35] The BME's repertoire quickly expanded to include regional music by Oaxacan composers, which it performed not only during regular performances but also at the Sábados Rojos (Red Saturdays) and Domingos Culturales (Cultural Sundays).[36] At one such regional music festival on 12 October 1928, the BME performed for the United States ambassador to Mexico, Dwight Morrow (served 1927–1930), and his staff.[37]

For the next decade, a state project that emphasized music as a didactic tool for the creation of a new post-Revolutionary citizenry, especially for "the masses," took place. While the BME did not perform at all such state-sponsored events, it did begin to give didactic concerts at schools and performed at some of the Sesiones Culturales (Cultural Sessions). When the BME did not participate, other bands would fill in. For example, during Arbor Day celebrations in Juchitán on 5 June 1926, a local orchestra played the overture that opened the Extraordinary Cultural Session in which the tree was celebrated as "the protector of the peasant" and man's "best and most disinterested friend."[38] Other musical performances included children's choirs singing "regional" or "Oaxacan" songs such as "Canción Mixteca."[39] In December of the same year, the BME performed at the Fiesta del Niño Indígena (Festival of the Indigenous Child) for an audience estimated at almost six hundred.[40]

In 1927, Chief of the Department of Public Education in Oaxaca Policarpo T. Sánchez called for the organization of an orquesta típica to perform at the state's Cultural Sessions and charged Guillermo Rosas Solaegui to direct.[41] Rosas Solaegui invited twenty-eight musicians to join, asking them to arrive at the first rehearsal with their instruments and to please be punctual. The orchestra was named La Agrupación Musical Oaxaqueña de Charros (Oaxacan Charro Musical Group). The response was poor: only one musician, a violist, arrived. While some of the invitees complained that they had been given the wrong address for the rehearsal site, a letter dated 10 September 1927 indicates that perhaps another reason existed for the failed attempt to form the group: the musicians faced difficult economic circumstances and were often forced to seek outside employment, which prevented them from dedicating themselves solely to their art; they may also have been unwilling to work for state wages. Another attempt to organize failed as well. According to Rosas Solaegui, the insufficient number of musicians, most of whom played the guitar and (oddly enough) the banjo, meant that some other group would have to cover the schedule. In a third and final attempt to organize the Charros, Sánchez transferred two members of the BME to the Department of Public Education in order to perform with the ensemble. When the group still fell short of members, Rosas Solaegui suggested that the BME, already experienced in such performances, should cover the Cultural Sessions as it had in the past.[42]

The following year in Juchitán, the Instituto Educativo Istmeño (Isthmian Educative Institute) held another Cultural Session. An orchestra directed by one Professor Josué de la Cruz opened a program that included musical pieces for piano and violin performed by Professor Samuel Mondragón Noriega, himself a composer of regional music.[43] A group of "pretty girls" sang such regional songs as "La Juchiteca" and "El Huipil," evoking a strong response from the audience.[44] Children from the Institute closed the program with a rendition of the "Himno Socialista Regional" (Regional Socialist Hymn).[45]

The "Regional Socialist Hymn" (music composed by Alberto Vargas, lyrics by Herbierto Sánchez) was copyrighted in Oaxaca in 1926. On 30 June 1928 Governor Vásquez decreed that the work be adopted as the official state hymn of Oaxaca.[46] The decree required that the Mexican national anthem be played at official civic ceremonies when the president of the Republic or the governor of Oaxaca was in attendance. When both men were present at an event, the "Regional Socialist Hymn" would immediately follow the national anthem. On 12 September 1928 the governor reminded the Inspector General of the Police (then in charge of the BME) to make sure the hymn was played at the upcoming 16 de Septiembre celebrations.[47] The hymn is played "marziale e grandioso" (in a style that is martial and grandiose).

The cover of the sheet music for the hymn is of the Mexican social realist style (see fig. 10). Possibly referencing the classical

FIG. 10. "Himno Socialista Regional" sheet music cover. Fondo Educación, Sec. Cultural y Artistica, Serie Musical, 1926–1930, Archivo General del Ejecutivo Poder del Estado de Oaxaca.

influence overlaid on the indigenous (or Vasconcelos's architectural project), the foreground contains what appears to be a marble pedestal erected upon a Mesoamerican pyramid block.[48] Two male *campesinos* (peasants) kneel on one knee, one facing forward, the other to the rear, their arms raised skyward. Both are dressed in typical *ropa de manta* (clothes of rough cotton). The campesino facing forward has a pick in one hand, an open book bearing the phrase "Amor omnia vincit" ("Love conquers all" in classical Latin) in the other. A tricolor block frames the song title. The horizon holds images that represent the ideals of modernization and revolution: a school in the classical architectural style; a highway full of modern automobiles; and a steamship, airplane, and dirigible rising from a semitropical foreground. A stylized rising sun encircles the image of the school. Such graphics must not have been reproducible in Mexico, for the bottom-left corner contains the inscription "Made in the USA," an irony perhaps lost on the Oaxacan government. The reverse of the sheet music includes photographs of Governor Vásquez, the composers Vargas and Sánchez, and the complete lyrics, finishing with a shout of "Death before a Life as Slaves!" (See fig. 11.)

Cultural sessions included musical performances, as they did in 1927 at the Fifty-Second Cultural Session in Oaxaca, when the BME opened with the overture from Carl Otto Nicolai's *Merry Wives of Windsor*. Students from local schools sang the "Hymn to the Highway," and the program concluded with a conference entitled "The Social Renovation of the School."[49] In December 1935, the Secretary of Public Education in Oaxaca held a songwriting contest for "revolutionary" songs. The call for submissions described song as the "surest vehicle of the people's artistic sentiment" and asserted that the songs would inform the state's children "of the idea of social justice and of the liberation of the masses." The purpose of the contest was "to educate the masses"; the governor sought for the contest winner a work of "socialist orientation" that would lead to "a greater valuation of the vernacular song."[50]

The important role of music in the state's educatory project meant that no single band could fill the state of Oaxaca's need for musical instruction. New songs imbued with socialist ideology entered the BME's repertoire. Its performance schedule expanded to include

FIG. 11. "Himno Socialista Regional" sheet music cover, reverse. Fondo Educación, Sec. Cultural y Artistica, Serie Musical, 1926–1930, Archivo General del Ejecutivo Poder del Estado de Oaxaca.

appearances at festivals and schools. Thanks to the increasing eminence of music's role in post-Revolutionary Mexico and the demands of an increasingly dense performance schedule, newly created bands proliferated; many of them operated at the municipal level and competed with the BME for performance opportunities.[51] Those bands and the BME's temporary status as a municipal band are the subjects of the next chapter.

6 Municipal Control to Innes's Reign

> The free municipality is the democratic base of the organization of the Mexican State; it is the root of its institutional life.
>
> Governor Alfonso Pérez Gasga

The BME's performance schedule grew with the addition of new didactic responsibilities and Revolution-inspired additions to the civil-religious pantheon. So great was the expansion of musical production within the state project that bands proliferated to fill the need. From 1937 to 1947, the BME was placed under municipal control and was known as the Banda de Música Municipal. After an intense expansion of the performance schedule while under municipal control, the BME then reverted to state control.[1] Then the BME undertook a new (economic) mission aimed at furthering Oaxacan culture internationally, distinguishing itself, with a special emphasis on tourism, from a number of newly formed bands at the municipal level.

Precedents for and Proliferation of Municipal Bands

Today, nearly one-fourth of the *municipios* (municipalities) in the entire nation of Mexico are in the state of Oaxaca.[2] Their multiplicity is a result of the land-tenure patterns in place in the state since the colonial period. As the political administrative districts in the state, the municipios of Oaxaca arose from native groupings of *cabeceras* (head towns) and hamlets rather than from the large hacienda complexes that developed, for example, in northern Mexico. In Oaxaca, peasant societies found corporate strength in their village communities. Furthermore, the relatively small number of Spaniards residing in Oaxaca during the colonial period allowed indigenous villages to maintain a certain level of continuity—and, to a degree, autonomy.[3] Oaxaca's isolating geography further contributed to the proliferation of municipalities within the state. But how, in such a setting, was the state to maintain its presence? Historically, one way was to provide municipalities with musical instruments for their bands, a relatively inexpensive means of maintaining loyalty to the state or the political party in power.

The state government quickly realized the importance of music to its citizens. A precedent had been established as early as 21 August 1857, when then-governor Benito Juárez received a request from the School of Music in San Felipe del Agua, a village on the outskirts of Oaxaca City, for $217.00 to purchase musical instruments. In his letter to the governor, director Gregorio Loaesa asked Juárez for an ophicleide (a bass-keyed tuba), a bugle, clarinets, a requinto, a piccolo, and various drums and percussion instruments so that the ten students might complete their lessons. Loaesa also requested compensation for music professor Eugenio Lanson.[4]

Perhaps in response to the expanded civic calendar and the primacy of education within the Revolutionary ideology, the archival records for the 1920s contain numerous similar requests from municipalities seeking state assistance in forming bands. On 14 November 1922 Fidel Leal, the municipal president of Ahuehuetitlán, confirmed receipt from the state government of musical instruments for his municipal band.[5] In 1927 the state government furnished the municipality of Cuquila with instruments. (See fig. 12.) But municipalities faced human-resources problems as well as financial obstacles; in addition to the sizable economic investment required, the small populations typical of Oaxaca's

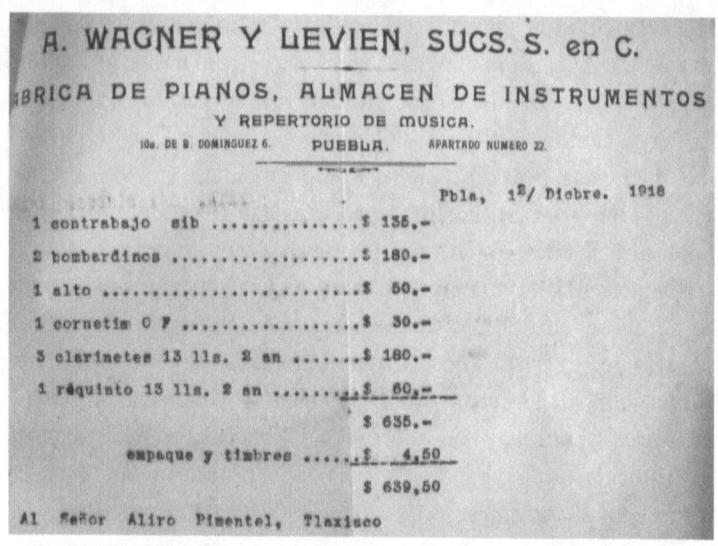

FIG. 12. Invoice for the purchase of various musical instruments from Wagner y Levien for the municipality of Tlaxiaco, Oaxaca. Dep. Gob., 1927, Exp. 39, Leg. 224, Archivo General del Ejecutivo Poder del Estado de Oaxaca.

municipalities may have made it difficult to muster the necessary personnel to form municipal bands. For example, in March 1921, the municipal president of Nochixtlán attempted to organize a band and visited Oaxaca City to procure governmental funds. While the results of his visit remain unclear, the band did not form at the time due to a lack of musicians.[6]

The year 1923 marked the 102nd anniversary of Mexican independence, and during the two-day celebration the state of Oaxaca resounded with musical performances. In the capital, the BME accompanied the requisite speeches, poetry readings, and parades, and played extended serenatas per its contractual obligation. The programs for the celebration reflect an official history of nationalist aesthetics and national identity through the expression of essential *mexicanidad* (Mexicanness), the presence of cultural chieftains and mediators, and a close association of (musical) nationalism with the state.

That year numerous municipal bands performed on Independence Day in their own hometowns. Municipalities communicated their plans and programs for the celebrations to the state capital; most of the events were organized along the lines of those programmed by the Junta Patriótica in the capital. Not surprisingly, the plans, programs, or descriptions of each municipality's celebration are rife with quasi-religious terminology and symbols such as altars, flags, regional and nationalist music, children's choruses, and poetry. Apparent in many of the programs is the nationalistic notion that nations and citizens are forged, tempered, and then united in blood and battle.

In a letter addressed to the Junta Patriótica in the state capital, Ysidro Gaspar, the president of the Comisión de la Fiesta Pátria (National Festival Commission) in Amatlán, confirmed that on 15 and 16 September his town "had celebrated the patriotic festivals with all complete solemnity" in honor of the iconic "caudillo of Independence," Father Hidalgo, the "venerable ancient priest of Dolores who 113 years ago sacrificed his life to make us independent."[7] Accompanying the religious terminology were the now-familiar symbols of Independence Day programs: altars, children's choruses, commemorative wreaths, and military honors. The flag was central to all celebrations. In San Mateo Riohondo, the village band performed throughout the festivities, providing musical pieces such as overtures, marches, and dianas. At the end of the day, the band accompanied a public dance.

Villa Alta is a district well known for its musical production. Located in the Sierra Juárez, it counts Zapotecs and Mixes among its indigenous citizens. The Mixe Indians are renowned for their bands, especially their children's band. To this day, participation in local bands may count toward community service, and musical training begins at an early age.[8] As might be expected, a musically rich and diverse program accompanied the 1923 Villa Alta municipality of Zoochila's Independence Day celebration. Bell ringing and dianas signaled the commencement of the festivities. Then one Adalberto G. Alcázar directed the municipality's band in parades, matinee performances, and flag raisings, as well as the seventeen different musical numbers listed in the program, including marches, pasos dobles, waltzes, polkas, fox-trots, danzones, and zarzuelas. A military band joined the municipal band for the national anthem.[9]

Where no municipal band existed, private orchestras, *cuerpos filarmónicos* (philharmonic ensembles), or bands were contracted. For example, unidentified bands played in the municipalities of San Lorenzo Cacaotepec, Suchixtlahuaca, and Etla. A cuerpo filarmónico performed at Tonaltepec, and in San Miguel "the intelligent director Citizen Ismael Ramos" directed the orchestra's performance of the national anthem. The state committee permitted the town of Putla to have a *jaripeo* (a type of rodeo) so long as order was maintained.[10]

The program in Cuicatlán was spread over 15, 16, 17, and 18 September. On 30 September the city held a celebration commemorating the anniversary of the birth of Independence hero José María Morelos. Events during the festival included a baseball game; a soccer match; a parade featuring floats with allegorical representations of Commerce, Agriculture, and Industry; and speeches, recitations, military parades, and serenatas. The night of 30 September featured a "serenata monstruo" (an "extraordinary serenade") performed by the Orquesta Abundio Martínez and dedicated to "Morelos, the Great Liberator."[11]

In at least two municipalities, celebrations took place at the town kiosk. In Santa María Yucuhite the new kiosk and plaza were inaugurated during the *fiestas pátrias*. In Ixcatlán, a long letter describes the festivities that took place in an improvised kiosk. The band assembled there after bells rang and fireworks filled the sky, calling the citizens to the festival, where "the best musical pieces" preceded "*el Grito de Independencia*" and were followed by a parade through all the town's streets. The entire program was repeated the following day. A patriotic altar was erected, and the local band accompanied a children's poetry reading. Other towns included speeches, piñatas, and late-night dances in their galas.[12]

Three years later, in 1926, Governor Vásquez invited at least nineteen municipal bands to perform at a regional exposition in Oaxaca; he even offered to pay half of their traveling expenses. Apparently the response was so poor that the governor later had to force some of the bands to participate. The tenuous nature of bands at the local level, especially given the poverty levels throughout the state, is reflected in responses indicating that some bands simply could not afford the trip. Any such travel would also mean that the musicians would not be available to work their fields, making such a journey a double economic hardship.[13]

Municipalities kept the governor apprised of their efforts to form bands. For example, on 13 March 1923, the municipal president of La Ollaga informed the governor that "a local society" had acquired "various musical instruments from the Casa de Wagner y Levien in Mexico City in order to organize our band."[14] An invoice dated 12 December 1918 from the Casa de Wagner y Levien branch in Puebla was attached (perhaps to indicate the estimated costs of the musical instruments) to a 1927 letter from the municipal president of Cuquila requesting the equivalent of $800 for the purchase of unspecified musical instruments.[15]

A newspaper editorial on 24 April 1924 urged the governor not to dissolve the BME in the face of mounting competition for finite audiences, nor to do so for merely fiduciary reasons.[16] The editorial did, however, describe the lamentable situation of the "artist employees," now forced to look for outside work because the treasury lacked sufficient funds to pay them. Furthermore, much had changed in the organization after the Revolution. Numerous other bands now entertained around the state, and an expanded civic calendar put pressure on the BME to fulfill its obligations.

The Return of Canseco

The BME persevered, and finally, on 8 October 1924 at 9:00 a.m., Germán Canseco took his oath of office and reassumed directorship of the BME. "Do you swear to protect and uphold the political constitution of the Mexican United States, the constitution of the state of Oaxaca, and the laws of both, and to remain loyal to the duties charged to the Director of the BME?" "I swear," Canseco replied. The presiding official at the ceremony then said, "If you should not, that the nation and the state should so demand." The position came with a salary of five pesos per day.[17]

In April 1925 Canseco turned in a work order for repair of the kiosk's handrails. In his memo to the municipal secretary responsible for the kiosk's upkeep, Canseco described the lamentable, almost ruinous condition of the iron handrails. He wrote that many musicians had already fallen from the bandstand and that he himself had fallen on 2 April 1925. (One wonders whether his fall was the result of a pre-existing condition, since he had originally left the band for medical reasons, or whether it was just an unfortunate mishap.) An inspection report of the handrail's condition deemed it necessary not only to replace twenty sections of the ironwork but also to construct a rail specifically designed to guard against further falls. In May the town council authorized payment of $35 to repair the kiosk.[18]

The final year of Canseco's tenure included an expanded civic calendar and the new responsibilities of the Revolutionary educatory project. In 1928 the BME performed an "official act" at the Normal School on 7 February, accompanied a literary session at ICA and then paraded with the students on 17 March, performed at the inauguration of the Benito Juárez School on 17 and 19 July, played again at ICA on 7 September, and performed at the Institute's festival on 9 October. The band's role as a cultural and educational mediator of the state had been cemented. In 1928, the BME also played at a reception for Mexican president Emilio Portes-Gil, honored Mexican aviators flying through Oaxaca, performed at a labor-union sports festival, and also played at a Charro Festival, to name but a few of the civic functions at which it appeared.[19] The BME also continued to perform its usual serenatas and dominicales.

On 19 April 1929 the governor ordered the army's Fifty-Eighth Battalion Band of Oaxaca to replace the BME for the Wednesday and Friday night serenades at the kiosk. A weekly Saturday performance at the General Hospital replaced the previously required Friday-night serenata. If the BME was also performing its traditional Tuesday- and Thursday-night serenades, this meant that five weekly musical performances were occurring in Oaxaca at the kiosk alone. The few extant memos from 1929 concerned BME performances at the Oaxaca Rotary Club (an early sign of the BME's developing role in Oaxaca's economic life) and for "The Week of the Child."[20]

On 26 April 1929 Moisés Baltazar Velasco became interim director of the BME, bringing to an end the nearly three decades of Canseco's service. The following month, on 18 May 1929, Agustín Hernández Toledo replaced Baltazar.[21] When Baltazar transferred the inventory to Hernández, it included twenty different musical instruments belonging to the BME, along with nine others "in bad condition."[22] The inventory of sheet music and arrangements extended to four single-spaced pages, including in its listing 5 zarzuelas, 23 overtures, 48 fantasies, 58 marches and pasos dobles, 19 waltzes, 12 polkas, 5 mazurkas, 107 "diverse pieces," and 33 "useless pieces" that were no longer performed.[23] The effects of the decade-long effort to incorporate regional music into the BME's repertoire is clear, for among those identified as "diverse pieces" were numerous compositions by Oaxacan composers including Samuel Mondragón, Guillermo Rosas Solaegui, and José Alcalá.

Municipal Control

Professor Agustín Hernández Toledo directed the BME from 1928 to 1936. On 1 December 1936 Capitán Próspero A. González replaced Hernández, and in 1937 the BME passed from state to municipal control, where it remained until 1947.[24] (See fig. 13.) A 1937 roll of municipal employees lists the forty-seven members for the BME (now renamed the Banda de Música Municipal), including the director, the músico mayor, and the *cita papelero* (a secretary-archivist). The roll sheet referred to the musicians as *agentes municipales* (municipal agents).[25] Unfortunately, the rolls do not include the

FIG. 13. The BME, ca. 1947. Courtesy of Archivo de la Banda de Música del Estado de Oaxaca.

instruments that the musicians played. Such information would aid the analysis of changes within the band's instrumentation. Besides the director and the músico mayor, there were four soloists; twenty musicians first-class; eighteen musicians second-class; and three musicians third-class. The position of subdirector did not appear. Classification was likely based upon skill levels and tenure. The class system was eventually discontinued in the 1990s in favor of the labor-union style of classifications of "de confianza" and "por contrato," discussed in "Artist as Laborer in the Socialist State II" below.

A brief list of *audiciones extraordinarias* (extraordinary, or special performances, as opposed to *audiciones ordinarias*, regularly scheduled performances such as serenatas) during the municipal period demonstrates not only the continuity of the civic religious calendar but also an increase in singularly Mexican "holidays." Among the BME's extraordinary performances during the municipal period were the following:

The anniversaries of Juárez's birth and death (21 March and 18 July, respectively)
Day of the Martyrs of the Revolution (anniversary of the deaths of Madero and Pino Suárez, 22 February)
Carnaval
May Day (1 May)
The anniversary of Hidalgo's death (30 July)
Independence Day (16 September)
The anniversary of the Revolution (20 November)
The anniversary of the Promulgation of the Constitution of 1917 (5 February)
Day of the Soldier
Day of the Child
Mother's Day (10 May)
Arbor Day
Employee's Day (20 or 21 October)
Flag Day (24 February)
The anniversary of the Battle of Miahuatlán (3 October)
The anniversary of Zapata's death (10 April)
Woman's Day (8 March)
Guelaguetza
Lenten Fridays
Anniversary of the Battle of Puebla (5 May)[26]

The preponderance of "extraordinary" performances must have put a strain on the BME, taking into account the rehearsal schedule and the "ordinary" performances. Ordinary performances still included the serenatas on Tuesdays, Thursdays, and Saturday evenings, as well as two Sunday performances, one during the afternoon and another at night. The distinction between "ordinary" and "extraordinary" is discussed below in the section on BME regulations. Nevertheless, the trend to expand the calendar continued until the governor was finally forced to divide and distribute the performances for the extensive civic religious calendar and didactic functions among other bands. In 1946 alone, the BME played approximately 136 extraordinary performances![27] Clearly, not all of these engagements were extensive; some required the BME's participation only for a flag-raising ceremony or an overture, but they still required that the band mobilize, organize, and arrive at the performance site prepared to perform with its customary precision.

In post-Revolutionary Mexico, patriotic festivals increasingly included sports exhibitions during the afternoons, as they did in Oaxaca on Constitution Day 1937. The state included sports in its education curriculum, viewing them as an alternative to alcohol consumption and even as a replacement for Sunday Mass.[28] During the presidency of Plutarco Elías Calles (1924–1928), Constitution Day festivities in Mexico City began to include civic sports parades, as Calles considered sports parades an effective tool in the construction of Mexican corporatism. Lorenzo Meyer has asserted that sports parades of the era demonstrated a maturing political process and associated the legitimacy of Calles' Partido Nacional Revolucionario (National Revolutionary Party, PNR) with the origins of the Mexican state.[29] The BME also performed for the PNR, the "official party" (and predecessor of the present-day PRI), and continued its didactic role in various city schools. For example, in 1937 the BME provided the musical accompaniment for daily classes in regional dance.

The program for 1937's Día de la Revolución (the anniversary of the Mexican Revolution, 20 November) began with the BME parading through the streets from 6:00 a.m. until 7:00 a.m. At 9:00 a.m. the BME performed with a school choir, and at 10:00 a.m. the official program, including overtures, speeches, and poetry readings, took place. At 4:00 p.m. the BME accompanied the *Tarde Deportiva* (Sports Afternoon), and its day ended with a three-hour serenata featuring unspecified "national music."[30]

Such scheduling likely put a strain upon the BME's members, but the frequent intervals during performances may have contributed to another problem: alcohol consumption. When placed in the context of an exuberant citywide festival, the resulting behavior is not difficult to predict.[31] The problem of inebriety (or at least the documentation of its incidence) first appears in the archival record during the municipal period. On 23 March 1946 the municipal president expressed his displeasure to director Anastacio García Santos. "It has come to my attention," the president wrote, "that frequently musicians [of the band] either miss their services completely or appear drunk for their services. Anyone repeating these irregularities will be sanctioned economically."[32] A loose document found at AHMCO entitled "Reglamento de Disciplina Interna de la Union de Filarmónicos de la Banda de Música Municipal" ("Internal Discipline Regulations of the Philharmonic Union of the BMM"), likely from 1944, details behavior unbecoming a band member and applicable fines for infractions. Article 1, Section 8 states that "any fellow worker that presents himself in an alcoholic state at any service or rehearsal will for the first infraction be fined one day's pay, and after four such infractions will be asked to resign in order to maintain the prestige of this Corporation and this Union." The union (UF) and the state's own Reglamento, published in 1948 are discussed in "The Return to State Control" below.

Violence also occasionally affected the BME, although in the following case alcohol is not mentioned as a possible contributing factor. Like any other group of humans, a band is subject to the expected rivalries, disorders, factions, and interpersonal antipathies that may arise. On 5 October 1939 musician first-class Prisciliano Martínez Mota presented himself to the municipal secretary to file a complaint against Director González. According to Martínez, that morning, during a BME performance at the Paseo Juárez, the director had attacked him for no reason, cutting the musician's left cheek with his knife! After assaulting the musician, González had inflicted such a beating that Martínez had feared for his life. According to the complainant, the attack took place not only in front of his fellow band members but also in front of the public assembled for the performance. The municipal secretary asked that charges be brought against the director.[33] Because no further records for the incident appear in the archives, nor were any reports published in the local newspapers, it is impossible to determine what might have caused such a violent outburst during a performance or how the case was adjudicated. Both men remained in the BME, probably after intervention or arbitration.

Artist as Laborer in the Socialist State II

By 1939, the BME's members belonged to the Union de Filarmónicos de la Banda de Música Municipal (Philharmonic Union of the Municipal Band, UF). Its motto was "For the Union and for the Betterment of Music."[34] Founded in 1919, the union followed the founding of the Confederación Regional Obrera Mexicana (Regional Confederation of Mexican Workers, CROM) by one year.[35] Ostensibly a state–labor alliance, the CROM arose from the battering that unions took in the latter years of the Revolution.[36] After returning to state control, the musicians belonged for many years to the Sindicato de Trabajadores del Estado (State Workers Union). Unless they are temporarily contracted, after a provisional period, today's BME musicians are "de confianza" (serving at the pleasure of the governor), and do not enjoy the protection of rights afforded to labor-union members under the Constitution. Although nonunion status is not specified in the regulations, band members are counseled against belonging to unions, given the importance of their roles in the state's premier musical organization and the resulting bad publicity that a strike might cause the state.

During the municipal era the UF fulfilled members' needs in a manner not unlike that of the colonial sodalities. It provided assistance to band members' widows, as well as interment assistance that included perpetual rights to crypts in a municipal mausoleum.[37] The UF also had its own internal regulations regarding admission, members' rights, and discipline.

On 6 February 1938, faced with increased service hours, the UF addressed a lengthy letter to the authorities that alluded to the ambiguous role of the artist as a civil servant. The petition opened by explaining the ongoing efforts to improve individual skills within the band, as well as the increasing public acclaim as testified by the ever-growing attendance at BME performances. Apparently (no confirming document appears in the historical record), the municipality had requested longer service hours. The musicians wrote that the extended hours made them "tired, both physically and morally, and we do not have the same enthusiasm. You [the Municipal Council] know that when dealing with Art, once the spirit is dulled, one is not able to continue with the same energy. [With a correspondingly extended break] we will be able to return . . . to our Cultural and Artistic labor."[38] Forty-nine members of the BME signed the letter.

Director Próspero González resigned on 15 May 1942 and handed the baton to Professor Anastacio García Santos. On 1 June 1942 the BME performed at celebrations for Día de la Marina (Mexican Navy Day). The BME paraded with bandas de guerra to start the day, and later a musical and literary program was held at the Teatro Macedonio Alcalá. School children danced to "Sobre las olas," and that afternoon schoolgirls sang regional music, including compositions by Mondragón and Rosas Solaegui.[39] A later payroll sheet dated 1943 listed fifty-eight members, but again did not include instrumentation. Monthly pay ranged from a high of $180.00 for the director to $48.00 for the musicians third-class.[40]

In 1944 Leopold Stokowski visited Oaxaca and served as guest conductor of the BME.[41] The great conductor of the Philadelphia Symphonic Orchestra was well known for his travels (and exploits) in Mexico and the rest of Latin America, and the performance with the BME added to his notoriety. Previously, in January 1931, Stokowski had traveled to Mexico for the first time, but he did not visit Oaxaca at that time. However, Marian Tyler, a journalist for the *New York Times* covering Stokowski's 1931 visit to Mexico City, wrote that should the conductor chance upon "the Oaxaca city band performing the *Eroica* in the plaza of an evening [it] would please even his ear with balance, shading, and real musicianship."[42] It was not to occur in 1931, for on 15 January a terrible earthquake struck southern Mexico, including the state of Oaxaca and its capital city. Stokowski, along with Mexican composer, violinist, and conductor, Julián Carrillo Trujillo, held two benefit concerts in Mexico City as part of the relief effort for the devastated state.[43]

Stokowski did visit the Isthmus of Tehuantepec in 1932, "where he was impressed by the local musical ideas."[44] He likely visited the city of Oaxaca on that trip, for Stokowski's friend and biographer Oliver Daniel writes that when, on 9 May 1944, the conductor drove his Oldsmobile from Mexico City to Oaxaca, he again "fell in love with the town" and later recalled fondly "the green-tinted cathedral" and the ruins of Mitla that he had seen on an earlier trip accompanied by Mexican composer and conductor Carlos Chávez.[45]

For the 1944 performance, Stokowski led the BME in the *1812 Overture* and "scared the wits out of Oaxaca."[46] According to coverage in *Time* magazine (which along with the *New York Times* seemingly covered every step that the peripatetic Stokowski took), with Tchaikovsky's bellicose and rousing work, the conductor "figured he would give his audience the works: real church bells, real rifle fire, dynamite blasts to simulate the cannon." The police chief, *Time* continues, "unaware of the esthetic goals, rounded up the sound effects shooters and blasters [and] had them safely behind bars by the time Stokowski beat out the last bar."[47] To the present day, when performing the *1812 Overture*, the state contracts cannoneers to accompany the BME and to enhance the performance, perhaps in homage to Stokowski.

The Return to State Control: Reorganization and Regulation

On 2 January 1947 the BME reverted to state control, and its name was changed back to La Banda de Música del Estado de Oaxaca (BME). That day, the BME passed the inspection of governor-elect Eduardo Vasconcelos (1947–1950).[48] On 24 June 1947 Capitán Amador Pérez Torres, per an agreement between Vasconcelos and the Secretary of National Defense, left his position as subdirector of the Artillery Band to become director of the BME, replacing García

Santos. Pérez Torres was born in Zaachila, a village south of Oaxaca City famous for its wind musicians. He was an acclaimed trombonist as well as a prolific composer.[49]

In February 1947 the BME celebrated the "virile attitude" of Francisco Madero and José María Pino Suárez on Martyr's Day, and two days later participated in the Día de la Bandera (Flag Day) celebration. For Flag Day, the BME performed Franz von Suppé's *Poet and Peasant Overture* and also accompanied a schoolchildren's choir for the "Himno a la Bandera" ("Hymn to the Flag"). The overture from Giuseppe Verdi's *Aida* punctuated the familiar speeches and poetry readings. The afternoon featured civic acts at all local schools, and the day concluded with a serenata. Citizens were encouraged to drape their homes in the colors of the Mexican flag—red, green, and white.[50] In October 1947 the BME's performance hours changed: Sunday concerts would be held from noon until 2:30 p.m., and the Tuesday and Thursday serenatas would run from 8:00 p.m. until 10:30 p.m.[51]

In 1948 Governor Vasconcelos mentioned the BME in his annual *Informe* (Report),[52] writing that the BME was undergoing a "period of reorganization," both technical and administrative, in order to improve its service to the state. First, soloists and musicians first-class were singled out for more strenuous qualification standards. Second, new (unspecified) compositions to be "constantly practiced" were added to the repertoire. Finally, Vasconcelos imagined a clearer, more formal state role for the BME: "So that the Band maintains the level to which it corresponds as a serious state institution, its services are availed only in acts of formal character." For all other classes of events that required musical pieces, a marimba band at the governor's service would perform.[53] The marimba, while popular throughout the state, is most associated with the Isthmus of Tehuantepec. The addition of these performances might be interpreted as an attempt to integrate the distant (and sometimes separationist) *Istmeños* into the state. Vasconcelos also specified that the BME should perform twice on Sundays: the traditional matinee as well as a nighttime performance.[54]

Reorganization included publication of the first *Reglamento de la Banda de Música del Estado* (Regulations of the BME), issued on 16 February 1948.⁵⁵ Chapter 1 outlined the organization of the BME, including the duties of the director, subdirector, músico mayor, soloists, and musicians first- and second-class, as well as the position of *cita papelero*. It also listed the requirements for holding each of the positions. Chapter 2 specified rehearsal schedules: they were to be held Tuesday through Saturday from 10:30 a.m. until 1:00 p.m. Attendance was mandatory, and roll was to be taken daily by the músico mayor; tuning was not to exceed thirty minutes of rehearsal time.

Chapter 3 defined the types of service, classified either as "Ordinary" or "Extraordinary." Ordinary services included Sunday matinees from 12:30 p.m. until 2:30 p.m. and evening performances on Sunday, Tuesday, and Thursday nights from 7:30 p.m. until 9:30 p.m. All others were "Extraordinary" services and could only be scheduled by the governor. All members were to be present thirty minutes before all performances. Chapter 3 also included "General Dispositions" such as salaries and vacations. In addition, it prohibited the members of the BME from wearing their uniforms at "political rallies, taverns, or other centers of vice," or at any occasion that was not an officially sanctioned service. Regulations required the BME to assemble on the first day of each month to pass the governor's (or one of his representatives') inspection, at which time uniforms would be checked for neatness and instruments for condition.⁵⁶ During inspection, each member had the opportunity to express grievances and to confirm that he had received his pay.⁵⁷ Also during inspection, musicians were allowed to request the opportunity to fill a vacancy within the band; any honors they had achieved would be awarded at that time. All BME members were made *empleados de confianza* (trusted employees), meaning that they were not allowed to join a union or go on strike.

Chapter 4 of the Reglamento listed sanctions, which included warnings, fines, suspensions, and terminations. Tardiness, unexcused absences, disobedience, and inebriation, along with general "lack of probity, honor, and morality," were all causes for disciplinary action, suspension, or even termination. Violence, threats, or injuring or poorly treating fellow musicians, even outside of BME events, were also listed as grounds for disciplinary action.

In his 1949 *Informe* Vasconcelos wrote that the BME had improved technically thanks to a five-month course funded by the governor. Vasconcelos had also purchased for the BME two sets of new uniforms, one formal and one semiformal. According to the governor, the BME achieved "great advancement in rhythmic technique and music reading."[58] The BME performed outside the city at least twice in 1949: in May 1949, the band traveled to the Isthmus, playing in various towns and honoring Mexican president Miguel Alemán's visit to the region; and on 3 October the BME took part in the anniversary celebration and festivities commemorating Porfirio Díaz's triumph over Interventionist forces at the Battle of Miahuatlán.[59]

The Arrival of Diego Innes

On 2 August 1950 the newspaper *Provincia* reported that the current director of Oaxaca's Escuela de Música y Declamación (School of Music and Speech), Diego Innes Acevedo, had been designated the new director of the BME, replacing outgoing director Amador Pérez Torres.[60] Innes, like former director Germán Canseco, was from Ejutla de Crespo. A classically trained violinist and conductor, Innes had spent the previous thirty-five years in the United States, where he had served for a time as associate conductor of the Wisconsin WPA Symphony Orchestra.[61] Innes went on to serve as the director of the BME for the next twenty-four years.

Physically imposing and of stern demeanor, Innes wore a uniform of belted tunic with epaulets, brass buttons, braids, and a braided officer's cap. (See fig. 14.) The new director announced that his first acts would be to fill BME vacancies caused by a shortage of instruments and to provide each musician with a copy of the Reglamento in order that it be "strictly observed." It was up to the BME's director to enforce all the regulations, and Innes fulfilled his duty with zeal. According to Vasconcelos, Innes's appointment

FIG. 14. Director Diego Innes (right) with Bulmaro Yescas Vázquez. Courtesy of Archivo de la Banda de Música del Estado de Oaxaca.

held the promise of renewed prestige and acclaim, but as Innes's first remarks indicated, his tenure would be one of strict regulation, conformity, and discipline.[62] Innes himself was subject to the strict guidelines put forth regarding the director's position: they required that the director have five years' experience in musical

FIG. 15. The BME in 1951. Innes appears in a suit, center front. Courtesy of Archivo de la Banda de Música del Estado de Oaxaca.

direction, that he know the rules of instrumentation, and that he have at least six months' experience leading "a premier band somewhere in the Republic of Mexico." Furthermore, the director must be of "notorious good conduct."[63]

During Innes's first days as director, the BME rehearsal site moved from the ex-Convent of San José to the ex-Convent of Santo Domingo, which, like the former facility, served as an army barracks.[64] (See fig. 15.) I believe, though I am unable to verify, that the BME remained in Santo Domingo until the early 1950s, when it relocated briefly to the Government Palace. The theme of liminality is especially evocative when considering a former military band practicing in a former convent concurrently occupied by a standing army. The BME's colonial vestiges are interconnected, not delimited, and deeply rooted.

The following week, Innes promised to improve the BME archive. Lack of attention had rendered some scores damaged and unusable, while others were incomplete or lost.⁶⁵ Innes's quest to bring order to the archives was perhaps spurred by the "discovery" in the BME archives a few years earlier of a "lost" waltz by Macedonio Alcalá. The "beautiful" waltz, entitled "Solo Díos en el cielo" ("Only God in Heaven"), had just debuted in partial form at a BME performance. According to some who heard the rendition, the piece had the sentimentality and musical tempo of "Díos nunca muere." One audience member remarked that if "Díos nunca muere" had not existed, then "Solo Díos en el cielo" would "surely have been the Hymn of Oaxaca."⁶⁶

Innes premiered as director on 13 August 1950, sharing the baton with subdirector Moisés Baltazar Velasco. Baltazar led the BME in the first four and final two selections, while Innes conducted selections five through eight. The new director told the press that he hoped to have microphones and amplifiers installed in the kiosk to enhance the public's listening experience, changing forever the nature of the performances. Innes was responding to the modern soundscape in which the BME now performed. Adding the amplified output of electric loudspeakers would confront the challenge posed by the organic noises that always accompany human activity, while also responding to the new kinds of noises that accompany urbanization.

Innes further stated that he had encouraged the band members to provide him with their own compositions so that they might be added to the BME's repertoire, and that each musician would also receive the opportunity to conduct a BME performance. Innes concluded the interview by stating that the pieces he would conduct were "specially selected" for the public's enjoyment: a medley of four dances from *The Nutcracker* by Tchaikovsky, the overture to Franz Schubert's *Rosamunde*, selections from Bizet's *Carmen*, Leon Jessel's "Parade of the Wooden Soldiers," and Johann Strauss Jr.'s waltz "Tales from the Vienna Woods."⁶⁷

In 1953 interim governor Manuel Cabrera Carrasquedo (served 1952–1955) spent $7,600 for new khaki uniforms for the BME and another $11,762 for formal uniforms to be used during the *fiestas pátrias*.⁶⁸ The following year Cabrera acknowledged that the reorganization from the previous decade, along with Innes's service, had contributed to great improvement in the BME. Furthermore, the governor said, "I am able to affirm, without any fear of being mistaken, that the BME has recovered the place it formerly held as one of the best bands in the Republic."⁶⁹ According to the governor, arrangements were being made to provide the BME with a new rehearsal site at Guerrero 22, a property adjacent to the governor's palace overlooking the Jardín de la Constitución.⁷⁰

The BME archives for Innes's first decade have unfortunately been lost, but beginning in 1960 a picture of daily life within the BME begins to emerge, thanks to better (or more extensive) record keeping and conservation. Before examining the BME's own institutional archives for the first time in this work, however, we must look at the transformation of the BME's mission during the second half of the twentieth century. We begin with the history of the Guelaguetza (gay-lah-GHET-sah), a pre-Hispanic tradition but now Oaxaca's largest annual (ticketed) tourist event, which for years included the BME's accompaniment; as well, we will consider the role of the BME in the development of the state of Oaxaca's tourism project.

7 From Political Proselytizer to Economic Engine

> Guelaguetza mine
> The hop shocks one's senses
> The color and gardens of the tehuana
> Where the white cotton trousers and the braids
> Enlaced
> Carry us away with the harmonious dances
> A heel-clicking love
> For my patria
> "La Guelaguetza," unknown poet

Whether or not the BME had completed its task of "teaching" Oaxacans to be citizens of a social democratic state is not verifiable—nor, by the mid-twentieth century, was it apparently as important to the state government. Although the civil-religious calendar still dominated the BME's performance schedule, the state government of Oaxaca looked to tourism to expand its economic base. Foreign institutions like the United Nations, as well as foreign investment, helped transform the state into one of Mexico's most visited destinations. Oaxaca's cultural and musical heritage became the focus of the state's tourism initiative, and it makes sense that the state would find at its disposal the musicians needed to press this new economic program forward. Crafting the program required great attention to the state's diversity in order both to preserve and to exploit this valuable commodity. The BME assumed the accompanying role in the project and in the Guelaguetza, which at once protects and profits from Oaxaca's musical patrimony.

The BME Joins in the Guelaguetza

The Guelaguetza has become one of Oaxaca's most important annual cultural events, drawing visitors from around the world.[1] The BME performs the extensive program (which includes songs and dances from each of Oaxaca's regions) twice for the *Lunes del Cerro* (Mondays on the Hill), on the penultimate and last Mondays of July. The second performance may be postponed until the first Monday in August if the date falls on Juárez's birthday. The Guelaguetza is so popular that modified versions may be performed for visiting dignitaries, in remote villages, or even for the president of the republic, as it was for President Adolfo López Mateos in Mexico City in 1961.[2]

The modern-day music and dance festival known as "la Guelaguetza" has its roots in pre-Hispanic times.[3] After the Aztecs subjugated the Central Valley of Oaxaca, they built a temple near the foot of the Cerro de Fortín, where the Carmen Alto church is located today. During the period that comprises the modern months of June and July, the Aztecs celebrated their Corn Goddess, Centeotl, and local Zapotecs joined in the celebrations. During the colonial period, Zapotec and Mixtec villages appropriated sites near the Cerro to honor their ancestors. The Carmelite order recognized the site's importance to the indigenous inhabitants and erected Carmen Alto there between 1679 and 1700.

By 1700 an annual Christian procession took place each year on 16 July in honor of the new convent's patron, St. Carmen. The procession, a hybrid of Spanish and indigenous celebrations, included fireworks, costumes, and Catholic songs accompanied by indigenous musicians and instruments. The procession ended at the doors of Carmen Alto. Celebrants carried food with them and picnicked on these Mondays, now known as Lunes del Cerro. The secularizing effects of the Reform tempered the spontaneous religious joy of such celebrations but did not end their observance.

"Guelaguetza" is a Zapotec word meaning "reciprocal exchange." Anthropologist Lynn Stephen asserts that Guelaguetza provides a framework for participation in ritual.[4] Not unlike social-support systems such as *cofradías* (sodalities) and *compadrazgo* (fictive kin), Guelaguetza moderates difference and creates connections and common ground for the exercise and development of a shared common identity, usually between intermarried families but often across communities.[5]

Sometime in the early twentieth century, a festival celebrating *indigenismo* (indigenism, or the valorization of indigenous culture), institutionalized as a state project after the Revolution, came to be celebrated in conjunction with Lunes del Cerro. Anthropologist Deborah Poole identifies a 1932 celebration called the "Homenaje Racial" (Racial Homage) as a predecessor of today's well-known Guelaguetza festival: "Organized as part of the four-hundredth anniversary of the founding of the city of Oaxaca, this predecessor [was described] by its scenographer Alberto Vargas as a 'great festival of the races to the Sultaness of the South' and was to consist of five delegations of 'racial ambassadresses' and their indigenous entourages. Each delegation, supposedly representing a discrete cultural territory within the state, paid homage to the city of Oaxaca."[6]

However, the AGEPEO Revolutionary-era files contain a memo from the governor of Oaxaca's secretary asking the BME to make its services available for an event called the "Fiesta de la Raza" (Festival of the Race) scheduled for 13 October 1918.[7] Whether or not the Fiesta de la Raza is a predecessor to Poole's Homenaje Racial is unclear. Furthermore, historian Rick López identifies a similar event that also predates Poole's: the "India Bonita" ("Pretty Indian Girl") contest in Necaxa, Puebla. Though no documents record the origins of the Necaxa event, it seems to have begun around

1921, when a girl named María Bibiana won the India Bonita contest. Mexican president Álvaro Obregón visited the town for the contest.[8]

Regardless of the event's genealogical uncertainty, Rosas Solaegui writes that in Oaxaca in 1932, "to end the Homenaje Racial, for the first time 'The Guelaguetza' was performed," and notes that the choreography included the offerings that give the festival its present name: "The unbelievably picturesque parade typical of the Valley: each Indian carrying in [his] hands the offering of clothing, kitchen utensils, serapes, jars, cups, glasses, toys, knives, machetes, sugar, and a great quantity of fruit and flowers."[9] Dancing pairs from Oaxaca's different regions, accompanied by immortal indigenous songs like the Isthmian "La Sandunga,"[10] provided a festival full of color, love, light, and happiness, according to Rosas Solaegui. If the 1918 event to which the BME was invited was indeed a predecessor of the 1932 festival, it is possible that the BME performed "The Guelaguetza" in 1932 as well.

The song "La Sandunga" and its connection to Isthmian identity merit a brief digression in order to explain its importance to the region's sense of patria chica. The title may be from the Isthmian Zapotec dialect for "profound music." When the BME plays the song of unrequited love, the audience does not have to be from the Isthmus to find its feelings of patria chica stirred. Oaxacans in general are already familiar, for example, with the Juchiteca, her (perceived) dominant cultural role, and her renowned beauty. If they are not themselves from the Isthmus, they might not hold the extreme sense of patria chica that the Juchiteco holds, but they might well recognize their own regional variation of it:

> While protective of their autonomy, the juchitecos feel themselves part of the Mexican nation and know how to conjugate their ethnic loyalty with their national loyalty. But their sense of belonging to the nation is peculiar: they integrate into the national community not as citizen-individuals, as liberal republican ideology requires, but as ethnic, to the point that the

national history that they share and celebrate is in good part the history of the juchitecan contributions to the construction and glorification of the nation: the victorious fight against the French in 1866, the juchitecan battalions in the Revolution, their men of letters, their artists, and above all, their painters of world renown.[11]

The passage does not mention music specifically, but the listener to "La Sandunga" recognizes the process at work—the tool, if you will, that constructs the connection to one's region, reinforces it in the memory as the music plays. Citizen and state are part of the process, and music torques the relationship between the two actors. A sense arises of unity within diversity, which the (political) state largely lacks but which it requires to remain viable. The Guelaguetza therefore functions in the same way for every Oaxacan when his or her region is represented during the performance.

Archival evidence indicates that performances of the Guelaguetza were held more or less regularly by the late 1920s.[12] In 1928, the Lunes del Cerro were postponed until August as Mexico was shaken by the assassination of former president, then president-elect, Álvaro Obregón.[13] The BME continued to play at the Guelaguetza during the municipal period: a 1946 performance took place in the Rotunda Azucena (White Lily Rotunda), then only a stone amphitheater carved on the Cerro del Fortín.[14]

Tourism: A "Concerted" Effort

As early as 1927, the Mexican federal government had formally expressed its dedication to, and involvement in, the development of tourism, but the hangover from the Revolution and the resultant bad press, along with a fractured national economy, delayed the project's success by nearly twenty years.[15] After World War II, however, the efforts paid off as large profits and crowds of visitors transformed Mexico into a tourist destination. The Mexican government envisioned a federal tourism project that would offset trade deficits, create jobs, and generate revenue with minimal infrastructure improvements and investment.[16] The quest for tourist dollars transformed the BME's mission, eventually making it one of the most visible (and audible) entities in the state. The exploitation of Oaxaca's cultural patrimony,[17] including BME performances, is now inextricably linked to tourism, and the advent of commercial aviation helped connect Oaxaca to the tourist world at large.

In his *Informe* of 1960, Governor Alfonso Pérez Gasga (served 1956–1962) wrote that the Lunes del Cerro celebrations had grown so popular that local hotels could no longer accommodate the influx of tourists. The governor also wrote that his offices would cooperate with the private sector (homes renting out rooms and the like) in any way possible in order to procure sufficient lodging for the anticipated influx of tourists.[18] By 1960 the annual governor's reports in Oaxaca clearly linked the state with the promotion of indigenous ritual life and tied Oaxacan cultural production, including the BME, to tourism.

Oaxaca also benefited from efforts made by the United Nations, which held its first Conference on Tourism and International Travel in 1963.[19] Governor Fernando Gómez Sandoval's (served 1970–1974) *Informes* of 1972 and 1973 contain photographs of the Rotonda de las Azucenas under construction but nearly completed.[20] The new, modern stadium replaced the stone amphitheater dug out of the Cerro de Fortín. The governor's accompanying written exposition directly linked the annual Guelaguetza festival, for which the BME provided musical accompaniment, to his state's tourism project:

> Among the plans we elaborate for the economic development of the State [of Oaxaca], those dedicated to the development of tourism occupy a notable place. With the end of strengthening our economy and with the purpose of enriching the spiritual ties that reciprocity generates between people, with great care the means are organized to facilitate this to the utmost, that whether nationals or foreigners visit and stay with us, they would be able to enjoy the sedate tranquility of our province, to admire

our pre-Columbian and colonial monuments, and to enjoy the natural beauty of the landscape and the traditional hospitality of the Oaxacan people.[21]

The new stadium was an essential part of the economic development project and contributed to the Guelaguetza's growth as Oaxaca's most important annual event for both tourists and locals. The festival and the stadium brought new visibility (and audibility) to the BME.

Nestor García Canclini notes that capitalism transformed Latin American "traditional peasant fiestas" and points out the advent of tourism as an economic enterprise of the state. García Canclini differentiates the traditional fiesta from the "urban fiesta," with its traits founded in capitalism, by at least seven different characteristics. The modern Guelaguetza, although based upon pre-Hispanic tradition, was constructed by the state to valorize the "peasant" contribution to Oaxacan culture and exhibits characteristics of the urban fiesta.[22]

The "traditional" fiesta took place within a carnivalesque "rupture of normal time," while its urban counterpart integrates the fiesta as a complement to, or compensation for, quotidian life. Traditional fiestas bore a collective character, with no exclusions based on class, but the urban fiesta is strongly privatized, exclusive, and selective: tickets must be bought to attend the Guelaguetza in Oaxaca. Furthermore, where traditional fiestas took place in great open spaces, the Guelaguetza, like the urban festival, is held in a private stadium, an enclosed space. While the Guelaguetza dates to at least early colonial Oaxaca, it was based on a pre-Hispanic agricultural calendar, and though the current festival's dates may approximate traditional dates, they now are subject to capitalist penetration, lack spontaneity, and therefore rely less on a classical calendarization. For example, weather events, civic holidays, or even social unrest can cause the Guelaguetza to be rescheduled. Finally, where the original fiesta-purpose of the Guelaguetza depended on an agricultural calendar marked by seasonal production, the urban form is now based on spectacle, the "logic of exchange value, conceived in the function of consumption," and is no longer a participatory celebration.[23]

Garcia Canclini's analysis, however, may not be perfectly suited to the Guelaguetza. For example, the paradigm ignores the strong emotional sense of regional pride that the performance arouses in the spectators. Nor can it account for the palpable and audible phenomenon of thousands of voices singing in joyful unison. Nevertheless, the schematic helps to identify the eternal (and politically constructed) processes at work in modern life, as well as a culture's acceptance of, or resistance to, those processes.

Cultural Patrimony, the United Nations, and the BME

Archeologist Roberto García Moll traces the origins of the Mexican state's project of historical preservation to the Revolutionary era, which produced similar state emphases on the fine arts, education, nationalism, and indigenism. In 1875 the Mexican government first established the Inspectorate of Monuments, and from 1917 to 1934 the government greatly expanded legislative control of Mexico's historic monuments. New legislation in the 1930s (concurrent with the first scientific excavations at Monte Albán) provided for the protection and conservation of the cultural patrimony, including archeological and historical monuments, "typical" villages, and sites of natural beauty. In 1972 a new federal law protecting the cultural patrimony was enacted and remains in place today.[24]

On 24 October 1966, the city of Oaxaca celebrated the twenty-first anniversary of the United Nations with great fanfare. At 11:00 a.m. the governor of Oaxaca, Rodolfo Brena Torres, along with the state delegation of UNESCO (the United Nations Educational, Scientific, and Cultural Organization), convened at the Teatro Macedonio Alcalá. Distinguished guests included representatives of Universidad Autónoma Benito Juárez de Oaxaca (Benito Juárez Autonomous University of Oaxaca, UABJO), representatives of the SEP, military officers, and government officials, as well as select members of Oaxaca's elite. The Banda de Guerra del Internado

"General Ignacio Mejia" presented the colors, marching down the theater's center aisle, first with the Mexican flag and then with the UN flag and the flags of its member nations.[25] Speakers at the event expressed Mexico's desire for peace, its unity with the UN, and its desires for non-intervention and for the self-determination of Mexican pueblos.[26]

The BME played the Mexican national anthem, then the overture from *O Guaraní* by the nineteenth-century Brazilian composer Antônio Carlos Gomes.[27] Then a choir from the Escuela de Bellas Artes (School of Fine Arts), directed by Herbierto Sánchez Tovar, performed "Mi casita del pinar" ("My Little House in the Pine Grove") by José Guadalupe Velázquez. A journalist covering the festivities observed the BME's military roots as fundamental to its ability to perform Franz Schubert's "Military March" so well. The BME also accompanied a recitation of Nicaraguan poet Rubén Darío's "La marcha triunfal" ("Triumphant March") with Chopin's "Military Polonaise." The BME closed the ceremony with the "Himno a la ONU" ("United Nations Hymn") by Oaxacan composer Gabino García Aranda. The United Nations Day ceremony, with its pomp, indigenist and military overtones, and inclusion of education officials, school choirs, and the BME, aptly represented Oaxaca's diversity within the program's themes.

Was there an ulterior motive for the celebration? Archival records, though incomplete, indicate that United Nations Day may have been celebrated annually in Oaxaca. While it seems unusual that the state of Oaxaca would celebrate the UN, it is possible that the annual celebration was part of a concerted effort to gain UNESCO recognition of Oaxaca's historical zones.[28] Furthermore, the effort dovetailed nicely with the government's gaze toward the foreign traveler for its tourism project, as well as with the BME's role within the project. The two-time BME director, Major Amador Pérez Torres (introduced below), even composed a hymn entitled "UNESCO"![29]

Ten years later, on 15 March 1976, Mexican president Luis Echeverría declared the colonial center of Oaxaca City and Monte

Albán "historic monument zones." In the official decree, the president detailed the historical significance of the state's pre-Hispanic civilization and monument zones.[30] A decade later, on 2 December 1986, the International Council on Monuments and Sites (ICOMOS), an advisory council to UNESCO, recommended that the historic center of the city of Oaxaca and the archeological site of Monte Albán be included on the World Heritage list, citing the "universal value" of the two sites.[31] The culmination of these events took place the following year on 10 December 1987, when, at the XI Meeting of the UNESCO Cultural Patrimony Committee, UNESCO added the city of Oaxaca to its list of honor for the city's contribution to the "Cultural Patrimony of Humanity." The BME's accompanying role in the achievement of this honor during the decades-long process attests to its importance in Oaxaca's tourism project.

Sixties Gigs: Itinerancy, Recording, Some Very Old Flags, and Oil

Meanwhile, the BME continued its daily routines. In his 1963 report on the BME from his annual *Informe*, Governor Raul Brena Torres (served 1962–1968) wrote, "Art has the virtue of uniting all men."[32] Brena Torres reported that within the previous year, the BME, now "of well-established prestige," had toured the country and participated in events in the National Auditorium in Mexico City for the Feria del Hogar (Home Tradeshow); in the Instituto Politécnico Nacional (National Polytechnic Institute), also in Mexico City; in Durango for the four-hundredth anniversary of its founding; and in the state of Guerrero for the Congreso de Anáhuac. The BME had also toured extensively within the state of Oaxaca, performing in Ejutla, Juchitán, and Loma Bonita. For Brena Torres, the BME's travels within the state served to "keep intact our affection [for those places]" and to "emotionally maintain unity within the state through the manifestations of art."[33]

The governor also reported that the BME had recorded various LPs on the Peerless label that were now available for sale[34] and that the proceeds would help to improve the BME's instruments and its members' preparation, as well as award the musicians with better individual economic compensation. The governor stressed that the recordings had been made not simply to create a business but to "diffuse our music and achieve at the same time the improvement of the BME."[35] One of the recordings was *Guelaguetza Oaxaqueña*, a double LP with gatefold cover featuring liner notes by Castro Mantecón. The studio recording reproduces an entire Guelaguetza.

Shortly after noon on 15 July 1964, a military plane landed at the federal airport in Oaxaca. A group of navy cadets escorted the plane's cargo to the Government Palace, where they delivered it to a group of military and civil leaders. But this was no ordinary cargo, as the civic fervor, parades and programs, and assembled groups attending the cargo's arrival that day attested. The cargo consisted of three Mexican military flags, captured by French Interventionist forces over a century before and now finally returned to their fatherland. Newspaper accounts described the flags as metaphorical "prisoners" from a time "when the Mexican national destiny was in the hands of a group of patriots, including some esteemed Oaxacans."[36] Headlines shouted that both "civic fervor" and "austere solemnity" accompanied the return of the flags. The words "fervor" and "solemnity" are not necessarily contradictory, nor are the emotions mutually exclusive. In fact, the headline writer paired two nouns that perfectly express the sentiments of civic religion. Such an event called for a celebratory program, and the BME provided the music for the occasion.

A quarter of a century earlier, on the evening of 18 March 1938, Mexican president Lázaro Cárdenas (served 1934–1940) had presided over Mexico's most significant nationalist event of the twentieth century when he nationalized Mexico's petroleum reserves and expropriated the equipment of the foreign oil companies in Mexico. The announcement inspired a spontaneous six-hour parade in Mexico City and was followed by a national fund-raising campaign to compensate the companies. Oil nationalization was

Mexico's greatest display of revolutionary economic nationalism.[37] At the celebrations, the Mexican flag prevailed over labor's red-and-black flags as the national colors, but anti-imperialism was only a minor current feeding "into the grander patriotic mainstream."[38] The act was accompanied by popular reactions, calls for unity and sacrifice, and unprecedented popular demonstrations, but the "reactions" were carefully organized events: labor unions, teachers, village commissions, veterans' associations, and Masonic lodges all mobilized in a patriotic effort in which many Mexicans participated and took national pride.[39] The date became known as Día de la Expropiación Petrolera (Petroleum Expropriation Day), and the BME led the celebrations—as it did, for example, in Oaxaca on 18 March 1966.[40] That the day was enshrined as a national holiday (and one displaying the characteristic Mexican patriotism) speaks to the importance of Mexican musical (and economic) nationalism.

Longing and Song: The Absent Oaxacan

La Semana del Oaxaqueño Ausente (Week of the Absent Oaxacan) reflects both continuity and change within the state and band contexts. The weeklong festival's events celebrate those Oaxacans who live abroad, some of whom return home for the celebration. The expatriate population residing in Mexico City, for example, is so large that a magazine entitled *Oaxaca en México* is published to keep absent Oaxacans informed of political and cultural happenings in their home state.[41] But the diaspora is not a solely modern occurrence: the pyramids at the Olmec monument zone at Teotihuacán north of Mexico City contain evidence of a Zapotec enclave. Conversely, visitors from Teotihuacán were received at the Zapotec royal seat of Monte Albán.[42]

Twentieth- and twenty-first-century realities have contributed to the creation of a new festival: The Week of the Migrant.[43] Oaxaca's extreme poverty has led to depopulation through mass migration to the United States, so much so that remittances from the United States are one of Oaxaca's main sources of income. Since

1966 the BME has played tribute to its migrant brothers (and sisters) during the weeklong remembrance, including *calendas* (street processions) in Oaxaca City, as well as at regional performances throughout the state. In 2001 a bureaucrat from the State Coordinator for Migrant Attention suggested that the BME perform "pieces related to the theme of migration [such as] "Al filo de la frontera" (On the edge of the border), "Ya no vengan para acá" (Don't come here anymore), "Al sur del Bravo" (South of the Rio Bravo), and, of course, "Canción Mixteca."[44]

After Innes: The Dance of the Directors

At 10:30 a.m. on 3 December 1974, the Innes era ended when the BME's director of a quarter century passed the baton to subdirector Prisciliano Martínez Mota.[45] Martínez served briefly as *encargado* (interim, or in charge) before the return of Major Amador Pérez Torres, who had served in the band as director from 1947 to 1950. Martínez had already served for nearly fifty years when he took charge, and he retired just four months after handing the baton to Pérez, in March 1975.[46] Pérez himself served only one more year. He became ill in January 1976 and, within a few weeks of taking sick leave, died in the Central Military Hospital in Mexico City on 30 January 1976. On 1 February the BME dedicated its Sunday performance to Pérez's memory. Pérez was a respected composer, and the BME opened and closed that day's performance with perhaps his most famous piece, the danzón "Nereidas." The memorial performance included a funeral march.[47] Among Pérez's works still found in the BME sheet-music archives are waltzes, corridos, hymns, pasos dobles, and marches.

Upon Pérez's death, músico mayor José Bautista Martínez took over as director, but he remained in the BME only until September 1976, when he resigned, ostensibly to attend to family matters. Instability in the director's position resulted in a loss of prestige for the band as it floundered during the first few years after Innes's departure. In a 1978 newspaper article[48] with the headline "The BME Better Each Day," Rosas Solaegui, who for some time had been writing about the BME, wrote of a recent and noticeable improvement within the BME: its uniforms were now crisp, its instruments polished—both sights unseen, according to Rosas Solaegui, for a long time. Rosas Solaegui alluded to the BME's malaise, suggesting that it had floundered under ineffective musical or administrative leadership. More than once in the article, Rosas Solaegui described a former director as "that unfortunate subject not worth mentioning by name," blaming the unnamed director for the BME's decline and resultant loss of prestige. Rosas Solaegui wrote, "For a long time the BME had been performing without pleasure, only to fulfill its duties," and noted that its uniforms had been "moldy from their filth."[49]

Two months later, Rosas Solaegui wrote an article describing his experience as a judge in the selection of the BME's new músico mayor. Also on the judges' panel was the Oaxacan historian Jorge Fernando Iturribarría, along with another journalist and a professor. The aspiring participants interpreted Verdi's "La fuerza del destino," and all three acquitted themselves well.[50] Leodegario Martínez Vásquez, a popular trumpeter in the BME, was awarded the position and eventually rose to the position of director in 1988. Martínez had played and served as captain in the Banda de Música de la Ciudad de México.[51]

Rosas Solaegui also wrote that the members of the BME, once divided and abused, all now sought to surpass previous heights and to discipline themselves in order to improve. Self-discipline, according to Rosas Solaegui, was the basis of success for all organizations. Rosas Solaegui addressed the poor condition of the instruments provided by the state, which meant that most musicians had to furnish their own; he also decried the deplorable conditions of the BME's new installations.[52]

The article raises some questions. Because Rosas Solaegui was writing to a contemporary audience, he chose his words carefully so as not to identify anyone by name. Was he referring to Innes's tenure as one of degeneration? Or was he referring to the "dance of directors" that had followed Innes? Could Pérez have been responsible in less than a year for the conditions that Rosas Solaegui described as having persisted "for a long time"? Logic suggests that Pérez could not have presided over such a precipitous loss of prestige in so short a time. On the other hand, evidence from the BME's own archives portrays Innes's twenty-four years of service as an era of bureaucratic zeal, interpersonal problems, and persistent turmoil within the organization, which might have given rise to disgruntled musicians and a resulting loss of professional demeanor.

An interview with Zoilo Solis Félix, who was at that time subdirector of the BME, provides details that give us a more complete view of the BME during Innes's later years. Solis joined the BME in 1971. His father was a bandleader in Yalalag, a suburb of Oaxaca, and his brother also played in the BME. One of Solis's sons, a clarinetist, represents the third generation of the family's service in the BME. According to Solis, Innes wielded absolute power within the BME. Rehearsal schedules were brutal: the BME practiced five times a week for two and a half hours each session. Innes's behavior during rehearsals could be unprofessional: as a classically trained symphonic violinist, Innes seemed unable to cope with the musical particularities of a wind band, often screaming during rehearsals when unsatisfied with the musicians' performance.[53]

No breach of the regulations went unnoted, either. The archival record is full of almost daily citations for tardiness, absences, and insubordination. The conditions under Innes, along with the extensive services required of the BME, led many musicians to leave the ensemble. Some sought to further their artistic interests and joined bands in Mexico City. For them, life in the BME had become less an artistic endeavor than a joyless bureaucratic routine. Further exacerbating the already difficult conditions, Innes often left his subdirector in charge so that the director could spend time in his newly constructed beachfront home on Oaxaca's Pacific coast. Solis says that it was rumored that Innes purchased the home by withholding some of the per diems granted to the musicians for travel. Outright venality was not unknown: Innes sometimes sold positions in the BME in lieu of auditioning musicians for the band.

Innes was also jealous of his more popular musicians; in fact, he refused to play Amador Pérez's compositions even though some were crowd favorites.[54]

As the state employees' union delegate for the BME, Solis was privy to a conversation that Innes had with an unidentified governor in the early 1970s. According to Solis, Innes told the governor that the musicians did not need a pay raise: they were peasants, had a patch of land to work, and would probably just get drunk on the increased pay.[55] Innes threatened the musicians with the loss of their positions if they ever took the opportunity granted them by the governor to air grievances during monthly inspections.

Band members' inebriation was a continual problem for Innes. For example, Agustín González Martínez of Teotitlán del Valle, Tlacolula, was a well-liked and proficient drummer. Innes began reprimanding him for (apparently alcohol-related) absences as early as 1962.[56] For the next five years González missed at least three performances a year. Maybe he was just working a loophole (the regulations allow up to three excused absences per year), but González's absences were never "excused." Was he such a good musician that it was worth putting up with his absences?[57] In 1967 González was suspended for striking another musician during a performance,[58] and through 1970 he continued to miss work without appropriate excuses. In 1971, González was cited for reporting to work while drunk.[59] In 1974 González asked for a leave of absence, which was granted, but he failed to return to work for the scheduled New Year's Eve performances. Innes cited him for abandoning his position and asked for his immediate termination. In January 1975 the state fired González,[60] but that was not the end of him: after Innes's retirement, González reappeared as a musician in 1986 under director Cosme Cruz. Sadly, the same problems persisted, and the drummer was fired again shortly after returning to the BME.

Elipedio Medina Tovar's tenure as director (1979–1981) was not without problems either. The archives allude to a possible lack of respect for the director, or at least to an ongoing disciplinary or morale problem among the musicians. Medina noted an incident during a performance at the Hotel Presidente in early 1981 by writing reprimands for musicians for what the director considered "acts of sabotage directed [at Medina] personally."[61] In an undated reprimand, Medina accused Joaquín Ortiz Rubio of dropping his part during the "Jarabe Mexicano" and claimed that the public had immediately recognized the silence. Medina wrote that he was "convinced [that Ortiz knew his] responsibilities and must duly comply, for the contrary is to take the attitude of rebel and to sabotage the work of others."[62]

Future BME director Leodegario Martínez Vásquez (who served as director from June 1988 to October 1992) was cited for the same incident. In the reprimand, Medina wrote that Martínez's entire trumpet section went quiet and that Martínez had "tried to prejudice [Medina] personally" as well. The director continued: "I am not the master of the Band; we owe [our positions] to the State Governor [and] to the people that we must serve with fidelity and care."[63]

Perhaps the years of duress under such stern taskmasters as Innes and Cruz (Cruz served from May 1983 to June 1988) lifted Martínez to the directorship. Cruz's forbidding comportment and harsh discipline eventually led to his forced resignation.[64] Rogelio Martínez Hernández, a tuba player with more than twenty-five years' service with the BME, recalls Cruz's skills as a clarinetist but also notes his terrible treatment of the musicians.[65] Cruz often kept his military sidearm on the desk of his office during meetings. His rage for order bordered on the "neurotic," and, according to Martínez, Cruz sometimes even threatened the musicians during public performances. At least ten members resigned from the BME during his tenure, citing the director as the reason for their departure. Eventually the governor intervened, visiting the rehearsal hall to hear the musicians' complaints against Cruz. When the governor heard that Cruz had once physically removed a musician from the hall by picking him up and carrying him to the street, the governor asked for Cruz's resignation.[66] Later, in a meeting between the governor, the BME syndicate delegate, and other members of the BME, complaints were lodged against the director.[67] The musicians called Cruz a "despot," describing him as one who saw himself as infallible and always blamed others for mistakes. The governor told the musicians present that they could choose the new director themselves, as he wanted to avoid any possible further problems with a nominee of his own. Because no section leader really wanted the position, after a thirty-minute meeting those present nominated Martínez. Although the BME members liked him personally, they saw him as ineffectual and unthreatening and perhaps nominated him in a moment of selfishness. The musicians thought that selecting such an *esponjoso* (spongy) leader would avoid the problems that might arise with a more dictatorial director.[68]

Though the government entities responsible for the BME oscillate between involvement and lack of interest depending on the personalities in power and the vagaries of bureaucratic administrations, the BME continues rehearsing and performing regardless of the political atmosphere. But is the government able to effectively direct what is at its core an artistic corporation? When bureaucrats become involved, bad, or at least funny, things may happen. In preparation for the visit to Oaxaca of the Spanish ambassador to Mexico during "Spanish Culture Week," the Director of Cultural Development (an Orwellian appellation if ever there was one) asked that the BME, instead of playing the same old Spanish saws "Granada" and "España Caní," perform "Spanish music, like 'Spanish Eyes.'"[69] The unwitting bureaucrat was apparently unaware that the German composer Bert Kaempfert is responsible for composing "Spanish Eyes," and the song contains only a pop-modulated reference to "authentic" Spanish music![70] The incident, though amusing, aptly demonstrates the danger involved when an uninformed bureaucrat attempts to play the role of cultural mediator in the realm of art. It also warns that music may not always be effectively wielded as a tool in the hands of the state.

Conclusion
Gauging the Political Tool

> Music creates order out of chaos; for rhythm imposes unanimity upon the divergent, melody imposes continuity upon the disjointed, and harmony imposes compatibility upon the incongruous.
> Yehudi Menuhin, *Theme and Variations*

> How could a unified whole be assembled from so many heterogeneous pieces?
> Jean Meyer, "Mexico"

The Last Colonial Vestiges

The last archival record of a request for the BME to perform at an ecclesiastical event is dated 12 March 1975. In a letter directed to director Amador Pérez, the chaplain of the Basilica de la Soledad requested that the BME perform on Good Friday in the procession of the Holy Virgin of Soledad. The performance was scheduled to take place in the atrium of the Minor Basilica, and the BME was asked to provide music to the procession "to provide the utmost prestige to the solemn act."[1] Whether or not the BME performed is not clear. While the BME does continue to perform at patron-saint festivals, it no longer enters any religious edifice or participates in any religious procession.[2]

Sometime between 1983 and 1988, although exactly when cannot be verified, a dustup occurred between BME director (and former army officer) Guillermo Cosme Cruz and a serving military officer. The BME performed at a breakfast event on Día del Ejército (Army Day, on or about 19 February), attired in their military-style uniforms. Cruz tried to give orders to some soldiers in the Twenty-Eighth Regiment of the Mexican Army. The soldiers, not knowing with whom they were dealing, sought out their superior to tell him that Cruz was ordering them around. Upon ascertaining that Cruz was not an army officer but a civilian bandleader, the regiment's leader went to the governor, complaining that attiring nonmilitary men in military-style uniforms had caused confusion among his troops. The officer and Cruz argued in front of the governor; the officer asked, "¿Quién es éste que se burla de los militares?" ("Who is this that mocks the military?").[3] The officer won out when, shortly thereafter, the BME's uniforms changed forever. No longer would they wear military-style uniforms. Instead, to this day, the BME dresses for gala events in that most bureaucratic of uniforms, the navy blue suit.[4]

Eliseo Martínez García, the BME's director since May 1995, is a classically trained pianist and organist. (See fig. 16.) Governor Diodoro Carrasco Altamirano (served 1992–1998) appointed Martínez, who at the time was Director of the School of Fine Arts at UABJO. Martínez studied at the School of Fine Arts at UABJO, at the National Conservatory of Music in Mexico City, and at the Pontifical Institute of Sacred Music in Rome. In addition to his work directing the BME, Martínez has performed in chamber groups and as a featured organist in cathedrals throughout Mexico. Martínez's father was an organist, and he continues to serve as the concert organist for the National Conservatory. "Maestro Cheo," as he is affectionately known by the public, also serves as professor of Music Theory and Harmony at UABJO's School of Fine Arts, and is Titular Organist at Santo Domingo Cathedral in the city of Oaxaca.[5]

An organizational chart from 1997 describes the BME hierarchy in its present form. The director remains at the top of the

FIG. 16. Maestro Eliseo Martínez García, Italy, 2014. Courtesy of Archivo de la Banda de Música del Estado de Oaxaca.

organization. Below the director are the *gestor* (manager) and two administrative assistants, who fulfill some of the duties of the former cita papelero position. Next is the ranking musician, known as the assistant director, a position usually filled by the first-chair clarinetist. An artistic coordinator, apparently the replacement for the former position of músico mayor, is next in the hierarchy, ranking directly above the other musicians. The 1997 incarnation of the BME included twenty-eight woodwinds, twenty-seven brass, and four percussionists. The chart called for a total of sixty-five musicians; the band apparently had four vacancies at the time.[6] In 2003 the BME represented the Republic of Mexico at Il Festival Bandistico Internazionale Città di Besana (The City of Besana International Wind Band Festival) in Italy. Participants included twelve other bands from around the world, including bands from Italy, Holland, Germany, Spain, Australia, Hungary, and the Czech Republic. Over 850 musicians performed twelve concerts and marched in three parades to a total spectatorship of over 60,000 music lovers. Finally, after 135 years, the BME had performed outside of Mexico to international acclaim.

The BME and the Present-Day *Fiesta Patronal*

On the afternoon of 7 December 2005, half of the BME's members gathered in front of Guerrero 406 to board a bus that would carry them to the municipality of Concepción Pápalo[7] in the Cañada (Canyon region) for the town's annual festival honoring La Inmaculada Virgen de la Concepción (The Virgin of the Immaculate Conception). The Cañada, bordering on the state of Puebla, is Oaxaca's northernmost region, a hot, low-lying canyon situated between the higher, cooler valleys of Oaxaca and the Puebla and Central Mexico basin.[8] As the name Cañada suggests, it is mountainous and rocky: Concepción is reachable only via a final ascent on a series of steep and unpaved switchback roads. The precipitous drops are unprotected by any form of guardrails, and the road's narrow gauge makes passing difficult and dangerous. Though Concepción is about 112 miles from the capital, the journey took some four hours, with most of that time spent traveling the final 12.5 miles. The altitude within the municipality rises from a minimum of 3,000 feet above sea level to a maximum of 10,500 feet! Concepción is the prototypical Oaxacan municipality: varied, geologically fractured, "accidental."

The BME was scheduled to perform an abbreviated version of the Guelaguetza at 8:00 p.m. Accompanying the performance was a student dance troupe from UABJO. At 7:00 a.m. the following day, the BME would arrive back in Oaxaca City, giving the band just two hours before it had to leave again to perform at another festival, this time in the Sierra Juárez at San Miguel Cajonos.

Concepción is a small town with a population of slightly more than three thousand. It is an agricultural town with a cowboy feel; many of the male inhabitants have adopted the style of the North American west: pickup trucks, cowboy hats and boots, and big belt buckles. The small arena built in the town center for the festival's jaripeo adds to the ambiance. The festival air that day was palpable: itinerant vendors parked their trucks on the sides of the narrow streets that wind throughout the town, selling pots and pans, electronic toys from China, leather goods, pottery, and knives. Arcades, games, and amusement park rides numbered among the attractions. From somewhere the sounds of an unseen brass band echoed. High above the already altitudinous town of Concepción sat the inevitable bandstand.

The band's late arrival did not matter, as the religious portion of the festivities had not yet concluded. A contracted private band was performing the services inside and outside the church, as the BME is no longer permitted to perform at specifically religious ceremonies. That two distinct bands were performing that day demonstrates the parallels between the religious organization of the town's church and patron saints and the secular state government. Wax flowers festooned the church entrance where the contracted band, led by the clergy, was entering the church for Mass as the BME descended from its bus. The band contracted to provide the accompaniment to Mass, and the procession within and without the church, could have been any Mexican band—likely a family or neighborhood band, consisting of brass, woodwinds, and percussion. A representative of the mayordomo, a congregation official responsible for governing the festivities, received the BME and ushered the musicians to the mayordomo's house, a vaguely modern concrete building that also serves as the town's community center. The band sat down to plates of *mole negro* and tortillas, followed by *pan dulce* and *café de olla*.

After dinner the Mass still not concluded, the BME members gathered their instruments and made their way to the venue, the town's open-air basketball courts. A pick-up game ensued between the musicians while they awaited their performance. (Interestingly, the town has four basketball courts and only one soccer field.) Once the folkloric dance group from UABJO had arrived and begun to don their costumes, people began to assemble. By 11:00 p.m. the gym was packed. The BME performed the Guelaguetza, a feat requiring about two hours of continuous music, with brief respites while the dancers changed costumes. Finally, there was time to grab a couple of cold beers and some fair food before returning to the bus for the journey back to Oaxaca City.

Within a performance like that night's in Concepción, all the history and heritage of the BME can be found: colonial military and religious vestiges surface, as do the liberal, post-revolutionary didactic role and the valorization of Oaxaca's ethnic heritage. The BME's liminal role, like that of its predecessors, has placed it on a sacred threshold, yet the secular band was not permitted to enter the church. The only thing lacking was the European repertoire, but the night called specifically for the Guelaguetza, and that was clearly what the crowd wanted. Perhaps most important, however, is the BME's relationship to the people: far from the Central Valleys, isolated by geography and poor modes of transportation, the people of Concepción awaited *their* BME.

Music accompanied the sociopolitical practices of both of the peoples who met when Spain invaded Mexico. The Spanish and the indigenous alike employed music to organize their invading troops and to intimidate and frighten their enemies. Both peoples employed music in their respective religious practices, which were difficult to separate from their bellicose traditions. Music performed for sacred purposes also functioned to unite the participants and offer praise to their deities. Finally, music could be spontaneous and celebratory, as in moments of victory or during rituals. The same musicians often participated in all these types of events. Musicians were required to bridge different worlds: the civilian and the military, the sacred and the secular, that of power and that of populace. When these peoples met and intermingled, so did their musical practices. The resulting people and practices were the progeny of a new, unique mestizo world. Musicians bridged the fissure that arose from that hybrid history. Neither Spanish nor Indian, neither Christian nor pagan, neither military nor civilian, the musicians who crossed the thresholds between Old World and New lived a liminal experience and were forced to adapt.

The new political realities that emerged in New Spain and later in Mexico added to the hybrid nature of musical practices. When the Bourbon regime suppressed the sodalities in the late eighteenth century, many previous sites of musical performance were closed. After independence and during the fitful growth of the liberal Mexican nation, religious venues for music suffered the same fate. The liberal nation filled the resulting vacuum with its own practice, a civil religion, which instead of sovereigns and deities enshrined both state and individual in a rapidly expanding pantheon replete with solemn and celebratory practices echoing with music. Like the imperial powers before it, the Mexican state realized music's importance.

Is music, deployed as a political tool, necessary at various stages of national development? While liberalism preferred militias made up of citizen-soldiers and abhorred the notion of a standing army, the same was not true of a standing military band, whose roots in Mexico were directly connected to the nation's bellicose history: the band as a state organization persisted and proliferated at all political levels, from municipal to federal. For nineteenth-century Mexican liberals, music helped unify the diverse populations into a single democratic community. It helped build both the conformity and heterogeneity required in a democracy. It taught a language of national symbols and values, contributing to the order and the work ethic required under capitalism; it taught respect for the power of the state and the individual's role within it. Music as a political tool in Oaxaca functioned as part of that civilizing and modernizing project. Later, music furthered the institutionalization of the social aspects of the Revolution. Finally, the late twentieth-century (capitalist) state government in Oaxaca found music an effective tool in marketing itself to the world and used many of the same social aspects important in the Revolution as a marketing tool—specifically, the valorization of mestizaje ethnically, culturally, and musically.

The BME is part of a broad process that has located it as a component of the modern state of Oaxaca. The state government "wields" the BME as part of its vast popular and political repertoire of practices. But what of the individual's response to state-sponsored musical practices? What of human motivation or simple enjoyment? Researchers often overemphasize power in their analyses. Historians must take care not to project personal values onto other peoples' cultures or overinterpret what might be emotional responses. The senses of community and ecstasy are present in music's military function, its religious function, and its role as simple entertainment. Besides providing order amid disorder, music can be pleasurable, and when pleasure reaches extremes, ecstasy ensues. Music can melt the boundaries of the self and reveal bonds to the external: the community, the state. Its rational order is a metaphor for social cohesion and order. When the citizens of Oaxaca hear their band, they wax ecstatic.

Throughout its existence as an independent country, Mexico's entrance on the international scene has followed an arduous path. Diverse projects—some failures, some successes—that have allowed Mexico to consolidate itself as a sovereign and autonomous nation in both its domestic and foreign politics have always had the same objective: to safeguard the nation's national sovereignty. Clearly, in the case of music, many influences have come from abroad, but an equal portion of the nation's musical repertoire has arisen from indigenous and hybrid mestizo influences. In Mexico, the use of music as a political tool illuminates the singular trajectory of the Mexican state, allowing its citizens to reflect on the challenges that political life has held for them in its past and to sing toward a more equitable and democratic future.

Can music actually function as an effective political tool, bringing unity to a state as diverse as Oaxaca? Recent political and social unrest may indicate otherwise: Oaxaca remains a vastly unequal state politically, socially, and economically. Unity shines through, however, in the form of patria chica, when the regional songs of Oaxaca sound forth, apparently inspiring all the state's inhabitants regardless of their native region.

Multiple sound images resonate from the BME today: memories of a bellicose, violent, and militaristic past, as well as the menace of the janissary; the reedy, voice-like clarinets bespeaking yearning beyond words; the tropical sound of the timbale. The multiplicity of sounds, instruments, and repertoire are the exclusive products of neither the Old World nor the New; instead, they are the triumphant refrains of a liberal promise made to a marginalized majority, the joys and tears of the complex cascade of history, of social forces that have sounded from the Sierra to the Central Valley and south to the Isthmus for hundreds of years.

E. P. Thompson writes, "Once a social system has become set, it does not need to be endorsed daily by exhibitions of power (although occasional punctuations of force will be made to define the limits of the system's tolerance); what matters more is a continuing theatrical style."[9] This work has not attempted to construct an "alternate modernity" for the diverse citizens of Oaxaca. The state's deployment of the BME as a political tool, and its accompanying "punctuations" of brass, woodwind, and percussion, all contribute to a theatrical style meant to provide unity and sustain the social system.

On 3 December 2013 the BME celebrated its 145th anniversary with a gala concert, free to the public, at the Teatro Alcalá. Maestro Eliseo Martínez García led his seventy musicians in renditions of Modest Mussorgsky's *Pictures at an Exhibition* and Tchaikovsky's *Concerto for Piano and Orchestra*, the latter accompanied by Oaxacan pianist Antonio Manzo D'nes. Before raising his baton, Maestro Cheo confirmed to those in attendance his continued commitment to collaborate with all artistic and cultural organizations within the Secretaría de las Culturas y Artes de Oaxaca (Secretariat of Culture and Art of Oaxaca). He then recognized the contributions of each musician and asked the audience to now "revel in their talent." And, as if to remind us of the BME's governmental role, he added that under his direction, the band would "continue its policy of openness and constant dialogue."

The history of the BME is that of musicians at the service of the state. Various bands through the ages have sounded imperial attacks in the quest for territory and precious metals, have performed and recorded in order to market the state and its products. But what of the response? How effective is the "tool of music"? It is difficult to gauge music's effectiveness as a tool, largely because of the multiplicity of emotional responses it inspires. The musicians of the BME have filled the fissures that appear on the continuum of the history of Oaxaca, have filled the empty air, connecting two spheres: the political and the personal. The BME's repertoire reflects the values, expectations, and implicit rules that express and shape the collective intentions of its fellow citizens. Its practices and performances, a result of cultural hybridity, a reaction to the violence of noise, enable creativity and agency on the part of both performer and listener, but that does not mean that the social and political systems in Oaxaca are equitable or yet consolidated. Integrating musical issues into political history is an elusive but important task for understanding the role of music in everyday experience, political life, and local economies. Studying the political use of music helps us to recover the aural experience of life in Oaxaca, the sounds that waft throughout all the state's regions. *It is impossible to ignore a wind band.* In that way, at least, the BME has been a consistent and unifying force for 146 years, one that the state must still find useful.[10]

APPENDIX 1

BME Directors

January 1868–April 1868	Pablo Vásquez (Batallón Zaragoza)
January 1868–October 1868	Bernardino Alcalá (Batallón Guerrero)
July 1868–1875	Francisco Sakar
1876–1880	Bernabé Alcalá
February 1880–April 1880	José Dominguez Castro (Provisional)
19 April 1880–December 1882	José Alcalá
1882–1892	José María Velasco
August 1892–April 1897	Lieutenant Gabriel Garzón
1 May 1897–August 1915	Germán Canseco
1915–1924	Professor Daniel Baltazar
8 October 1924–1928	Germán Canseco (four months solista Moises Baltazar Velasco, encargado)
1928–1936	Professor Agustín Hernández Toledo (one month músico mayor Moises Baltazar Velasco, encargado)
1936–1942	Captain Próspero A. González
1942–1947	Prof. Anastacio García Santos (by 15 May 1942)

1947–1950	Capitán Amador Pérez Torres (10 days Subdirector Moises Baltazar Velasco, encargado)
1950–3 December 1974	Professor Diego Innes Acevedo (briefly Subdirector Prisciliano Martínez Mota)
1975–January 1976	Major Amador Pérez Torres
January 1976	Músico Mayor Jose Bautista Martínez, encargado
1976–1979 (perhaps continuing to 1981; record unclear)	Elipedio Medina Tovar (by 1 February)
1981	Bulmaro Yescas Vásquez
21 December 1981–October 1982	José Bautista Martínez
October 1982–May 1983	Lucas Hernández Martínez
May 1983–June 1988	Guillermo Cosme Cruz
June 1988–October 1992	Leodegario Martínez Vásquez
November 1992–December 1994	Abel Jiménez Luis
January 1995–April 1995	Zoilo Solís Félix, Subdirector encargado
May 1995–Present	Eliseo Martínez García

Sources: Archivo de la Banda de Música del Estado de Oaxaca, Oaxaca, Mexico (ABME); Archivo General del Ejecutivo Poder del Estado de Oaxaca, Oaxaca, Mexico (AGEPEO); Castro Mantecón, *Efemérides*, n.p.; *Memorias Administrativas del Ciudadano gobernador Albino Zertuche 1889, parte expositive. Provincia.*

APPENDIX 2

Oaxaca Military and National Guard Units, 1846 and 1848

Military Units in Oaxaca, 1846
1. Cuerpo de Plana Mayor
2. Piquete de Artillería
3. Batallón de Oaxaca
4. Piquete de Tamiltepec
5. Batallón de Tehuantepec
6. Auxiliares de Tehuantepec
7. Depósito de Tropa
8. Regimiento actívo de Caballería
9. Tropa retirada
10. Auxiliares de Huajuapam
11. Auxiliares de Tonalá
12. Departamento de la Comandancia general
13. Batallón Trujano

National Guard Units in Oaxaca, 1848
1. División de Teotitlán del Camino
2. Batallón Lealtad de Tehuantepec (three companies)
3. División de Huajuapam de León
4. División de Tlaxiaco
5. División de Tuxtepec
6. Mayoría de Ordenes de Oaxaca

7. Caballería Permanente
8. Artillería
9. Batallón Ligero Guerrero (four companies, one piquete de artillería)

Source: Archivo General del Ejecutivo Poder del Estado de Oaxaca (AGEPEO), Concentración, Guerra 1846 and 1848.

APPENDIX 3
BME Dependencies

1868–ca. 1907	Ramo de Guerra
1907–1937	Secretaría de Gobernación, Inspector General de la Policía, Ramo de Guerra y Seguridad Pública
1937–1947	Municipio de la Ciudad de Oaxaca
1947–ca. 1969	Secretaría de Gobernación

Departments within the Secretaría de Gobernación Responsible for the BME

1969–1984	Departamento de Información, Relaciones Públicas, y Cultura
1984–1987	Dirección General de Educación, Cultura, y Recreación, Secretaría de Desarrollo Económico y Social
1987–1992	Dirección General de Educación, Cultura, y Bienestar Social
1992	Consejo Estatal para la Cultura y las Artes
ca. 1993–2003	Instituto Oaxaqueño de las Culturas
2004–2010?	Secretaría de la Cultura
2010–present	Secretaría de las Culturas y Artes de Oaxaca

Sources: Archivo General del Ejecutivo Poder del Estado de Oaxaca, Oaxaca, Mexico (AGEPEO); Archivo Histórico del Municipal de la Ciudad de Oaxaca, Oaxaca, Mexico (AHMCO); Archivo de la Banda de Música del Estado de Oaxaca, Oaxaca, Mexico (ABME).

APPENDIX 4

Extraordinary Performances, 1966 (Partial)

Graduation Ceremony, UABJO (19 January)
Presidential performance for President Díaz Ordáz (Mexico City, 22 January)
First day of classes, UABJO (26 January)
Constitution Day (5 February)
Carnival (12, 19–22 February)
Commemoration of the monument to Guerrero in Cuilalpam (14 February)
Woman's Day (16 February)
Army Day (19 February)
Martyr's Day, anniversary of the deaths of Madero and Pino Suárez (22 February)
Flag Day (24 February)
Congress of the Ophthalmologists' Academy (6–10 March)
Oath of the Oaxaca Student Federation (7 March)
Petroleum Expropriation Day (18 March)
Juárez's birthday in Guelatao (20–21 March)
Infant Games and Rounds (26 March)
Welcoming the President to the Isthmus (31 March–1 April)
Lenten Festival and Easter (six consecutive Fridays, March–April)
American Indian Day (April)
Improvers of the Rural Home (18 April)

May Day, or Workers' Day (1 May)
Teachers' Day (3 May)
Batalla de Puebla (5 May)
Mothers' Day (8 May)
Students' Day (21, 23 May)
Week of the Absent Oaxacan (23–29 May)
La Guelaguetza (June–July)
Arbor Day (11 July)
Bastille Day (14 July)
Anniversary of Juárez's death (18 July)
Commemoration of the Battle of de Juchitán de Zaragoza (5 September)
Commemoration of the Defense of Chapultepec Castle (13 September)
Independence Day (15–16 September)
Anniversary of the Battle of Miahuatlán (3 October)
Commemoration of the Battle of La Carbonara (18 October)
United Nations Day (24 October)
Vocational School Graduation (15 November)
Anniversary of the Revolution (20 November)
Fourth National University Basketball Championship (12 December)
Night of the Radishes (23 December)

No date given

Centenary of the Taking of Oaxaca in 1866
Congress of Medical Surgeons
Cornerstone-laying ceremony, School of Medicine
Employees' Day
First day of classes, primary school
First day of classes, Vocational School
Inauguration of the Artisans' School
Miss Normal School Pageant
National Dance Contest (Mexico City)
Race of the Symbolic Fire (in celebration of the Olympics)

Source: Compiled from Archivo de la Banda de Música del Estado de Oaxaca (ABME), 1966. The BME performed at least fifty extraordinary performances, some involving multiple sets and travel, in 1966. It should be remembered that this list does not include an additional 138 ordinary performances at serenatas and dominicales. While some performances might have been abbreviated—for example, only requiring the national anthem for a flag-raising ceremony—the BME still had to prepare and perform. Performances in 1966, not including rehearsals, numbered more than two hundred. A number of other bands have now assumed the duties of many of these performances, providing not only performance opportunities for the new symphonies, orchestras, and bands that have emerged within the state but also respite for the BME.

NOTES

INTRODUCTION

1. The BME has undergone various permutations that have led to a variety of names, some vague, others specific. The name changes are discussed below. Unless otherwise specified, I will refer to the band as the "BME." All translations are my own.
2. The song was written in 1917 by Oaxacan composer José López Alavés (1889–1975). López Alavés began his career at the age of ten, playing the guitar and mandolin; one year later, he was playing the *requinto* (E-flat clarinet) for the children's band in his village of Huajuapan. After studying at the National Conservatory of Music in Mexico City from 1907 to 1913, where he won first prize while seated as first clarinet, he played in various bands. López Alavés was nearly shot during the Revolution and later found safe employment accompanying silent motion pictures in Mexico City cinemas. From 1928 to 1955, López Alavés performed in various military and police bands in Mexico City. He composed more than three hundred pieces and is credited as one of the progenitors of the foxtrot in Mexico City. See Bustamante Gris, *Cancionero de música popular oaxaqueña*, 95–96.
3. The state is a "type of very strong, usually highly centralized government with a professional ruling class, largely divorced from the bonds of kinship that characterized simpler societies. It can wage war, draft soldiers, levy taxes, and exact tribute. It has public buildings, works, and services of various sorts, usually implemented through professional architects, engineers, and bureaucrats. Among these will usually appear public works of a religious nature, attended by full-time specialists maintaining a state religion." See Flannery, "The Cultural Evolution of

Civilizations," 403–4. I have chosen Flannery's definition as the result of his extensive work in the Valley of Oaxaca. Although he does not specifically include the role of musicians within his definition, such an inclusion is contextually and thematically appropriate for the purposes of the present work. Flannery's definition also highlights the characteristics of the pre-Hispanic Mesoamerican, Spanish Imperial, and (Western) modern states. By "modern" I mean the age in which the separation of church and state resulted in the dominance of science and increasing secularism. Those developments, however, are paralleled by, and at times in conflict with, the mobilization of religious rhetoric and ideologically driven worldviews.

4. See Chance, *Conquest of the Sierra*, and Chassen-López, *From Liberal to Revolutionary Oaxaca*, 39.
5. The majority of the members of the BME self-identify as being of Serrano Zapotec descent, a few others as being of Mixtec descent. An even smaller number are unaware of or choose not to identify their descent.
6. Paddock, *Ancient Oaxaca*, 2.
7. Gerhard, *Guide to the Historical Geography of New Spain*, 48.
8. Gerhard, *Guide to the Historical Geography of New Spain*, 50.
9. Gerhard, *Guide to the Historical Geography of New Spain*, 50–51.
10. The national *Partido Revolucionario Institucional* (Institutional Revolutionary Party, PRI) has held sway in Oaxaca for decades.
11. The term is not pejorative: the state government used the term to describe the state's topography on government websites.
12. Bellah, "Civil Religion in America."
13. Bellah, "Civil Religion in America."
14. Rousseau, *Social Contract*, 123–25.
15. Gellner, *Nationalism*, 1–2.
16. Attali, *Noise*, 33, 60–62.

1. CLOSING THE COLONIAL PAST

1. Tehuantepec is the name given to the Isthmus and is derived from the Nahuatl for "hill of the beast." See Bradomín, *Toponomía de Oaxaca (Crítica Etimológica)*, 250.
2. The history of Oaxaca's founding is based on Brioso y Candiani, *La evolución del Pueblo Oaxaqueño*, 11–16.
3. Rodríguez Pérez, "Estudio y Proyecto para la Plaza Mayor," 38.
4. Brioso y Candiani, *La evolución del Pueblo Oaxaqueño*, 59.
5. Pérez Herrero, "El México Borbónico," 136–37.

6. Pérez Herrero, "El México Borbónico," 136–37.
7. Marchena Fernández, *Oficiales y soldados*, 332–35.
8. Gay, *Historia de Oaxaca*, 430.
9. Gay, *Historia de Oaxaca*, 430.
10. Gay, *Historia de Oaxaca*, 430.
11. "The Spanish soldier of the colonial period was a good military man when animated by religious passion, the love of his country, or personal ambition. He was too individualistic to subject himself to the tedious discipline of the barracks. [Later, the] Mexican soldier needed analogous impulses to crystallize his own military spirit" (quoted in Velázquez, *El estado de guerra*, 233).
12. Velázquez, *El estado de guerra*, 430.
13. On officers' training, see Marchena, *Oficiales y soldados*, 239–48.
14. The list appears in Castro Mantecón, *Efemérides*, n.p.
15. Service in the militia may have mitigated the importance of caste barriers for people of color. Indeed, military service carried with it a degree of social status, and musicianship likely did as well.
16. *1er Censo De Población De La Nueva España, 1790*, 159.
17. Aurelio Tello argues that "mestizo music" defies just such categorizations as "profane," "popular," or "folkloric." Some affirm that the term "popular," socioculturally speaking, is an individual creation subject to characteristics or patterns that a community accepts and that are incorporated into a people's repertoire. "Folkloric," on the other hand, is defined by some as part of a long tradition that a people makes its own by adding variation to the lyric or melody, converting it into "an anonymous expression, transmitted across generations." The different types of Mexican music may perhaps be better described as that "which arises *in* the breast of the people, and that which is made by others *for* the people." See Tello, "El patrimonio musical de México," 86–87.
18. "Música," *Enciclopedia de México*. Only the initials "S. R. G." identify the author of the entry. While those initials do not appear in the credits, the author is probably Silvino Robles Gutiérrez (1914–1990), the late director of the Escuela Superior de Música de León.
19. Brading, *Miners and Merchants*, 27.
20. According to Gunter Kahle, the Mexican army lost the moral and disciplinary compass that had guided Spain's royal army in New Spain. The Mexican soldiers' persistent egotism and venality contributed to the chaos of early post-independence Mexico, but the army nevertheless

remained omnipotent; every region in Mexico fell under the control of military men. With the Mexican military completely beyond civil control and power and in a permanent state of revolt, the institution formed an obstacle to political and economic development. See Kahle, *El ejército y la formación del Estado*. One can imagine that the musicians became the personal tools of the powerful caudillos.

21. Campos, *El folklore y la música mexicana*, 197. With the advent of the Mexican nation, patriotism was added to, but did not replace, the colonial roots of popular (and political) culture.
22. Campos, *El folklore y la música mexicana*, 200.
23. Campos, *El folklore y la música mexicana*, 200.
24. Ruiz Torres, "Historia de las bandas militares en México," 115.
25. Ruiz Torres, "Historia de las bandas militares en México," 115.
26. Castro Mantecón, *Efemérides*, 2. My research failed to uncover what other musicians comprised the "military band."
27. Dublán and Lozano, *Legislación Mexicana*, 647.
28. Calderón de la Barca, *Life in Mexico*, 139.
29. The Durkheimian identification of the religious with the communal (in this case, the "imagined community" of the state) makes any republican assembly more or less religious. See Durkheim, *Elementary Forms of Religious Life*, 238–39.

2. INVASIONS AND INFLUENCES

1. Dublán and Lozano, *Legislación Mexicana*, vol. 5, 162.
2. Iturribarría, "El batallón de Oaxaca," 443–44.
3. Taracena, *Efemérides Oaxaqueñas*, 33.
4. *Leyes y Decretos*, vol. 1, 448–50.
5. *Leyes y Decretos*, vol. 1, 448–50. The currency for Mexico is the *peso mexicano* (MXN). The currency symbol for pesos mexicanos is the same as the U.S. dollar sign. Unless otherwise specified, all monetary amounts are expressed in pesos mexicanos.
6. Increased regimentation and a more developed military structure statewide characterized Oaxaca during the war with the United States and the subsequent years leading up to the War of the Reform. However, primary documents in the Archivo General del Ejecutivo Poder del Estado de Oaxaca (Oaxaca State Archives, AGEPEO) relating to the organization of the Guardia Nacional remain uncataloged, bundled simply in brown paper and labeled "Guerra 1846" and "Guerra 1848." I have compiled lists of the units activated from these files and included

them in the appendix to provide an idea of the state's military organization. The information on military music contained in these documents (musters, etc.) generally refers only to *bandas de ordenanza* (ordinance bands, or drum-and-bugle corps).

7. Iturribarría, "El batallón de Oaxaca," 446.
8. Iturribarría, "El batallón de Oaxaca," 446.
9. Vigil y Robles, *Rectificaciones y aclaraciones a las memorias del Gral. Porfirio Díaz*, 20. It is fascinating to imagine the young Díaz participating in such festivities. That the future president of Mexico participated in them as a raw recruit speaks to their important place in Mexican culture.
10. The bellicose nature of nation-states arguably drove the worldwide brass-band phenomenon. Music historian Jon Newsom argues that the presence of military bands in the United States after the Mexican War was on the wane, but the outbreak of the U.S. Civil War in 1861 "ended any hope or danger of the demise of brass bands" in the United States; see Newsom, "American Brass Band Movement.,"125. Newsom's article includes an 1863 lithograph by H. B. Dodsworth entitled "Central Park Music" depicting the view of the south end of the park. At the center are "participants in the idyllic scenes . . . unaware that the new principles of war from which many were probably the immediate economic beneficiaries" had gathered to enjoy a musical performance around the bandstand. See Newsom, "American Brass Band Movement," 115. See also Hindle-Hazen and Hazen, *Music Men*.
11. Carreño, *Jefes del ejército mexicano*, ccxix.
12. Alcaraz, *Other Side*, 342.
13. *Leyes y Decretos*, vol. 1, 483–84.
14. Pareyón, *Diccionario de música en México*, 321. The BME music archives (mistakenly?) attribute the hymn to Gabino García. The hymn as a song form is traceable to the march, and the word shares the same Latin root as the word "hymen," indicating that hymns have their origins in nuptial marches.
15. The war also spawned numerous compositions about battles and warriors north of the Rio Grande. A list of keyboard battle pieces and popular songs from the time of the war are listed in Arnold, *Music and War*, 95. Arnold writes that Mexican forces likely heard U.S. forces playing "Yankee Doodle," among other songs.
16. Dabbs, *French Army in Mexico*, 28–49.
17. Dabbs, *French Army in Mexico*, 86.

18. Circular 13, 17 March 1864, in *Leyes y Decretos*, 2nd ed., vol. 4, 66–69. The circular vilifies Emperor Napoleon III, who had installed Maximilian, as "the caudillo of that foreign group of clerics, soldiers, and men of the *ancien regime* who desire monarchy."
19. Whether or not the Independence Day celebration in 1813 described above was an "official" celebration is not clear.
20. *Leyes y Decretos*, vol. 2, 567–68.
21. Maillefert, *Directorio del comercio del imperio mexicano*, n.p.
22. *La Victoria*, Oaxaca, 17 December 1863, cited in Navarette Pellicer, "Las Capillas de música de viento," 7. As will be further discussed below, a government's readiness to eliminate military music as a cost-cutting measure often overlooks its nonrational (or entertainment) function and value. I am indebted to Sergio Navarette Pellicer for allowing me to cite this and the following references, as I was unable to find the archive that held this period's newspapers.
23. *La Victoria*, Oaxaca, 1 May 1864, cited in Navarette Pellicer, "Las Capillas de música de viento," 7.
24. *La Paz*, Oaxaca, 10 June 1866, cited in Navarette Pellicer, "Las Capillas de música de viento," 7.
25. Weckmann, *Medieval Heritage of Mexico*, 555.
26. Open-air musical performances date to antiquity, but the modern combination of several classes of wind instruments in which a properly arranged accompaniment sustained the melody belongs to the medieval Thurmer bands of Germany and Austria. Thurmer bands were charged with the performance of certain municipal duties, for which they enjoyed the privileges of a recognized guild. Their daily performances required a repertory of pieces consisting of hymns or chorales, melodies of popular songs, and dances. Complex arrangements, lengthy performances, and the continued introduction of new instruments and instrument technologies made it necessary to formulate some "rules" of instrumentation, the effects of which could be accurately estimated before performances. The Thurmer bands are yet another indication of the persistence and ubiquity of the world band phenomenon. See Kappey, *Military Music*, 67–68.
27. LeMoigne-Mussat, *La Belle Epoque*, 53–54.
28. Guy P. C. Thomson describes the popularity of bands among civilians as a transformative agent and describes their performances as offering citizens "a sense of urbanity within the wilderness," a phrase that

perfectly captures music's ability to bring forth order from disorder. See Thomson, "Bulwarks of Patriotic Liberalism," 31–68.

29. Attracting recruits and stimulating faith in—and support of—the troops is yet another political function of military music.
30. Cosío Villegas, "La vida cotidiana," 455–56. The absence of such evidence before 1868 in the Oaxaca archives forces me to include this example from Mexico City.
31. Cosío Villegas, "La vida cotidiana," 455–56. The *redowa* is a Czech variation of the waltz; the *cavatina* is a simple, melodious air, usually part of an operatic movement. The polka is a half-rhythm dance traceable to nineteenth-century Bohemia. The Strauss family of Vienna, the capital of the vast Hapsburg Empire, also composed many polkas. The form was included in classical repertoires and diffused worldwide, emerging with distinct regional variations. Twentieth-century Mexican versions of the polka form also may be found in the accordion-based *norteño* and *conjunto* music of the Mexican north and the U.S. southwest, respectively, the result of mid-nineteenth century German and Czech immigration to the region. The waltz in Mexico is discussed in Chapter 5.
32. Stevenson, *Music in Mexico*, 192.
33. Thomson, "Ceremonial and Political Role of Village Bands."
34. Hefter, *El soldado de Juárez*. Hefter's work is an excellent source for the history of Mexican military uniforms. For example, he cites a German firsthand account of a young Mexican drummer who, amid the vivid imperial uniforms, was dressed in nothing but a rag. See Hefter, *El soldado de Juárez*, 15.
35. Pénette and Castaingt, *La Legión Extranjera*, 103–6. One of the BME's first directors, Francisco Sakar, discussed below, was an Austrian officer who remained in Oaxaca after the Intervention.
36. Ruiz Torres, "Historia de las bandas militares," 170–79. Like Díaz, the Interventionists, even if only for the sake of public relations and entertainment, recognized the nonrational function of music as a political tool.
37. *Colección de Leyes y Decretos del Estado de Oaxaca* 2nd ed. vol. 4, 410–11. In March 1864 Díaz had mandated obligatory universal male service in the Guard. His decree, along with his brother's cited here, recalls the citizen-soldier nature of the Guard: now decommissioned, they should return to their "habitual exercises" (read "work"). Díaz's decree is found in the same volume of *Colección de Leyes y Decretos*, 70–71.

3. INCEPTION AND INSTITUTIONALIZATION

1. A complete list of BME directors is included in Appendix 1.
2. For example, see *Colección de Leyes y Decretos del Estado de Oaxaca*, 2nd ed., vol. 4, 528–29, for Félix Díaz's Cinco de Mayo program for 1868.
3. *Colección de Leyes y Decretos del Estado de Oaxaca*, 2nd ed., vol. 4, 387, 31 January 1868. The beautification project and material improvements to the plaza are discussed in detail below.
4. Castro Mantecón, *Efemérides*, n.p. Bernardino was the brother of Macedonio Alcalá (1831–1869), the distinguished musician and composer most famous for his waltz "Dios nunca muere" ("God Never Dies"), the unofficial state hymn of Oaxaca. Macedonio played and composed by ear and was known as a great improviser. He lived a bohemian lifestyle, fluctuating between poverty and illness, both likely attributable to alcoholism. The last two years of his life found Macedonio wandering the Sierra Mixteca searching unsuccessfully for a better life, although the musicians' social aid society, the Society of Santa Cecilia (patron saint of musicians), did offer moral and economic support. "Dios nunca muere" was commissioned by a group of Indians from Tlacolula, a pueblo near Oaxaca City, while Macedonio was gravely ill. He never was able to perform the composition on his own violin, as he had pawned it and could never recover it. Apparently another brother, Bernabé, attempted to take credit for the composition, but the Tlacolulans thwarted his efforts and made sure the song was properly credited to Macedonio. See Grial, *Músicos Mexicanos*, 25–26. A kiosk graces the cover of Grial's book, further evidence of its ubiquity in Mexican musical life.
5. Castro Mantecón, *Efemérides*, n.p , and González Esperón, *Perfiles de Oaxaca*, 204. Neither González Esperón nor Castro Mantecón provides any documentation or sources. An exhaustive search at the Archivo Histórico de la Secretaría de Defensa Nacional (AHSDN) failed to unearth any information on Vásquez, Sakar, or Bernardino Alcalá.
6. Originally published in the Mexico City periodical *El Orden*, May 1853. Cited in Ruiz Torres, "Historia de las bandas militares," 145–48. Riesgo's work in its entirety is on microfilm at The Nettie Lee Benson Latin American Collection of the University of Texas at Austin.
7. Riesgo cited "ugly emulation" among directors as the principal cause limiting the advancement of the bands. He was, however, unconcerned by the implications of "emulating" European models.

8. *Colección de Leyes, Decretos, Circulares*, vol. 10, 134.
9. The *diana* is a fanfare or flourish—that is, a short, loud piece of music usually sounded by trumpets or bugles that is meant to draw attention.
10. *Colección de Leyes y Decretos del Estado de Oaxaca*, 2nd ed., vol. 4, 433–35, 4 February 1868.
11. *Colección de Leyes y Decretos del Estado de Oaxaca*, 2nd ed., vol. 4, 525–26, 1 April 1868.
12. Along with Díaz, Zaragoza was a commander at the Battle of Puebla.
13. *Colección de Leyes y Decretos del Estado de Oaxaca*, 2nd ed., vol. 4, 528–29, 30 April 1868.
14. The programs were not unique to Oaxaca. For a description of a similar celebration in Mexico City in 1824, see Fernández de Lizardi's account in Carballo, *Las fiestas patrias*, 20. For an example demonstrating the continuity and similarity of such events, Porfirian-era Cinco de Mayo and Independence Day celebrations in Mexico City are described in Cosío Villegas, *Historia Moderna de México*, 700–705.
15. *Colección de Leyes, Decretos, Circulares 1871–1874*, vol. 6, 155–57.
16. *Colección de Leyes y Decretos del Estado de Oaxaca*, 2nd ed., vol. 4, 155–57, 29 July 1872.
17. For a discussion of Juárez's mythical legacy at the national level, see Weeks, *The Juárez Myth in Mexico*.
18. *Colección de Leyes, Decretos, Circulares 1871–1874*, vol. 6, 165–67, 10 October 1872. Another monument was ordered built in the city's main plaza, but it has since been relocated to the Paseo de Guadalupe, a park specifically dedicated to Juárez's memory.
19. Esparza, *Padrón de capitación de la ciudad de Oaxaca, 1875*, xiii. The 1842 census is analyzed in Chance, *Race and Class in Colonial Oaxaca*. Whether or not the musicians were military musicians is not clear.
20. *Colección de Leyes, Decretos, Circulares, 23 Septiembre 1874–21 Enero 1876*, vol. 7, 149.
21. *Colección de Leyes, Decretos, Circulares, 23 Septiembre 1874–21 Enero 1876*, vol. 7, 100.
22. Fortson, *Los gobernantes de Oaxaca*, 141–43.
23. The BME's role within the state's educatory and tourism projects is discussed below.
24. *Colección de Leyes, Decretos, Circulares, 23 Septiembre 1874–21 Enero 1876*, vol. 7, 362. The *partida* (line item) states "per contract." Extensive research failed to unearth this or any other of the seemingly apocryphal

"contracts." In one case, the contract cited in the *Colección de Leyes, Decretos* actually pertained to municipal ordinances for the refrigeration of cuts of meat!

25. Martínez Gracida. *Efemérides Oaxaqueñas*, 138.
26. Castro Mantecón, *Efemérides de la Banda*, n.p.
27. *Colección de Leyes, Decretos, Circulares 21 Enero 1876–3 Abril 1877*, vol. 8, 75–77.
28. As a raised structure on which to place sacrificial offerings to a deity, the altar is another important civil-religious symbol.
29. *La Victoria*, 4 May 1877, 2.
30. Castro Mantecón, *Efemérides*, n.p.
31. The influence of the Alcalá family on Oaxacan music is great. Further research into their family archives might help us paint a more complete picture of the BME in its formative years.
32. *La Victoria*, 2 March 1877, 1.
33. During Esperón's term, Meixueiro and Hernández had conspired against the governor from the Sierras. As governor, Meixueiro faced a battle in the Isthmus between the towns of Juchitán and Tehuantepec, the former supporting Díaz and the latter supporting Lerdo. At the same time, the *borlados*, or moderate liberals, hoped that Meixueiro and Hernández would be punished for deposing Esperón. See Chassen-López, *From Liberal to Revolutionary Oaxaca*, 355–58.
34. *Granada* is Spanish for both "grenade" and "pomegranate," the former's design inspired centuries ago by the latter.
35. *Colección de Leyes, Decretos, Circulares*, vol. 10, 143–50. Though I have condensed the decree (which in the original is some ten pages long), I hope that the uniform's elegance emerges.
36. Meixueiro, *Memorias que el C. General Francisco Meixueiro*, 32–33 and supplement.
37. Díaz chose General Manuel González to run for president; González easily won the four-year term.
38. *Colección de Leyes, Decretos, Circulares*, vol. 11, 24–25. The deactivation of the Guard immediately saved $100,000. See Fortson, 117.
39. *Colección de Leyes, Decretos, Circulares*, vol. 11, 145.
40. *Colección de Leyes, Decretos, Circulares*, vol. 11, 455. By this time, the perceived lack of any foreign threat meant that the War Branch was increasingly responsible for domestic policing and public security.
41. Berry, *Reform in Oaxaca*, 30.

42. *Colección de Leyes, Decretos, Circulares,* vol. 11, 73.
43. *Colección de Leyes, Decretos, Circulares,* vol. 10, 249.
44. *Colección de Leyes, Decretos, Circulares,* vol. 10, 249.
45. *Colección de Leyes, Decretos, Circulares,* vol. 10, 252.
46. See Wagner, Box, and Morehead, *Ancient Origins of the Mexican Plaza.*
47. Ricard, *The Spiritual Conquest of Mexico,* 139–40.
48. Ricard, *The Spiritual Conquest of Mexico,* 139–40.
49. Ricard, *The Spiritual Conquest of Mexico,* 140.
50. On the history of the plaza in Mexico, see Prieto and Rodríguez Carballar, *Arquitectura popular mexicana,* 22–49. On the nature of the activities that define the plaza and the ubiquity of the chessboard and grid in colonial Latin American city design, see Martínez Lemoine, "Classical Model of the Spanish-American Colonial City." That most towns in Spain lacked a plaza is due to the country's hilly geography, which often conspired against their construction.
51. Marjorie Becker writes, "Landlords, priests, and the government had devised a host of inducements to look upward. To follow that gaze is to find that towering over this tawdry collection of sideshows was the plaza, dominated by a central building, the church." See Becker, *Setting the Virgin on Fire,* 13.
52. None of the Mexican cities or towns analyzed by the Secretaría of Asentamientos Humanos y Obras Públicas lacks a plaza—83 percent have one plaza and 13 percent have two plazas—but one usually assumes central importance and is larger in size and social stature, while the second is situated in an outlying or developing neighborhood. Second plazas become necessary as populations increase, new construction advances, and new (commercial) interests arise. Elements found in the plazas may include trees, grass, and gardens, as is true of 90.79 percent of Mexican plazas. Vegetation is often integrated into the central area of cities to express harmony between nature and man's works and to soften the urban edges. Plazas benefit from botanical additions, which ease the plaza's contours and help clean the polluted urban air. Such vegetation is usually regional (in Oaxaca, poinsettias and laurel trees are employed), but depending on the local climate, non-native ornamental choices are possible, highlighting the possible differences between regions, populations, and areas and reflecting the variety that one finds in the distinct Mexican regional landscapes. See Prieto and Rodríguez Carballar, *Arquitectura popular mexicana,* 22.

53. Low, *On the Plaza*, 240. Low demonstrates the historical importance (and persistence) of the plaza in case studies from the Caribbean, Central America, and South America.
54. The Zócalo in Oaxaca comprises the Alameda de León (named for the General) and the Jardín de la Constitución (Garden of the Constitution), two adjoining plazas. The Jardín de la Constitución is the former Plaza de Armas. The cathedral opens onto the Alameda, while the government palace overlooks the Jardín de la Constitución. Mark Brill pointed out in a personal conversation that the Oaxaca plaza is unusual among Mexican plazas in that the cathedral does not directly face the Government Palace. The kiosk sits in the Jardín de la Constitución. The nomenclature may be confusing: the Plaza de Armas in Oaxaca has been alternatively called "Plaza Benito Juárez," "Zócalo," "Jardín," and "Plaza de la Constitución."
55. During the political and social unrest in Oaxaca between May and November 2006, the Zócalo became the city's most contested site. Protesters seized the site early on, and when it was finally "recaptured" by the government, the retaking of the Zócalo was seen as a "victory" for the government forces. During the crisis the BME was forced to suspend performances, and the kiosk was vandalized. Upon realizing the public-relations nightmare perpetrated when the beloved bandstand fell victim to the political violence, both parties in the conflict blamed the other. The kiosk itself suffered little permanent damage, but the arcade beneath the platform suffered extensive damage by vandals. Protestors blamed the military forces that had expelled them from the plaza for the damage. A day-by-day account of the seven-month-long siege may be found in *Oaxaca: Tiempo Nublado*, no. 17 (November 2006), published by PROAX, a foundation for the defense and conservation of Oaxaca's cultural patrimony.
56. Prieto and Rodríguez Carballar, *Arquitectura popular mexicana*, 23.
57. The history of kiosks is found in LeMoigne-Mussat, *La Belle Epoque des Kiosques à Musique*.
58. These enduring and quaint "acoustic boxes" are reminders of not only small-town life in our own country, but also of the prevalence of nineteenth-century bands and their importance in our communities.
59. Chanfón Olmos, *Historia de la arquitectura y el urbanismo mexicanos*, book 3: *El México independiente*, vol. 2: *Afirmación del nacionalismo y la modernidad* (México: Universidad Nacional Autónoma de México, 1998), 456–57.

60. Lastra, *Sound Technology and American Cinema*, 4.
61. The concept of a new aurality as a component of modernity is found in Kahn, *Noise, Water, Meat*, 4, 9.
62. Architectural acoustics like those incorporated in kiosk design had become a science by the beginning of the twentieth century. For a history of architectural acoustics and its role in modern life, see Thompson, *Soundscape of Modernity*.
63. Calderón Martínez, "Un recorrido," 5.
64. Cruz Aguillón, *Oaxaca*, 35.
65. Calderón Martínez, "Un recorrido," 8. Beyond their ornamental function, fountains complement the environmental requirements of public space. Together with the fresh air, sunlight, and vegetation, water contributes to the plaza's microclimate and generates a feeling of well-being that is especially important in warmer climates such as that of Oaxaca. Nevertheless, the percentage of Mexican plazas with fountains is very low. Fountains in the Oaxaca plaza have been removed, then replaced; there are fountains today, but water rarely flows. On the other hand, more than half of Mexico's plazas contain monuments, usually of historic personages, a detail that indicates the presence of a considerable popular civil cult. The most common monuments in Mexico are dedicated to Benito Juárez, Miguel Hidalgo, and Emiliano Zapata, as well as to "the mother" as a symbol of life and social fortitude; see Prieto and Rodríguez Carballar, *Arquitectura popular mexicana*. While monuments to the state's civil religion are ubiquitous, the most fundamental aspect of human life, water, is difficult to come by in Oaxaca, not only due to prolonged drought but also to governmental inefficiency, ineptitude, and simple lack of concern.
66. *Colección de Leyes y Decretos del Estado Libre de Oaxaca*, vol. 1, 47–48.
67. Calderón, "Un recorrido," 8.
68. *Colección de Leyes y Decretos del Estado Libre de Oaxaca*, vol. 1, 387. See also Cruz Aguillón, *Oaxaca*, 35.
69. Bueno Sánchez, *Efemérides Oaxaqueñas*, 115. A complete analysis of Oaxaca's late nineteenth-century Porfirian urbanization project, including the gardens and plazas, is found in Lira Vásquez, "La ciudad de Oaxaca."
70. Aguillón, *Oaxaca*, 35. Castro Mantecón writes only, "González ordered the old kiosk fixed, giving it a better aspect and making it more beautiful;" *Efemérides*, np. Unfortunately, I was unable to locate any primary

sources pertaining to the construction of the kiosk in Oaxaca. The kiosk has been remodeled or replaced at least once since then.
71. *Memoria Constitucional*, vol. 1, n.p. Apparently Meixueiro had ordered the Plaza de Armas remodeled before Jiménez's term. The kiosk replaced the Plaza's central fountain, and benches of iron and wood surrounded the kiosk so that the public could rest comfortably during the band's performances. Unfortunately, I found neither the original work orders nor specific references to these improvements in my research. Even in his *Memorias Administrativas* from 1881, Meixueiro only listed paving and cobblestoning of the streets around the Plaza and the Palacio Municipal. Jiménez did, however, credit Meixueiro with the remodeling and renovations.

4. PORFIRIATO AND REVOLUTION

1. Castro Mantecón, *Efemérides*, n.p. During the French Intervention Oaxaca became home to a number of Frenchmen, Hungarians, Zouaves, and Austrians who, like former director Francisco Sakar, may have contributed to the introduction, dissemination, and growing popularity of European music in the state.
2. Castro Mantecón, *Efemérides*, n.p. By 1884 Mexican bands were playing to international audiences at world's fairs and exhibitions, sent along as cultural ambassadors with Mexican delegations as part of the Porfirian project of enhancing Mexico's image abroad. See Tenorio-Trillo, *Mexico at the World's Fairs*, and Yeager, "Porfirian Commercial Propaganda," 230–43.
3. The ambivalent nature of the BME's nomenclature continues here: even the governor himself is unable to decide what to call it.
4. *Memoria que Presentó el C. general Luis Mier y Terán*, 90.
5. *Memoria que Presentó el C. general Luis Mier y Terán*, 91. Mier y Terán wrote that the new Tehuantepec National Guard band would be initiating its duties. The identity of the third band is unclear, but the reference is important, as the proliferation of bands, discussed below, corresponds to the increasing importance of Mexican civil religion.
6. *Memoria que Presentó el C. general Luis Mier y Terán*, 37.
7. *Memorias Administrativas del Ciudadano gobernador Albino Zertuche*, n.p.
8. The roll is found in *Memorias Administrativas del Ciudadano gobernador Albino Zertuche*, n.p.

9. The *pistón* is a valved metal instrument, in this case possibly a cornet. The *octavina* is a small flute. The *requinto* is an E-flat clarinet. A *gira* may be either a spinning percussion device or the transport mechanism for the large drums.
10. Castro Mantecón, *Efemérides*, n.p.
11. Archivo Histórico de la Secretaría de la Defensa Nacional, Mexico City (AHSDN), Expediente xi/111/9/21709.
12. González Esperón, *Perfiles de Oaxaca*, 207–8.
13. Burke, "Marche Fúnebre." 81–82, 390–395. The military march is a distinct type of musical construction, consisting at first of just one or two parts of a strongly marked melody, usually in common or 6/8 time. Besides the funeral march, there are the slow march, the quick march, and the double-quick march. Kappey writes, "While marching had always been the military's most common form of mobility, it became a habit and was practiced during parades to demonstrate the drill, uniforms, and other displays of military pomp that became the earmarks of a successful sovereign. The stepping together of large bodies of men in exact rhythm to the sounds of loud musical instruments was carefully taught and became a military habit." See Kappey, *Military Music*, 68–69.
14. See Kastner, *Manuel général de musique militaire*, 335.
15. Wagner was especially aware of the tonal power of wind instruments, as his music demonstrates. See Wagner, *My Life*, 359–60.
16. Hilfiger, "Funeral Marches, Dirges, and Wind Bands," 2.
17. The quoted term is from Ozouf, *Festivals and the French Revolution*, 95. Ozouf demonstrates the persistence of civil religious manifestations during the French Revolution, identifying Republican festivals as sites of "the transfer of sacrality" from the church to the state.
18. In Mexico City in November 1559, a multiday commemoration was celebrated to honor the Holy Roman Emperor Charles V, who had died the previous year. Music mixed with other sensory stimuli not only to bridge the temporal and the eternal, the living and the dead, but also to reinforce a sense of colonial power and concomitant cultural hierarchy. See Wagstaff, "Processions for the Dead," 167–80.
19. Canseco's biographical information is found in Grial, *Músicos Mexicanos*, 29, and in Pareyón, *Diccionario de música en México*, 93.
20. In 1866 the Sociedad Filarmónica Mexicana (Mexican Philharmonic Society) was established in a building of the Universidad de México with the intent of eventually creating a musical conservatory.

Instructional subjects were *solfège*, piano, strings, woodwinds, harmony, instrumentation and orchestration, composition, Spanish language, French, music history and biography, acoustics, physiology of voice, history of instruments, and aesthetics. In January 1868 classes were held in the Academia de Música del Presbítero (Presbyter Music Academy) with Agustín Caballero, a priest, as director. In 1877 the government assumed full responsibility for the Sociedad and changed its name to the Conservatorio Nacional de Música. The act may be seen as part of the Liberal penchant for education as well as an early attempt at musical nationalism, but the curriculum was modeled on that of Italian conservatories. Student and faculty musical programs consisted mainly of operatic arias, duos, and piano works of operatic excerpts.

21. See Castro Mantecón, *Efemérides*, and González Esperón, *Perfiles de Oaxaca*.
22. Rosas Solaegui, *Un hombre en el tiempo*, 116–23. Rosas Solaegui, a renowned Oaxacan composer in his own right, was born in 1897. A feeling of nostalgia for his experiences as a youth listening to the BME under Canseco's direction may have led him to refer to the director's tenure as "the Golden Age" of the BME. The qualities he describes have likely led other *cronistas* like Castro Mantecón and González Esperón to adopt the same appellation. Rosas Solaegui's military service probably contributed to his appreciation for band music. Biographical information on Rosas Solaegui is found in Bustamante Gris, *Cancionero de música popular oaxaqueña*, 99–100.
23. The details are found in Rosas Solaegui, *Un hombre en el tiempo*, 116–23.
24. Rosas Solaegui, *Un hombre en el tiempo*.
25. Rosas Solaegui, *Un hombre en el tiempo*, 117.
26. Based on budgets found in *Colección de Leyes, Decretos, Circulares*, vol. 11.
27. *Memorias Administrativas del Licenciado Emilio Pimentel*, n.p. The 37-centavo wage for regular musicians in the BME compares favorably to that of the military musicians attached to a regular National Guard company, who received 38 centavos per day.
28. *Memorias Administrativas del Ciudadano gobernador Miguel Bolaños Cacho*, document numbers 28 and 29 respectively.
29. The presence of timbales in the BME appears to be another deviation from European models, as well as an indication of hybrid instrumentation.

30. The paso doble is based on marches from the bullfight arenas that were modified into dance form in the nineteenth century.
31. The schottische (in Spanish, *chotis*) is similar to a slow polka. Along with the paso doble and the waltz, it was an indispensable part of Mexican band repertoires. The form reached great popularity during the Mexican Revolution, and Mexican composers such as Agustín Lara (1900–1970) had great success with it. Lara's most famous chotis is "Madrid." So prolific was Lara that he is sometimes referred to as *el Schubert jarocho* ("the Schubert of Veracruz"). At least seven works by Lara—including his homages to Iberia, such as "Granada"—appear in the BME sheet music archive and enjoy great popularity among the BME's audiences.
32. The zarzuela is a song form from the important Spanish opera form of the same name; while not limited to comedy, it is similar to *opera buffa* in its play on dialogues. More than forty zarzuelas are included in the BME sheet music archive. The mazurka is a lively dance of Polish origin. (The Polish national anthem is an example of a mazurka.) Three mazurkas are found in the BME sheet music archive.
33. Mentz, Radkau, Scharrer, and Turner, *Los pioneros del imperialismo alemán*, 78. Originally cited in Ruiz Torres, "Historia de las bandas militares."
34. Mentz, Radkau, Scharrer, and Turner, *Los pioneros del imperialismo alemán*, 195. Promotional materials from the period suggest the predominance of European musical instruments from the "best and most modern European factories, expressly selected for various distinguished artists." A catalog dated 1896 from Nagel H. Sucesores included among its offerings the expected polkas, waltzes, and schottisches, as well as indexed collections for "Los ecos militares para banda military." See Saldívar, *Bibliografía*, 307. An ad for the firm Proveedor del Ejército (Provider to the Army) featured among the group's products drums and drum accessories, batons for drum majors, and clarinets. See Maillefert, 18. Originally cited in Ruiz Torres, "Historia de las bandas militares," 220.
35. Saldívar, *Bibliografía*, 275, 316. Originally cited in Ruiz Torres, "Historia de las bandas militares," 222.
36. Stevenson, *Music in Mexico*, 205. Originally cited in Ruiz Torres, "Historia de las bandas militares," 222.
37. See, for example, Archivo General del Ejecutivo Poder del Estado de Oaxaca (AGEPEO), 1927, Dep. Gob., Exp. 39 Leg. 224.

38. Ruiz Torres, "Historia de las bandas militares," 222.
39. Lamb, "Waltz." I would also like to thank Mark Brill for his help with the history of the waltz.
40. Archivo General de la Nación (AGN), 1810, *Grupo Documental Inquisición*, vol. 1449.f. Exp. Fojas, 187–88.
41. AGN, 1810, *Grupo Documental Inquisición*, vol. 1449.f. Exp. Fojas, 187–88.
42. Saldívar, *Historia*, 216.
43. See Stewart, "Mexican Band Legend," and Brenner, *Juventino Rosas*.
44. The *quinceañera* is a fifteenth-birthday celebration for girls; it celebrates the symbolic passage from childhood to womanhood.
45. Chassen-López, *From Liberal to Revolutionary Oaxaca*, 401–47.
46. *Memorias Administrativas del Licenciado Emilio Pimente*, vol. 2. Extensive research failed to uncover this and other apocryphal band contracts that might hold information on the organizational structure of the BME. See Iturribarría, *Oaxaca en la historia*, 256.
47. Chassen-López, *From Liberal to Revolutionary Oaxaca*, 479.
48. The programs are found in Mantecón, *Efemérides*, n.p.
49. *Memorias Administrativas del Licenciado Emilio Pimentel*, 98. While the sum of $15,479.00 appears to be almost twice that of previous budgets, it must be remembered that the Monetary Reform Act of 1904 greatly devalued the Mexican peso; see MacLachlan and Beezley, *El Gran Pueblo*, 118.
50. The BME director regularly sent reports on his organization up the chain of command. These reports usually cataloged absences, disciplinary problems, requests for leave, and the like.
51. Castro Mantecón, *Efemérides*, n.p.
52. Chassen-López, *From Liberal to Revolutionary Oaxaca*, 499.
53. Knight, *Mexican Revolution*, vol. 1: *Porfirians, Liberals, and Peasants* (Lincoln: University of Nebraska Press, 1986), 234.
54. Rosas Solaegui, *Un hombre en el tiempo*, 121. Though Rosas Solaegui does not clearly identify "Mr. Brill," it is likely George Martin Brill (1845–1906) of the J. G. Brill Company of Philadelphia, an American railcar and trolley manufacturing firm. The company dominated the world of trolley and undercarriage manufacturing and, during the Porfiriato, equipped at least one rail line in Oaxaca, the *Ferrocarril Agrícola de Córdoba a Tuxtepec*, with an innovative express, baggage, and mail car. G. M. Brill was president of the company during the early twentieth century and probably heard the BME while traveling in Oaxaca. He

died suddenly from "an attack of apoplexy" on 30 March 1906, not, as Rosas Solaegui states, in 1912. The earlier date also means that Emilio Pimentel, not Juárez Maza, would have been governor at the time. For G. M. Brill, his sudden demise, and his firm's Mexican interests, see Brill, *History of the J.G. Brill Company*, 109. Rosas Solaegui writes of previous plans for a BME trip to London that also failed to take place.

55. Rosas Solaegui, *Un hombre en el tiempo*, 121. The current director of the BME, Maestro Eliseo Martínez García, says that other bands, especially those from Mexico City, still attempt to recruit from the BME's ranks. Furthermore, some members migrate to Mexico City of their own volition, whether to hone their skills, gain experience, or play before larger audiences; but more than a few, according to Martínez, return to their *patria chica* and the ranks of the BME.

56. González Esperón, *Perfiles de Oaxaca*, 213–14.
57. AGEPEO, *Per. Rev.*, 1914, Leg. 30, Exp. 1.
58. AGEPEO, *Per. Rev.*, 1914, Leg. 30, Exp. 1.
59. National holidays increasingly included sports exhibitions after the Revolution. For example, President Plutarco Elías Calles included sports parades during Constitution Day celebrations in Mexico City; similar events in Oaxaca are discussed below.
60. AGEPEO, *Per. Rev.*, 1914, Leg. 30, Exp. 1.
61. The sovereignty movement, importantly bolstered by a new militia of Zapotec soldiers, is discussed in McNamara, *Sons of the Sierra*, 195–96.
62. *Periódico Oficial del Gobierno del Estado Libre y Soberano de Oaxaca*, 17 August 1916, vol. 3, no. 6, Decreto 62.
63. *Periódico Oficial del Gobierno del Estado Libre y Soberano de Oaxaca*, 19 February 1920, vol. 7, no. 8.
64. *Periódico Oficial del Gobierno del Estado Libre y Soberano de Oaxaca*, 28 December 1916, vol. 3, no. 25, 7.
65. Absent such political change or turmoil, bureaucratic reorganizations are a way for a governor to leave his mark on the state, and to this day Oaxacan governors continue to do so. The chief executive's propensity to reorganize has certainly contributed to the confusing array of dependencies to which the BME has pertained. See Appendix for a list of BME dependencies.
66. See, for example, *Informe del Gobernador Manuel García Vigil*, 16 April 1922, 7–8. In 1996 an actual "Police Band" was created, the *Banda de la Policía Preventiva* (Preventive Police Band).

67. See AGEPEO, *Revolucionario/Centro*, 1926, Gob., Exp. 25, Leg. 201, letter number 8841.
68. AGEPEO, *Sec. Gob.*, Lugar Centro, 1926, Exp. 25, Leg. 201.
69. "Grave accidente sufrió el señor Germán Canseco," *El Mercurio*, 2 October 1920, 4.
70. "Outside work" is a near-universal necessity of historical persistence for musicians, not just a challenge faced in Oaxaca. Military musicians fulfilled many duties besides the strictly martial, possibly for monetary gain. Sites of musical production such as the colonial sodalities imply that other labors likely accompanied musical pursuits. Furthermore, the cargo system (services owed to either the secular government or the religious organization of the church and patron saints; see Chassen-López, *From Liberal to Revolutionary Oaxaca*, 285–289) meant that tasks at the service of the municipality were required of musicians. Such tasks could include neighborhood vigilance or even service in political positions. However, neither of these types of "work" included the most prominent form of extramusical employment: subsistence labor. The economy in Oaxaca could only support a few, if any, musicians solely dedicated to the practice of their art; as a result, humble work in the *milpa* (cornfield) often competed with music as the musician's most important pursuit while ironically ensuring the viability of the art form. Finally, because music is not a broadly economically empowering career, many musicians simply sought to augment their incomes by taking outside engagements. All these forms of nonmusical work compete today with BME members' craft.
71. "Los Músicos de la Banda del Estado Estudian," *El Mercurio*, 12 February 1921, 2.
72. "La Reorganización de las Bandas Militares," *El Mercurio*, 25 November 1920, 2.
73. "El Director de la Banda del Estado Disfruta de la Confianza," *El Mercurio*, 26 October 1920, 2. One report from 13 October 1920, however, alludes to a public less than enthralled with the BME's performance. At a matinee during the Fiestas de la Raza Hispano Americana (Festival of the Hispanic American Race), the audience demonstrated "their indifference . . . and only one family was seen attending." Yet the article contradicts itself insofar as attendance is concerned, when it later states that "disorganization produced disgust among many families." Whether it was the fiesta or the BME that was disorganized is unclear.

74. "Enriquece su Repertorio la Banda del Estado," *El Mercurio*, 5 February 1921, 3.
75. That a foxtrot appears indicates an early penetration of (North) American popular culture into the repertoire. The foxtrot had premiered less than a decade earlier on vaudeville stages in New York. With alternating staggered slow and quick rhythms, the dance quickly became popular north of the border.
76. "La Banda del Estado Estrena 'El Osculo,'" *El Mercurio*, 9 January 1921.
77. The *danzón* is a Cuban dance that combines European ballroom forms with Afro-Cuban rhythms. It appeared in Cuba at the end of the nineteenth century, and in Mexico in the early twentieth century.
78. "Programa de la Audición Musical de hoy en la Mañana," *El Mercurio*, 23 January 1921, 1. On performance days, BME programs customarily appeared on the front page of local newspapers.
79. Vásquez, *Música popular y costumbres regionales*, 22. Vásquez played guitar and piano and was also a composer of marches, hymns, and rhapsodies dedicated to Oaxaca, its pantheon of heroes, and its culture. The BME music archives contain a number of his compositions.
80. Vásquez is a complex man and worthy of a full-length biography. He was an author, a composer, and an armchair anthropologist. He practiced a "soft" socialism, not the extreme form associated with his patron at the national level, president Plutarco Elías Calles. Nor was he, also unlike Calles, a virulent anticlerical. He sought unity in Oaxaca through cultural programs he himself designed, instituted, and even led, though they met with mixed results. These programs are discussed below. He was a cultural nationalist who maintained, however, a paternalistic attitude toward the indigenous of his home state. See Smith, *Pistoleros and Popular Movements*, 37–41.
81. See *El Mercurio*, 1, 22, and 23 January and 18 February 1921.
82. "Los viernes de Cuaresma en el Paseo Juárez," *El Mercurio*, 18 February 1921, 3.
83. The program included a work identified as "Los dioses desterrados," which Mark Brill believes is likely Siegfried's funeral march from Wagner's *Götterdämmerung*. Personal conversation.
84. Besides being known as "The Apostle of Mexican Democracy," Madero is also referred to by another quasi-religious sobriquet, "The Martyr of the Revolution."
85. "Homenaje Fúnebre al señor Don Francisco I. Madero," *El Mercurio*, 22 February 1921, 1.

5. THE SOCIALIST STATE

1. Brown, "Mexico's Constitution of 1917," 113.
2. Carpizo, *La constitución mexicana de 1917*, 72–73.
3. Carpizo, *La constitución mexicana de 1917*, 80.
4. Sierra, *Obras completas*, vol. 5, *Discursos*, 304.
5. Sierra, *Obras completas*, vol. 5, *Discursos*, 344.
6. Sierra, *Obras completas*, vol. 8, *La educación nacional*, 37–39.
7. Sierra, *Obras completas*, vol. 8, *La educación nacional*, 40.
8. Altamirano, *Obras completas VIII, Crónicas 2*, 447; cited in Ruiz Torres, "Historia de las bandas militares." "La Marseillaise" eventually entered the BME's repertoire; they performed it at least once on May Day 1924, as well as at annual Bastille Day celebrations. *El Mercurio* described the song as "a workers' hymn." See *El Mercurio*, 1 May 1924, 1. In fact, "La Marseillaise" was originally a hymn written for the Army of the Rhine and by the time of the French Revolution had circulated widely in France, even replacing the *Te Deum* at public celebrations. The revolutionary army supposedly sang "La Marseillaise" after it won its first battle. See Mason, *Singing the French Revolution*, 100–103. Mason argues that songs, even those considered frivolous and lowly by authorities that at once disdained and feared them, served as a potent means of simultaneously criticizing political, social, and cultural orders. She also identifies a strong pedagogical component especially concerned with patriotism within song culture. Though Mason does not address bands or musicians in her work, it is likely that musical groups accompanied many songs.
9. Altamirano, *Obras completas VIII, Crónicas 2*, 448.
10. Altamirano, *Obras completas VIII, Crónicas 2*, 448, 451–54.
11. Secretaría de Educación Pública, *La Educación pública*, 55.
12. Song and dance forms are included in the appendix. For a collection of Oaxacan songs, see Kuri-Aldana and Mendoza Martínez, *Cancionero Popular Mexicano*, vol. 1, 171–206.
13. Secretaría de Educación Pública, *La Educación pública*, 56.
14. Mexico's first "official" orquesta típica was founded in 1884 at the National Conservatory of Music. Largely made up of middle-class musicians, the "typical" folk ensembles consisted of violins, psaltery, mandolins, and contrabass. The orquesta típica links the erudite and its use of "European" instruments with the popular and its use of "indigenous" instruments. These mostly urban dance ensembles often took their music from upper-class salon music, as well as the popular forms

of pasos dobles, polkas, schottisches, and waltzes. See Stevenson, *Music in Mexico*, 191–92. That the orquesta típica was "mostly" urban is a result of the state's concentrated elite educational efforts within urban locales during the period. The orquesta típica transformed in the twentieth century in response to post-Revolutionary cultural developments, and their eventual adoption of charro costumes and mestizo folk elements expressed a spirit of *costumbrismo* (an art form giving particular attention to regional or national "typical" costumes). Interesting "rural" and "popular" counterparts to the orquesta típica are the *músicos callejeros* (street musicians), itinerant groups composed mostly of poor rural migrants. See Hayes, *Radio Nation*, 73. The formation of the orquesta típica offers a nationalist counterpoint to Riesgo's positivist and foreign gaze.

15. Secretaría de Educación Pública, *La Educación pública*, 153–55.
16. Vázquez de Knauth, *Nacionalismo y educación*, 151–56. While forming a six-year plan for the Partido Nacional Revolucionario (National Revolutionary Party, PNR) in 1933, one group of members wanted to use the term "rationalist" and another group "anti-religious" as a qualifier for "education." They compromised and chose the adjective "socialist," perhaps finding it a less provocative word.
17. *Constitución Política de los estados unidos Mexicanos*, 5–8 (italics mine).
18. Vaughan, *Cultural Politics in Revolution*, 45. Campos's work (discussed above) linked the advent of wind bands in Mexico with liberalism and nascent Mexican nationalism.
19. Archivo General del Ejecutivo Poder del Estado de Oaxaca (AGEPEO), Instrucción, Fondo Público, Legajo 2, Sección Cultura Artistica, Serie Banda de Música.
20. AGEPEO, Instrucción, Fondo Público, Legajo 2, Sección Cultura Artistica, Serie Banda de Música.
21. Vasconcelos, *Ulises Criollo*, 18–22. Vasconcelos studied law and joined a group of radical scholars known as the Ateneo de la Juventud (Youth Association), which used French spiritualism to formulate a critique of positivism in order to undermine the justifications given for the Porfiriato and propose a new relationship between the individual and society. Vasconcelos was also a member of the Anti-Reelectionist movement, and the totality of such experiences suggests that such insights on the Díaz regime likely carry a hint of sarcasm.
22. Vasconcelos, *Ulises Criollo*, 18.

23. Vasconcelos, *Ulises Criollo*, 68.
24. See Cárdenas Noriega, *José Vasconcelos*, 88–136.
25. Cárdenas Noriega, *José Vasconcelos*, 88–89.
26. Cárdenas Noriega, *José Vasconcelos*, 111–36.
27. From "Informe del Departamento de Cultura Indígena," *Boletín de la* SEP 1, 2 September 1922, 263; cited in Fell, *José Vasconcelos*, 224.
28. "Informe del Departamento de Cultura Indígena."
29. Anda Alanis, *La arquitectura de la revolución Mexicana*, 69–76.
30. Tenorio-Trillo, *Mexico at the World's Fairs*, 216.
31. Vasconcelos, *La raza cósmica*. Similar ideologies were being formed in other Latin American regions. For example, in Brazil, Mario de Andrade published *Macunaíma* in 1928. The novel juxtaposed the modern and the primitive, as well as the rural and the urban, and played out through the experiences of a shape-shifting Brazilian Indian. Often considered the cornerstone of Brazilian Modernist literature, the work was fiercely nationalistic and sought to valorize all aspects that contributed to "Brazilian-ness." In *Nationalizing Blackness*, Robin Moore analyzes the once-despised Afro-Cuban musical and cultural forms that a state project transformed into a symbol of national cultural identity.
32. Fell, *José Vasconcelos*, 224.
33. Fell, *José Vasconcelos*, 224.
34. Fell, *José Vasconcelos*, 225–69.
35. Fell, *José Vasconcelos*, 225–69.
36. AGEPEO, Fondo Educación, Sección Cultura y Artística, Serie Musical, 1926–1930.
37. González Esperón, *Perfiles de Oaxaca*, 216.
38. A band called simply "banda de música" did play that day also, but it is not clear whether it was the BME.
39. AGEPEO, 1926–1930, Fondo Educación, Sección Cultural y Artistica, Serie Música, Leg. 1.
40. AGEPEO, Instrucción Fondo Público, Sección Cultural y Artística, Serie BM, Música regional, sesiones culturales, Leg. 2.
41. I was unable to verify whether this was the same Policarpo Sánchez who worked in education in Michoacán and appears in Becker, *Setting the Virgin on Fire*.
42. The *Charros* correspondence is found in AGEPEO, Instrucción, Fondo Público, Sección Cultural y Artística, Serie BM, Música regional, sesiones culturales, Leg. 2.

43. Mondragón (1895–1962) began his musical career as a child singer in the choir of the Cathedral of Oaxaca. He studied voice in Oaxaca and later distinguished himself at the National Conservatory of Music. In 1907, he performed a tenor role in Verdi's *Rigoletto*. As pianist, arranger, composer, and singer, he traveled throughout both North and South America as part of the Orquesta Típica Miguel Lerdo de Tejada. See Bustamante Gris, *Cancionero de música*, 97.
44. The Juchiteca is the female native of Juchitán, an archetype of Mexican female strength, and is admired throughout Mexico for her beauty and strength; the huipil is her embroidered native blouse.
45. Bustamante Gris, *Cancionero de música*, 97. Along with Rosas Solaegui, Mondragón was an integral part of the state's mission to use music as a tool in post-Revolutionary education.
46. *Periódico Oficial del Gobierno del Estado Libre y Soberano de Oaxaca*, 7 July 1928, 1.
47. AGEPEO, Sec. Gob., 1928, Exp. 14, Leg. 236.
48. This pedestal-upon-pyramid image seems a direct reference to José Vasconcelos's mestizo ideology.
49. AGEPEO, Instrucción, Fondo Público, Sección Cultura y Artística, Serie BME, Legajo 2. Much of the period's governmental correspondence includes the motto "Nuestro estado es pobre por ignorancia y la falta de comunicaciones" ("Our state is poor because of ignorance and the lack of communication"), a phrase that echoes another Revolutionary refrain, "carreteras y escuelas" ("highways and schools"). The Spanish word for "communication" in this case connotes efficient modes of transportation and the integration of remote parts of the state into a highway system. Oaxaca's difficult terrain still conspires against state highway and road-construction projects. A source I am unable to recall credited the motto, I believe, to Governor Vásquez.
50. AGEPEO, Cultural y Artística, 1929, Fondo Educación, Sección Técnica, Serie BME, Legajo 3. The document is dated 1935. A supplement entitled "Música Oaxaqueña," perhaps included to demonstrate the types of entries desired, included titles such as the "Corrido del agrarista" ("Ballad of the Agrarian"), featuring music by Rosas Solaegui.
51. Municipal-band proliferation was neither new nor unique to Oaxaca. For a similar case in Zacatecas, see Romero, *La música en Zacatecas*.

6. MUNICIPAL CONTROL

1. "La Banda de Música Paso Ayer Revista de Ingreso al Gobierno del Estado," *La Voz de Oaxaca*, 2 January 1947, 1, 4.
2. See Secretaría de Gobernación y Gobierno del Estado de Oaxaca, *Los municipios de Oaxaca*. 13. Today there are 2,378 municipalities in Mexico, 570 of which are located in Oaxaca.
3. The history of indigenous municipalities (for in Oaxaca that is what they largely are) and governmental attempts in the twentieth century to reduce their political power by reducing their numbers, may be found in Díaz Montes and Ornelas López. *Problemática municipal de Oaxaca*. On the history of Oaxacan colonial land-tenure patterns and municipalities, see William B. Taylor, *Drinking, Homicide, & Rebellion*, and Taylor's *Landlord and Peasant*. Oaxacan historian Carlos Sánchez Silva demonstrates the nineteenth-century continuity of Taylor's patterns of land distribution in "Indians, Merchants, and Bureaucracy."
4. Archivo General del Ejecutivo Poder del Estado de Oaxaca (AGEPEO), Fondo Instrucción, Sección Instrucción de los Distritos, Serie Centro, 1857, Subserie Escuela de Música, Lugar San Felipe de Agua. To date no response from Juárez has been found. I am indebted to Selene García for sharing this document with me. Selene also found a request from 1884 from the *jefe político* (political boss) of Tehuantepec, who requested instruments in order to fulfill his duties in organizing national and local holidays. See AGEPEO, Fondo Instrucción Pública, Sección Instrucción de los distritos, Serie Cuicatlán.
5. AGEPEO, Dep. Gob., 1922, Exp. 18, Leg. 127.
6. *El Mercurio*, 5 March 1921, 1.
7. AGEPEO, Era Revolucionaria, Centro, 1923, Exp. 35, Leg. 135. At least two dozen other letters appear in the same file, indicating a concerted effort by the state, working down to the municipal level, to institutionalize and standardize the Independence Day programs. Almost all the programs feature a band of some sort. All of the 1923 Independence Day programs cited below are found in this file.
8. In a 2006 article about the Mexican singer Georgina Meneses's collaboration with a Mixe band, Elena Poniatowska provided interesting historical and literary insight into the region's musical traditions. See "Georgina Meneses canta en la sierra mix con la banda del pueblo de Santiago Zacatepec," *La Jornada* (México City), 21 January 2006, section *de en medio*, 1a, 7a.

9. Letters documenting these performances are found in AGEPEO, Era Revolucionaria, Centro 1923, Exp. 35, Leg. 135.
10. AGEPEO, Era Revolucionaria, Centro 1923, Exp. 35, Leg. 135.
11. AGEPEO, Era Revolucionaria, Centro 1923, Exp. 35, Leg. 135.
12. AGEPEO, Era Revolucionaria, Centro 1923, Exp. 35, Leg. 135.
13. AGEPEO, Sec. Gob., Centro, 1926, Exp. 17, Leg. 215.
14. AGEPEO, Sec. Gob., 1923, Exp. 41, Leg. 139.
15. AGEPEO, Dep. Gob., 1927, Exp. 39, Leg. 224. The proliferation of municipal bands required a commercial infrastructure that could meet the demand for instruments, sheet music, and equipment. One of the BME's important functions has been the dissemination of sheet music to other bands throughout Mexico.
16. *El Mercurio*, 24 April 1924, 1, 4.
17. AGEPEO, Tesorería General del Estado, Sección 2a, Exp. 86. The oath required of the director (and all musicians in the BME) is another interesting intersection of state and art.
18. Archivo Histórico del Municipio de la Ciudad de Oaxaca (AHMCO), Sección Públicas, Departamento Obras, Exp. 456, 7-F.
19. Memos documenting all these functions are found in AGEPEO, Sec. Gob., Distrito Centro, 1928, Leg. 236, Exp. 14.
20. AGEPEO, Sec. Gob., 1929, Exp. Fondo Educación, Sección Técnica, Cultural, y Artística, Serie BME, Leg. 3. During "The Week of the Child" the BME performed six different times at government offices, the plaza, and an orphanage.
21. AGEPEO, Exp. Fondo Educación, 1929 Sección Técnica, Cultural, y Artística, Serie BME, Leg. 3.
22. AGEPEO, Exp. Fondo Educación, 1929 Sección Técnica, Cultural, y Artística, Serie BME, Leg. 3.
23. Why these pieces were labeled "useless" is unclear. Perhaps the songs' popularity had waned or the sheet music was merely in poor physical condition.
24. Although during this period the BME had been renamed temporarily and bore the acronym "BMM" during this time, for the sake of clarity I will continue to refer to it as the "BME." Research failed to uncover any documentation explaining the change, though it may have been for fiscal reasons or attributable to the struggle over state and local control between various political factions at the time. See, for example, Smith, *Pistoleros*, 240–48.
25. AHMCO, Fondo Secretaría Municipal, Caja 91, 1937.

26. This list is compiled from various AHMCO files. It does not include other, more mundane events that appeared on the BME's schedule, such as various school and business openings or the welcoming of foreign dignitaries and political officials (and the subsequent send-offs at the train station or airport). See AHMCO, Caja 143, 1937, Exp. 36.
27. AHMCO, Caja 177, 1945–1946, Exp. 7/5.
28. Becker, *Setting the Virgin on Fire*, 89–90.
29. Mario González, "El tradicional Desfile del 20 de noviembre," *e-once Noticias*, 20 November 2006. In the article González interviewed Mexican historian Lorenzo Meyer, who noted the diminished role of sports parades and exhibitions in the 2006 Revolution Day events in comparison to the Calles period.
30. AHMCO, Caja 144, 1937, Exp. 39. It should be remembered that, in many cases, a functionary from the municipal offices "designs" the programs—thus the use of such vague genres as "national music." I assume that the selections were left to the director's discretion.
31. I am grateful to former BME subdirector Zoilo Solís Félix for insight on the matter of inebriation within the BME.
32. AHMCO, Hacienda, 1946, No. 1514. The fine for musicians' inebriation was usually loss of the day's wages.
33. AHMCO, Actas del Cabildo, 1939, Exp. 9, Caja 156.
34. AHMCO, Caja 156-B, 1939, Exp. 27.
35. *El Mercurio*, 23 February 1921. There is no evidence that a musician's labor union existed in Oaxaca before the UF. An archival source from sometime between 1929 and 1936 refers to a strike by the Liga Filarmónica Socialista (Socialist Philharmonic League) against the Teatro Juárez. Apparently the theater's introduction of new sound technology had at least partially displaced some musicians who had provided accompaniment to the previously silent reels. The introduction of the Vitafono, as the sound projector was called, meant a reduction in League workers' salaries. In an attempt to recoup some of their losses, the musicians asked the state if they could use the Teatro Luis Mier y Terán for one month in order to make some money. See AGEPEO, Servicios Intelectuales y Artísticos, 1929–36, Leg. 98. In 1924, the BME was performing inside cinemas, their music apparently alternating with the films. See *El Mercurio*, 8 May 1924, for example, where the BME was announced to be performing along with the screening of an unnamed "moral movie."

36. It is not clear whether the UF was part of the CROM, but this is an interesting avenue for further research.
37. See, for example, AHMCO, Actas de Cabildo, 1936, 192, 1r–12r, 10–11; and Actas de Cabildo, 24 August 1937, 194.
38. AHMCO, Caja 151, 1938.
39. AHMCO, Caja 165, 1942, Exp. 12.
40. AHMCO, Caja 170, 1943, Exp. 23.
41. Other guest conductors include flautist, conductor, and composer Theodore Paschedag of Illinois (numerous times from the late 1940s to 1979); violinist, conductor, and composer James Niblock of Michigan State University (1970); and Mexican composer and conductor Eduardo Mata.
42. Tyler, "Native Mexican Art."
43. Gibson, "Music of Ponce, Carrillo, and Chávez, 123.
44. "Stokowski Returning, Likes Mexican Music," *New York Times*, February 17, 1932.
45. Daniel, *Stokowski*, 472. In the early 1940s Carlos Chávez had performed in the United States with future director of the BME Diego Innes Acevedo a number of times in Milwaukee, Wisconsin.
46. *Time*, "People" section, June 5, 1944.
47. *Time*, "People" section, May 29, 1944.
48. "La Banda de Música."
49. González Esperón, *Perfiles de Oaxaca*, 217. Affectionately known as "Dimas," Pérez Torres's danzón "Nereidas" remains one of the most popular songs in the BME repertoire. The BME archive holds many of his works. He returned to lead the BME in 1975.
50. "En Torno de la Bandera Nacional se Congregarán Mañana Todos los Mexicanos," *La Voz de Oaxaca*, 23 February 1947, 1, 5.
51. "Nuevo Horario para las Audiciones de la Banda de Música del Estado," *La Voz de Oaxaca*, 5 October 1947, 1, 8. While the hours are shorter, the Sunday, Tuesday, and Thursday performances remain audiciones ordinarias for the BME. No reason for the change is given further than "por disposición del gobierno" (by order of the government).
52. *Informe del Gobernador Eduardo Vasconcelos*, 30–31.
53. The state's creation of a marimba band to share duties with the BME is not only a direct affirmation of the state's musical diversity (as the marimba is closely associated with the musical traditions of the Isthmus) but also an indication that the state considered its musical project worthwhile, if not quantifiable.
54. It is unclear when the Sunday evening performances ended.

55. "Reglamento de la Banda de Música del Estado," *Periódico Oficial del Gobierno del Estado Libre y Soberano de Oaxaca*, 13 March 1948, 75–80.
56. The practice of inspection, one of the last remaining military vestiges in the BME, ended in the early 1990s.
57. The use of the exclusively male pronoun is correct, as the BME remained an all-male organization until 1975, when one Veronica Pacheco Gomes became its first female member. Pacheco left within a year but rejoined, again only briefly, in 1985. See ABME, 4 October 1975 and 1 October 1976. Currently there are two female musicians in the BME, the first females since Pacheco.
58. *Informe del Licenciado Eduardo Vasconcelos*, 39.
59. *Informe del Licenciado Eduardo Vasconcelos*, 39.
60. "Se le Designó Director de la Banda de Música del Estado," *Provincia*, 2 August 1950, 1, 4.
61. González Esperón, *Perfiles de Oaxaca*, 217–18.
62. "Se le Designó Director de la Banda de Música del Estado."
63. "Reglamento de la Banda de Música del Estado." Research failed to indicate whether Innes had in fact directed another band in Mexico prior to his appointment in Oaxaca, though his experience in the Wisconsin WPA Symphony Orchestra was likely considered as fulfillment of the requirement.
64. "Los Conciertos Especiales de la Banda de Música del Estado el Próximo Domingo," *Provincia*, 6 August 1950, 1, 4.
65. "Se Hace Revisión al Archivo de la Banda de Música," *Provincia*, 9 August 1950, 1, 2. The position of archivist was never permanent and, probably due to economic conditions and the BME's limited budget, sometimes went unfilled. Today an administrative staff that is part of the government's civil service works full-time in the BME offices and, among other duties, attends to the music archives.
66. "Una Bella Composición Musical de sabor Netamente Oaxaqueño," *La Voz de Oaxaca*, 7 January 1947, 1, 3.
67. "Audición Musical de Hoy," *Provincia*, 13 August 1950, 1, 7.
68. *Informe Manuel Cabrera Carrasquedo*, 16 September 1953, 53.
69. *Informe Manuel Cabrera Carrasquedo*, 16 September 1954, 10.
70. I was unable to verify whether the move ever took place. Since approximately 1960 the BME offices and rehearsal hall have been located at Guerrero 406, Centro, just a few blocks off the Zócalo.

7. POLITICAL PROSELYTIZER

1. The design of Oaxaca's governmental website for culture and tourism from 2006 attested to this fact. The banner at the top of the web page was a photograph of a row of dancers performing the "Flor de piña" (Pineapple blossom) dance from the Tuxtepec region. That image dissolved into a close-up of a group of Asian tourists enjoying the performance.
2. For a filmed version of the performance, see *Oaxaca de la Colección de Imágenes de México de la Filmoteca de la UNAM*, DVD, ed. Jorge Vargas Hernández, Dirección General de Actividades Cinematográficas de la UNAM (Mexico City: Universidad Autónoma de México, 2005).
3. The pre-Hispanic and colonial roots of Guelaguetza are found in Castro Mantecón, *Las fiestas de los "Lunes del Cerro."*
4. Stephen, *Zapotec Women*, 194.
5. For an anthropological analysis of guelaguetza, see Cohen, *Cooperation and Community*, 90–93.
6. Poole, "An Image of 'Our Indian,'" 37–82. The quotes appear on page 76.
7. Archivo General del Ejecutivo Poder del Estado de Oaxaca (AGEPEO), Era Revolucionaria, Leg. 81, Exp. (illegible, either 24 or 27). Indicating that the celebration took place for at least two more years, *El Mercurio* reported that a bullring was built especially for the 1920 Fiesta de la Raza. The BME, "situated in front of the portico in front of the bullring[,] executed selections from their repertoire"; see "Seis Bravos Cornúpetos Harán La Alegría de esta Tarde," *El Mercurio*, 12 October 1920, 1.
8. López, "India Bonita Contest of 1921," 291–328.
9. Rosas Solaegui, *Un hombre en el tiempo*, 152–53. The 1932 festival was part of the festivities that year, celebrating the four-hundredth anniversary of the founding of the city of Oaxaca.
10. On Isthmian song and dance traditions, see Royce, "Music, Dance, and Fiesta," 51–60. For a traveler's account of musical practices in the Isthmus, see Covarrubias, *Mexico South*, 322, 335, and 378–80. Covarrubias, a Mexican painter interested in anthropology, rightly identified the opposing traditions of brass-band and marimba groups on the Isthmus, as well as the influence on both of jazz, polka, and popular dance arrangements, when he describes the "wild ad-libs of local orchestras

[the marimbas] lost in the Oompah-pah tunes." He also wrote of the lifestyle of *pura pachanga* (pure party): the intense Isthmian social activity; celebrations, religious and otherwise; the weekly village festivals and dances; the military authorities' converting ball courts at the local barracks into a dance floor, and so on.
11. Giménez, "Comunidades primordiales y modernización," 163.
12. For example, for the governor's orders for the BME to perform in 1926 and 1928, see AGEPEO, Era Revolucionaria, Exp. 27, Leg. 81.
13. *Diario del Sur*, 22 July 1928, 1.
14. See, for example, *La Voz de Oaxaca*, 3 July 1946, 1, 2.
15. On the history of tourism in Mexico, see Berger, *Development of Mexico's Tourism Industry*.
16. Clancy, *Exporting Paradise*, 41. Clancy writes that the UN sought to encourage governments and international organizations to promote international tourism, or at least to work to tear down barriers to its promotion.
17. "Cultural patrimony" may be understood as the set of chattel and real goods protected by legal instruments at the municipal, state, or federal level. This definition may signify the incorporation of an elite discourse that seeks to identify "noble" examples worthy of official recognition. For a study of the Brazilian government's cultural-patrimony project, see Miceli, "SPHAN." See also García Canclini, *Culturas populares en el capitalismo*. On the relationship between cultural patrimony, nationalism, monuments, and tourism, see Álvarez Ponce de León, *México Turismo y Cultura*.
18. *Informe del Gobernador Alfonso Pérez Gasga*, 16 September 1960, 15.
19. Clancy, *Exporting Paradise*, 41.
20. The stadium is also referred to as Estadio Guelaguetza (Guelaguetza Stadium).
21. *Informe del Licenciado Fernando Gómez Sandoval*, 23.
22. García Canclini, *Culturas populares*, 185.
23. García Canclini, *Culturas populares*, 185.
24. García Moll, "Protección del patrimonio cultural, 31–35.
25. The inclusion of a primary school banda de guerra may have increased the sentimentality and emotional charge of the ceremony.
26. "Oaxaca Envia Un Mensaje Fraternal Para Que El Mundo Viva Libre y En Paz," *El Imparcial*, 25 October 1966 1, 3. The Mexican desire for non-intervention was especially important given the political turmoil in the Dominican Republic and the escalating war in Vietnam.

27. The selection of the overture is interesting, for it encapsulates in one composition (albeit in a Brazilian context) some of the BME's essential twentieth-century themes. Gomes, a Brazilian liberal and patriot, based the opera on fellow Brazilian José de Alencar's *O Guarani*. Both novel and opera embodied the modern Latin American intellectual preoccupation with miscegenation and indigenism, and both also subverted the usual trope of the love between the European male colonizer and the indigenous woman. *O Guarani* told the less acceptable tale of the reverse: the encounter and subsequent love between a Portuguese noblewoman and an Indian male.

28. UNESCO is a specialized agency of the United Nations established in 1945. Its stated purpose is to contribute to peace and security by promoting international collaboration through education, science, and culture in order to further universal respect for justice, the rule of law, and the human rights and fundamental freedoms proclaimed in the UN Charter. See UNESCO, "Constitution," http://portal.unesco.org/en/ev.php-URL_ID=15244&URL_DO=DO_TOPIC&URL_SECTION=201.html (accessed 13 March 2014).

29. ABME, Sheet music inventory, entry no. 1999. The year of the composition is not given.

30. Velasco Pérez, *Oaxaca*, 7–12.

31. UNESCO, ICOMOS, No. 415, "World Heritage List," 2 December 1986, http://whc.unesco.org/archive/advisory_body_evaluation/415.pdf (accessed 13 March 2014).

32. *Primer Informe Raul Brena Torres*, 16 September 1963, 19.

33. *Primer Informe Raul Brena Torres*, 16 September 1963, 19.

34. Discos Peerless (Peerless Records) was founded in Mexico City in 1933. The label mostly released popular Mexican music, and included in its catalog are songs by José Alfredo Jiménez, Agustín Lara, and Lola Beltrán. In addition to Mexico, Peerless records were sold in other parts of Latin America and in some communities in the southwestern United States. Peerless issued some long-playing vinyl records starting in the 1950s, and the labels sometimes have text in both English and Spanish, as does the BME's *Guelaguetza Oaxaqueña*. Today Warner Music owns the Peerless catalog. Arturo Cruz Bárcenas, "Lanza Peerless Discos con temas remasterizados para festejar 80 años," *La Jornada*, 20 July 2013, http://www.jornada.unam.mx/2013/07/30/espectaculos/a10n2esp (accessed November 2014). See also Rust, "Peerless."

35. *Primer Informe Raul Brena Torres*, 16 September 1963, 20.

36. "Fervor Cívico y Austera Solemnidad Ayer en la Recepción de las Banderas," *El Imparcial*, 16 July 1964, 1.
37. Knight, *U.S.-Mexican Relations*, 141. Knight sees Mexican nationalism as the most visible form of patriotism.
38. Knight, *U.S.-Mexican Relations*, 106.
39. Knight, *U.S.-Mexican Relations*, 106.
40. ABME, Leg. Servicios, 1966.
41. A collection of *Oaxaca en México* may be found in Oaxaca at the Hemeroteca Pública de Oaxaca "Nestor Sánchez H."
42. Marcus and Flannery, *Zapotec Civilization*, 208, 217, and 220–21.
43. On Oaxacan emigration to the United States, see Klaver, *From the Land of the Sun to the City of Angels*. Male populations in smaller villages have been decimated, but the men do attempt to return home when possible, especially for the Christmas and New Year's holidays. This trend has given the state's migrants their own liminal status: to which world, exactly, do Oaxacan migrants belong?
44. Archivo de la Banda de Música del Estado de Oaxaca (State Band of Oaxaca Archives, ABME), Letter 000615, 7 December 2001.
45. ABME, 1956–1979, loose document.
46. ABME, 3 March 1975, no. 023.
47. The funeral program is found in ABME, 30 January 1976, no. 054, and 19 February 1976, no. 117.
48. "La Banda de Música del Estado: Mejor Cada Día," *El Imparcial*, 2 April 1978, Sunday supplement, n.p.
49. *El Imparcial*, 2 April 1978, Sunday supplement, n.p.
50. "La Banda de Música del Estado sigue Reintegrándose," *Oaxaca Gráfico*, 5 June 1978, n.p. Photocopy found in ABME 1978.
51. Curriculum Vitae, Professor Leodegario Martínez Vásquez, ABME, 8 November 1990, loose document.
52. *Oaxaca Gráfico*, 5 June 1978, n.p.
53. Zoilo Solís Félix, interview by the author, Oaxaca, 10 and 17 February 2006.
54. Again, as an organic structure, the BME is susceptible to the usual intrigues and antipathies. Given the discord that Rosas Solaegui noted, it is possible that Solis himself had difficulties with Innes, other musicians, and even other directors.
55. Although alcohol was a problem for the BME, Innes's comments recall an elite preoccupation since colonial times with alcohol consumption by the poor (indigenous) and its ensuing systemic social breakdown

characterized by violence and sex. See, for example, Taylor, *Drinking, Homicide, & Rebellion in Colonial Mexican Villages*. Taylor, however, disagrees with the colonial elites' connection between alcohol and violence and concludes in part that social breakdown was not an inevitable partner of drinking in peasant villages. Oaxacan villages, along with villages of central Mexico, are the focus of Taylor's research. Furthermore, while it is difficult (and perhaps dangerous) to ascribe personal prejudices to someone, if Innes was of Anglo extraction, as his name suggests (the surname is of Scottish heritage), his comments carry a paternalistic, if not derogatory, tone.

56. Innes documented at least three absences in 1962. See ABME, 22 April, 31 May, and 1 November 1962.
57. Solís believes that it was worth it to put up with Agustin's absences because he was a good percussionist and absenteeism, to a certain extent, was common among the musicians. Economic pressures often led to absences, as musicians were forced to stay at home to bring in a crop or to moonlight in other bands to help make ends meet.
58. ABME, Gob., Sec. Personal, no. 1818, 26 September 1966.
59. ABME, 30 May 1971; Innes no. 85, 31 May 1971.
60. ABME, no. 131, 7 January 1975 and no. 425, 24 January 1975.
61. ABME, 24 January 1981.
62. ABME (undated, perhaps 24 January) 1981.
63. ABME, no. 16, 24 January 1981. It should be noted that no such incident would ever occur under the present director, Maestro Eliseo Martínez García. Martínez's managerial style brooks no lapses in discipline, and disputes are resolved more on a personal, rather than bureaucratic, level.
64. Cruz also, at least for a time, contributed to the confusing nomenclature of the BME. He insisted on calling the BME "La Banda Sinfónica" (The Symphonic Band), saying he did so with gubernatorial permission. This quirk caused no small amount of consternation among the bureaucrats who dealt with the band. In a letter dated 4 May 1983, the secretary to the governor reminded Cruz that governor Eduardo Vasconcelos had in 1948 established the name of the BME by official decree. See ABME no. 933, 4 May 1983. The secretary admonished Cruz, saying that any name change required an act of the government and had to be published in the *Periódico Oficial del Gobierno del Estado Libre y Soberano de Oaxaca*. When Cruz finally appealed to the governor to clarify the BME's name, the governor admonished him for his pedantic

behavior. See ABME no. 150, 6 November 1985, and no. 181, 17 December 1985.
65. Rogelio Martínez Hernández, interview by the author, Oaxaca, 17 February 2006.
66. Maestro Eliseo Martínez García, interview by author, Oaxaca, 14 February 2006.
67. It appears that the BME had sought remedy from the governor during Medina's tenure as well. *Carteles del Sur*, 29 June 1979. For a complaint by a musician, see ABME "64"/169, 10 November 1983.
68. Interview with Solis Félix.
69. ABME, letter from Instituto Oaxaqueño de Cultura 1688/01, 16 October 2001.
70. The song originally was an instrumental entitled "Moon over Naples," and when lyrics by Eddie Snyder were added, Al Martino and Engelbert Humperdinck, among others, recorded the song, perhaps adding to the bureaucrat's cultural confusion. Kaempfert was a talented multi-instrumentalist and received formal training at the Hamburg Conservatory of Music. He is perhaps best known for the Frank Sinatra classic "Strangers in the Night." The BME music archive holds arrangements for "Spanish Eyes" as well as a Sinatra potpourri that includes themes from "Strangers" and the ever-popular, even in Oaxaca, "New York, New York."

CONCLUSION

1. Archivo de la Banda de Música del Estado de Oaxaca (ABME), 12 March 1975.
2. For example, in 2001 the BME performed at "The Honor of the Holy Virgin of Guadalupe" in Ocotlán de Morelos (12 December) and at the Parish of St. Mary of Guadalupe in Huajuapan (5 December). See ABME, December 2001.
3. At the time Cruz may have borne the four braids of a general on his uniform.
4. Interview with Zoilo Solís Félix. Other current uniforms include guayaberas and polo shirts with the BME's logo.
5. ABME, "Breve Curriculum Eliseo Manuel Martínez García," 19 September 2000.
6. ABME, 1997, loose document.
7. "Place of the Butterflies"; Bradomín, *Toponomía de Oaxaca*, 41.
8. For an archaeological monograph of the Cañada, see Spencer and Redmond, *Archaeology of the Cañada de Cuicatlán, Oaxaca*. The authors

argue that profound disruptions, both geological and political, within the region have forced major economic, social, political, and religious change.
9. Thompson, "Patrician Society, Plebian Culture," 389.
10. The present government's logo adorning all official state correspondence and government websites speaks to the ongoing, and still unconsolidated, goal of state unity. A map of the state, not unlike the map in this volume, is stylized with seven hand-holding figures (dancing?) across the state and dividing the seven regions. The motto reads, "Oaxaca de todos, un gobierno de todos" (Oaxaca of all, a government of all).

GLOSSARY OF SONG AND DANCE FORMS

chilena. A song and dance form for bands, imported from Chile, that first arrived on the coast of southern Oaxaca during the great migration northward to California during the Gold Rush. The couples dance mimics the courting ritual of chickens!

danzón. A ballroom dance song form based on European dance music as performed by Caribbean musicians.

fantasía. A musical composition in free form, or one based on motifs from an opera.

fox-trot. A dance form of alternating staggered slow and quick rhythms.

huapango. Another variation of the *son* (see below), generally associated with the southern state of Veracruz and often featuring a solo violin.

jarabe. A Mexican dance form of popular origin with great regional variation, perhaps based on Spanish Empire–era dances.

jarana. A popular dance form from southern Mexico, similar to the *son* but usually without lyrics.

mazurka. A lively dance of Polish origin.

paso doble. A song and dance form based on bullfight arena marches.

polka. A half-rhythm dance traceable to central Europe, probably nineteenth-century Bohemia.

schottische (*chotis* in Spanish). A round dance, similar to a polka, but slower.

son. A popular song and dance form, possibly with Spanish roots and also with great regional variation.

waltz. A gliding, whirling couples dance of close embrace in triple time.

zarzuela. A song form from the Spanish light opera of the same name.

BIBLIOGRAPHY

ARCHIVES
Archivo de la Banda de Música del Estado de Oaxaca, Oaxaca, Mexico
(ABME)
Archivo General de la Nación, Mexico City (AGN)
Archivo General del Ejecutivo Poder del Estado de Oaxaca, Oaxaca, Mexico
(AGEPEO)
Archivo Histórico de la Secretaría de la Defensa Nacional, Mexico City
(AHSDN)
Archivo Histórico del Municipal de la Ciudad de Oaxaca, Oaxaca, Mexico
(AHMCO)
Colección Porfirio Díaz, Universidad Iberoamericana, Mexico City (CPD)

UNPUBLISHED SOURCES
Informe del Gobernador Alfonso Pérez Gasga, 16 September 1960.
Informe del Gobernador Manuel García Vigil, 16 April 1922.
Informe del Licenciado Fernando Gómez Sandoval, 1972.
Informe Manuel Cabrera Carrasquedo, 16 September 1953.
Informe Manuel Cabrera Carrasquedo, 16 September 1954.
Informe Manuel Cabrera Carrasquedo, 16 September 1955.
Memorias Administrativas del Ciudadano gobernador Albino Zertuche 1889, parte expositiva.
Memorias Administrativas del Ciudadano gobernador Miguel Bolaños Cacho, Septiembre 16 de 1902.
Memorias Administrativas del Licenciado Emilio Pimentel presentadas al XXIV Legislatura el día 17 de Septiembre de 1907.
Primer Informe Raul Brena Torres, 16 September 1963.

PUBLISHED SOURCES

Alcaraz, Ramón. *The Other Side: Or Notes for the History of the War between Mexico and the United States*. Translated by Albert C. Ramsey. New York: John Wiley, 1850.

Altamirano, Ignacio Manuel. *Obras completas VIII, Crónicas 2*. Edited by Carlos Monsiváis. Mexico City: Secretaría de Educación Pública, 1986.

Álvarez Ponce de León, Griselda. *México Turismo y Cultura: Una aproximación al patrimonio turístico cultural*. Mexico City: Editorial Diana, 2000.

Anda Alanis, Enrique X. de. *La arquitectura de la revolución Mexicana: Corrientes y estilos en la década de los veinte*. Mexico City: Universidad Nacional Autónoma de México, 1990.

Andrade, Mario de. *Macunaíma, el héroe sin ningún carácter*. Barcelona: Seix Barral, 1977.

Arnold, Ben. *Music and War: A Research and Information Guide*. New York: Garland, 1993.

Attali, Jacques. *Noise: The Political Economy of Music*. Translated by Brian Massumi. Minneapolis: University of Minnesota Press, 2003.

Becker, Marjorie. *Setting the Virgin on Fire: Lázaro Cárdenas, Michoacán Peasants, and the Redemption of the Mexican Revolution*. Berkeley: University of California Press, 1995.

Bellah, Robert N. "Civil Religion in America." *Daedalus* 96, no. 1 (Winter 1967): 1–21.

Bereson, Ruth. *The Operatic State Cultural Policy and the Opera House*. London: Routledge, 2002.

Berger, Dina. *The Development of Mexico's Tourism Industry: Pyramids by Day, Martinis by Night*. New York: Palgrave Macmillan, 2006.

Berry, Charles R. *The Reform in Oaxaca, 1856–1876*. Lincoln: University of Nebraska Press, 1981.

Brading, David A. *Miners and Merchants in Bourbon Mexico 1763–1810*. London: Cambridge University Press, 1971.

Bradomín, José María. *Toponomía de Oaxaca (Crítica Etimológica)*. Mexico City: José María Bradomín, 1980.

Brenner, Helmut. *Juventino Rosas: His Life, His Work, His Time*. Warren MI: Harmonie Park Press, 2000.

Brill, Debra. *History of the J.G. Brill Company*. Bloomington: Indiana University Press, 2001. Brill, Mark. "Los maestros de capilla de la Catedral de Antequera." In *Cuadernos de Historia Eclesiástica 2 De papeles mudos a composiciones sonoras: La música en la Catedral de Oaxaca,*

Siglos XVII–XX, edited by Jesús J. Lizama Q. and Daniela Traffano, 21–40. Oaxaca: Archivo Histórico de la Arquidiócesis de Oaxaca, 1998.

Brioso y Candiani, Manuel. *La evolución del Pueblo Oaxaqueño desde la Conquista hasta la Consumación de la Independencia 1521–1821*. Mexico City: Tipógrafo Oaxaca en México, 1939.

Brown, Lyle C. "Mexico's Constitution of 1917." In *Revolution in Mexico: Years of Upheaval, 1910–1940*, edited by James W. Wilkie and Albert L. Michaels, 112–115. Tucson: University of Arizona Press, 1984.

Bueno Sánchez, José Manuel. *Efemérides Oaxaqueñas*. Mexico City: Costa-Amic Editores, 1980.

Burke, Richard N. "The Marche Fúnebre from Beethoven to Mahler." PhD diss., City University of New York, 1991.

Bustamante Gris, Manuel, comp. *Cancionero de música popular oaxaqueña*. Oaxaca: Instituto Oaxaqueño de las Culturas, 1998.

Calderón de la Barca, Madame Frances Erskine. *Life in Mexico during a Residence of Two Years in That Country*. London: Century Hutchinson, 1987.

Calderón Martínez, Danivia. "Un recorrido por la historia del Zócalo de Oaxaca: Primera Parte." *La Gaceta del Instituto Patrimonio Cultural* 1, no. 2 (July–September 2005): 4–11.

Campos, Rubén M. *El folklore y la música mexicana: Investigación acerca de la cultura musical en México (1525–1925)*. Mexico City: Publicaciones de la Secretaría de Educación Pública, 1928.

Carballo, Emmanuel. "Prólogo." In *Las fiestas patrias en la narrativa nacional*. Mexico City: Editorial Diógenes, 1982.

Cárdenas Noriega, Joaquin. *José Vasconcelos 1882–1982: Educador, Político, y Profeta*. Mexico City: Ediciones Oceano, 1982.

Carpizo, Jorge. *La constitución mexicana de 1917*. Mexico City: Editorial Porrúa, 1995.

Carr, Barry. "Labour and Politics in Mexico 1910–1929." PhD diss., Oxford University, 1974.

Carreño, Alberto Maria. *Jefes del ejército mexicano en 1847*. Mexico City: Secretaría de Fomento, 1914.

Castro Mantecón, Javier. *Efemérides de la Banda de Música del Estado*. Oaxaca: Casa de la Cultura Oaxaqueña, 1983.

———. *Las Fiestas de los "Lunes del Cerro."* Oaxaca: Instituto de protección a la infancia del Estado de Oaxaca, 1971.

Chance, John K. *Conquest of the Sierra: Spaniards and Indians in Colonial Oaxaca*. Norman: University of Oklahoma Press, 1989.

———. *Race and Class in Colonial Oaxaca*. Stanford CA: Stanford University Press, 1978.
Chanfón Olmos, Carlos, coordinator. *Historia de la arquitectura y el urbanismo mexicanos*. Vol. 3, *El México independiente. Book 2, Afirmación del nacionalismo y la modernidad*. Mexico City: Universidad Nacional Autónoma de México, 1998.
Chassen-López, Francie R. *From Liberal to Revolutionary Oaxaca: The View from the South, Mexico 1867–1911*. University Park PA: Penn State Press, 2004.
Clancy, Michael. *Exporting Paradise: Tourism and Development in Mexico*, Kidlington, Oxford: Elsevier Science, 2001.
Cohen, Jeffrey H. *Cooperation and Community: Economy and Society in Oaxaca*. Austin: University of Texas Press, 1999.
Colección de Leyes, Decretos, Circulares. Vol. 10. Oaxaca: Imprenta del Estado, 1893.
Colección de Leyes, Decretos, Circulares. Vol. 11. Oaxaca: Imprenta del Estado, 1887.
Colección de Leyes, Decretos, Circulares 1871–1874. Vol. 6. Oaxaca: Imprenta del Estado, 1879.
Colección de Leyes, Decretos, Circulares 21 Enero 1876–3 Abril 1877. Vol. 8. Oaxaca: Imprenta del Estado, 1880.
Colección de Leyes, Decretos, Circulares, 23 Septiembre 1874–21 Enero 1876. Vol. 7. Oaxaca: Imprenta del Estado, 1912.
Colección de Leyes y Decretos del Estado Libre de Oaxaca. Vol. 1. Oaxaca: Imprenta del Estado, 1909.
Colección de Leyes y Decretos del Estado Libre de Oaxaca. Vol. 2. Oaxaca: Imprenta del Estado, n.d.
Colección de Leyes y Decretos del Estado de Oaxaca. 2nd ed. Vol. 4. Oaxaca: Tipógrafo del Estado, 1898.
Constitución Política de los estados unidos Mexicanos. Mexico City: Ediciones Fiscales ISEF, 2005.
Corbin, Alain. *Village Bells: Sound and Meaning in the 19th-Century French Countryside*. Translated by Martin Thom. New York: Columbia University Press, 1998.
Cosío Villegas, Daniel. *Historia Moderna de México: El Porfiriato; La Vida Social*. Mexico City: Editorial Hermes 1990.
Cosío Villegas, Emma. "La vida cotidiana." In *Historia Moderna de Mexico La Republica Restaurada La Vida Social*, edited by Daniel Cosío Villegas, 453–525. Mexico City: Editorial Hermes, 1956.

Covarrubias, Miguel. *Mexico South: The Isthmus of Tehuantepec*. New York: Alfred A. Knopf, 1954.

Cruz Aguillón, Raúl. *Oaxaca: Nuestra ciudad, aspectos de su historia*. Oaxaca: Honorable Ayuntamiento de Oaxaca de Juárez, 1995.

Dabbs, Jack Autrey. *The French Army in Mexico, 1861–1867: A Study in Military Government*. The Hague: Mouton, 1963.

Daniel, Oliver. *Stokowski: A Counterpoint of View*. New York: Dodd, Mead, 1982.

Díaz Montes, Fausto, and José Luz Ornelas López. *Problemática municipal de Oaxaca: Los conflictos municipales y los municipios indígenas*. Oaxaca: Universidad Autónoma "Benito Juarez" de Oaxaca, Instituto de Investigaciones Sociológicas, 1987.

Dublán, Manuel, and José María Lozano. *Legislación Mexicana: Colección completa de las disposiciones legislativas expedidas desde la Independencia de la República*. Book 2 Mexico City: Imprenta del Comercio, 1876. CD-ROM.

Durkheim, Emile. *The Elementary Forms of Religious Life*. Translated by Karen E. Fields. New York: Free Press, 1995.

Encyclopedia of Mexico: History, Society & Culture. Vol. 2. Edited by Michael S. Werner. Chicago: Fitzroy Dearborn Publishers, 1997.

Esparza, Manuel. *Padrón de capitación de la ciudad de Oaxaca, 1875*. Oaxaca: Archivo General del Estado de Oaxaca, 1983.

Fell, Claude. *José Vasconcelos: Los años del águila (1920–1925), Educación, cultura e iberoamericanismo en el México postrevolucionario*. Mexico City: Universidad Nacional Autónoma de México, 1989.

Flannery, Kent V. "The Cultural Evolution of Civilizations." *Annual Review of Ecology and Systematics* 3 (1972): 399–426.

Fortson, James R. *Los gobernantes de Oaxaca*. Mexico City: J. R. Fortson, 1985.

Gage, Thomas. *The English-American: A New Survey of the West Indies, 1648*. Abingdon, UK: RoutledgeCurzon, 2005.

García Canclini, Nestór. *Culturas populares en el capitalismo*. Mexico City: Editorial Grijalbo, 2002.

García Moll, Roberto. "Protección del patrimonio cultural: Estado y sociedad civil." In *Temas y problemas*, edited by Armando Torres Michúa and Enrique X. de Anda Alanís, 31–35. Mexico City: Universidad Nacional Autónoma de México, 1997.

Gay, José Antonio. *Historia de Oaxaca*. Mexico City: Editorial Porrúa, 1982.

Gellner, Ernest. *Nationalism*. New York: New York University Press, 1997.

Gerhard, Peter. *A Guide to the Historical Geography of New Spain*. Norman: University of Oklahoma Press, 1993.

Gibson, Christina Taylor. "The Music of Manuel M. Ponce, Julián Carrillo, and Carlos Chávez in New York, 1925–1932." PhD diss., University of Maryland, 2008.

Giménez, Gilberto. "Comunidades primordiales y modernización." In *Modernización e identidades sociales*, coordinated by Gilberto Giménez and Ricardo Pozas H., 151–183. Mexico City: Universidad Nacional Autónoma Mexicana, 1994.

González Esperón, Luz María. *Perfiles de Oaxaca*. Oaxaca: Instituto Oaxaqueño de las Culturas, 2004.

Grial, Hugo de. *Músicos Mexicanos*. Mexico City: Editorial Diana, 1978.

Hayes, Joy Elizabeth. *Radio Nation: Communication, Popular Culture, and Nationalism in Mexico, 1920–1950*. Tucson: University of Arizona Press, 2000.

Hefter, Joseph, coordinador. "Crónica del Traje Militar en México del Siglo XVI al XX." *Artes de México* 15, no. 102 (1968).

———. *El soldado de Juárez, de Napoleón y de Maximiliano*. Mexico City: Sociedad de Geografía y Estadística Sección de Historia, 1962.

Hilfiger, John Jay. "Funeral Marches, Dirges, and Wind Bands in the Nineteenth Century." *Journal of Band Research* 27 (1992): 1–20.

Hindle-Hazen, Margaret, and Robert M. Hazen. *The Music Men: An Illustrated History of Brass Bands in America, 1800–1920*. Washington DC: Smithsonian Institution Press, 1987.

Índice Alfabético de la Colección de Leyes y Decretos del Estado de Oaxaca. Oaxaca: Imprenta del Estado, 1902.

Informe del Gobernador Eduardo Vasconcelos, 16 de Septiembre de 1948. Oaxaca: Talleres Gráficos del Estado de Oaxaca, n.d.

Informe del Gobernador Eduardo Vasconcelos, 17 de Septiembre 1949–16 de Septiembre 1950. Oaxaca: Talleres Gráficos del Estado de Oaxaca, 1950.

Informe del Licenciado Eduardo Vasconcelos rendido ante la XL Legislatura, 16 de Septiembre 1949. Oaxaca: Talleres Gráficos del Gobierno del Estado, 1949.

Instrucción para la Infantería del Ejército Mexicano. Mexico City: J. M. Lara, 1841.

Iturribarría, Jorge Fernando. "El batallón de Oaxaca." In *Oaxaca: Textos de su historia*, vol. 2, edited by Margarita Dalton, 444–453. Mexico City: Instituto de Investigaciones Dr. José Luis Mora, 1997.

———. *Oaxaca en la historia (de la época prehcolombiana a los tiempos actuales)*. Mexico City: Editorial Stylo, 1955.
Kahle, Gunter. *El ejército y la formación del Estado en los comienzos de la independencia de México*. Mexico City: Fondo de Cultura Económico, 1997.
Kahn, Douglas. *Noise, Water, Meat: A History of Sound in the Arts*. Cambridge MA: MIT Press, 1999.
Kappey, J. A. *Military Music: A History of Wind-Instrumental Bands*. London: Boosey & Co., n.d.
Kastner, Georges. *Manuel général de musique militaire: À l'usage de armées françaises*. Paris: Typographie de Firmin Didot Freres, 1848.
Klaver, Jeanine. *From the Land of the Sun to the City of Angels: The Migration Process of Zapotec Indians from Oaxaca, Mexico to Los Angeles, California*. Utrecht: University of Amsterdam, 1997.
Knight, Alan. *The Mexican Revolution*. Vol. 1, *Porfirians, Liberals, and Peasants*. Lincoln: University of Nebraska Press, 1986.
———. *U.S.-Mexican Relations, 1910–1940: An Interpretation*. San Diego: University of California, San Diego, 1987.
Kuri-Aldana, Mario, and Vicente Mendoza Martínez, eds. *Cancionero Popular Mexicano*. Vol. 1. Mexico City: Conaculta, 2001.
Lamb, Andrew. "Waltz." In *The New Grove Dictionary of Music and Musicians*, vol. 20, edited by Stanley Sadie and John Tyrrell, 200–206. London: Macmillan Reference, 2001.
Lastra, James. *Sound Technology and American Cinema: Perception, Representation, Modernity*. New York: Columbia University Press, 2000.
LeMoigne-Mussat, Marie-Clare. *La Belle Epoque des Kiosques à Musique*. Paris: Editions Du May, 1992.
Lira Vásquez, Carlos Antonio de Jesús. "La ciudad de Oaxaca: Una aproximación a su evolución urbana decimonónica y al desarrollo arquitectónico porfiriano." Master's thesis, Universidad Nacional Autónoma de México, 1997.
López, Rick. "The India Bonita Contest of 1921 and the Ethnicization of Mexican National Culture." *Hispanic American Historical Review* 82, no. 2 (May 2002): 291–328.
Low, Setha M. *On the Plaza: The Politics of Public Space and Culture*. Austin: University of Texas Press, 2000.
MacLachlan, Colin M., and William H. Beezley. *El Gran Pueblo: A History of Greater Mexico*. Upper Saddle River NJ: Prentice Hall, 2004.

Maillefert, Eugenio. *Directorio del comercio del imperio mexicano para el año de 1867*. Mexico City: Instituto de Investigaciones Dr. José María Luis Mora, 1992.

Marchena Fernández, Juan. *Ejército y milicias en el mundo colonial Americano*. Madrid: Editorial Mapfre, 1992.

———. *Oficiales y soldados en el ejército de América*. Seville: Escuela de Estudios Hispano-Americanos de Sevilla, 1983.

Marcus, Joyce, and Kent V. Flannery. *Zapotec Civilization: How Urban Society Evolved in Mexico's Oaxaca Valley*. New York: Thames and Hudson, 1996.

Martínez Gracida, Manuel. *Efemérides Oaxaqueñas, 1853–1892*. Mexico City: Tipografía de El Siglo XIX, 1892.

Martínez Lemoine, René. "The Classical Model of the Spanish-American Colonial City." *Journal of Architecture* 8 (Autumn 2003): 355–368.

Mason, Laura. *Singing the French Revolution: Popular Culture and Politics, 1787–1799*. Ithaca NY: Cornell University Press, 1996.

McNamara, Patrick J. *Sons of the Sierra: Juárez, Díaz, and the People of Ixtlán, Oaxaca, 1855–1920*. Chapel Hill: University of North Carolina Press, 2007.

Memoria Constitucional por el ejecutivo del Estado Libre y Soberana de Oaxaca al H. Congreso del mismo el 17 de Septiembre de 1882 sobre todos los ramos de la Administración Pública Mariano Jiménez. Vol. 1. Oaxaca: Imprenta del Estado en el Ex-Obispado, 1883.

Memoria que Presentó el C. general Luis Mier y Terán, Gobernador Constitucional del Estado al H. Congreso del Mismo, el 17 de Septiembre de 1885. Oaxaca: Tipógrafo del Estado en la Escuela de Artes y Oficios, 1887.

Memorias Administrativas del Licenciado Emilio Pimentel presentadas al XXII Legislatura el día 17 de Septiembre de 1903. Oaxaca: Imprenta del Estado, 1904.

Memorias que el C. General Francisco Meixueiro, Gobernador Constitucional del Estado Libre y Soberano de Oaxaca presenta a la 11a Legislatura del Mismo el dia 17 de Septiembre de 1881 sobre todos los ramos de la Administración Pública. Oaxaca: Imprenta del Estado en el Ex-Obispado, n.d.

Mentz, Brígida von, Verena Radkau, Beatriz Scharrer, and Guillermo Turner. *Los pioneros del imperialismo alemán en México*. Mexico City: Centro de Investigaciones y Estudios Superiores en Antropología Social, 1982.

Menuhin, Yehudi. *Theme and Variations*. New York: Stein and Day, 1972.

Miceli, Sergio. "SPHAN: Refrigério da cultura official." *Revista do Patrimônio* 22 (1987): 108–122.

Middlebrook, Kevin J. *The Paradox of Revolution: Labor, the State, and Authoritarianism in Mexico*. Baltimore: Johns Hopkins University Press, 1995.

Molière. *Le Bourgeois gentilhomme*. Paris: Librairie Génerale Française, 1985.

Moore, Robin. *Nationalizing Blackness: Afrocubanismo and Artistic Revolution in Havana, 1920–1940*. Pittsburgh: University of Pennsylvania Press, 1997.

Navarette Pellicer, Sergio. "Las Capillas de música de viento y los vientos de la Reforma en Oaxaca durante el siglo XIX." *Acervos* 6, no. 24 (Winter 2001): 4–13.

Newsom, Jon. "The American Brass Band Movement." *Quarterly Journal of the Library of Congress* (Spring 1979): 114–139.

Ozouf, Mona. *Festivals and the French Revolution*. Translated by Alan Sheridan. Cambridge MA: Harvard University Press, 1988.

Paddock, John, ed. *Ancient Oaxaca: Discoveries in Mexican Archaeology and History*. Stanford CA: Stanford University Press, 1970.

Pareyón, Gabriel. *Diccionario de música en México*. Mexico City: Secretaría de Cultura de Jalisco, 1995.

Pénette, Marcel, and Jean Castaingt. *La Legión Extranjera en la Intervención Francesa (Historia Militar) 1863–1867*. Mexico City: Sociedad de Geografía y Estadística Sección de Historia, 1962.

Pérez Herrero, Pedro. "El México Borbónico: ¿Un 'Éxito' Fracasado?" In *Interpretaciones del siglo XVIII mexicano: El impacto de las reformas borbónicas*, coordinated by Josefina Zoraida Vázquez, 109–152. Mexico City: Editorial Patria, 1992.

Poole, Deborah. "An Image of 'Our Indian': Type Photographs and Racial Sentiments in Oaxaca, 1920–1940." *Hispanic American Historical Review* 84, no. 1 (February 2004): 37–82.

Prieto, Valerio, and José Luis Rodríguez Carballar, coordinators. *Arquitectura popular mexicana*. Mexico City: Secretaría de Asentamientos Humanos y Obras Públicas, 1982.

1er [i.e., Primer] *censo de población de la Nueva España, 1790: Censo de Revillagigedo, "un censo condenado."* Mexico City: La Dirección, 1977.

Recopilación de leyes de los reynos de las Indias: Mandadas imprimir, y publicar por la Magestad católica del rey don Carlos II. 4 vols. Madrid: I. de Paredes, 1681.

Ricard, Robert. *The Spiritual Conquest of Mexico: An Essay on the Apostolate and the Evangelizing Methods of the Mendicant Orders in New*

Spain: 1523–1572. Translated by Lesley Bird Simpson. Berkeley: University of California Press, 1966.

Rodríguez Pérez, Sergio. "Estudio y proyecto para la Plaza Mayor de la ciudad de Oaxaca." Professional thesis, Universidad Autónoma Benito Juárez de Oaxaca, 1970.

Romero, Jesús C. *La música en Zacatecas y los músicos zacatecanos*. Mexico City: Universidad Nacional Autónoma de México, 1963.

Rosas Solaegui, Guillermo. *Un hombre en el tiempo*. Mexico City: B. Costa-Amic Editor, 1971.

Rousseau, Jean-Jacques. *The Social Contract*. Translated and edited by Charles Frankel. New York: Hafner, 1947.

Royce, Anya Peterson. "Music, Dance, and Fiesta: Definitions of Isthmus Zapotec Community." *Latin American Anthropology Review* 3, no. 2 (December 1991): 51–60.

Ruiz Torres, Rafael Antonio. "Historia de las bandas militares en México: 1767–1920." Master's thesis, Universidad Autónoma Metropolitana, 2002.

Rust, Brian. "Peerless." In *Encyclopedia of Recorded Sound in the United States*, edited by Guy A. Marco and Frank Andrews, 520–521. New York: Garland, 1993.

Saldívar, Gabriel. *Bibliografía Mexicana de Musicología y Musicografía*. Mexico City: CENIDIM, 1991.

———. *Historia de la música en México*. Mexico City: Secretaría de Educación Pública, 1987.

Sánchez Silva, Carlos. "Indians, Merchants, and Bureaucracy in Oaxaca, Mexico, 1786–1860." PhD diss., University of California, San Diego, 1995.

Secretaría de Educación Pública. *La Educación pública en México desde el 10 de diciembre de 1934 hasta el 30 de Noviembre de 1940*. Mexico City: Talleres gráficos de la nación, 1941.

Secretaría de Gobernación y Gobierno del Estado de Oaxaca. *Los municipios de Oaxaca*. Mexico City: Centro Estatal de Estudios Municipales de Oaxaca, 1988.

Sierra, Justo. *Obras completas del maestro Justo Sierra*. Book 5, *Discursos*. Edited by Agustín Yáñez. Mexico City: Universidad Nacional Autónoma de México, 1948.

———. *Obras completas del maestro Justo Sierra*. Book 8, *La educación nacional: Artículos, actuaciones, y documentos*. Edited by Agustín Yáñez. Mexico City: Universidad Nacional Autónoma de México, 1948.

Smith, Benjamin T. *Pistoleros and Popular Movements: The Politics of State Formation in Postrevolutionary Oaxaca*. Lincoln: University of Nebraska Press, 2009.

Spencer, Charles S., and Elsa M. Redmond. *Archaeology of the Cañada de Cuicatlán, Oaxaca*. New York: American Museum of Natural History, 1997.

Stephen, Lynn. *Zapotec Women*. Austin: University of Texas Press, 1991.

Stevenson, Robert. *Music in Mexico: A Historical Survey*. New York: Thomas Y. Crowell, 1952.

Stewart, Jack. "The Mexican Band Legend–Part II." *Jazz Archivist* 9, no. 1 (May 1994): 1–17.

Taracena, Ángel. *Efemérides Oaxaqueñas*. Oaxaca: n.p., 1941.

Taylor, William B. *Drinking, Homicide, & Rebellion in Colonial Mexican Villages*. Stanford CA: Stanford University Press, 1979.

———. *Landlord and Peasant in Colonial Mexico*. Stanford CA: Stanford University Press, 1972.

Tello, Aurélio. "El patrimonio musical de México: Una síntesis aproximativa." In *El patrimonio nacional de México II*, edited by Enrique Florescano, 76–110. Mexico City: Fondo de Cultura Económica, 1997.

Tenorio-Trillo, Mauricio. *Mexico at the World's Fairs: Crafting a Modern Nation*. Berkeley: University of California Press, 1996.

Thompson, Emily. *The Soundscape of Modernity: Architectural Acoustics and the Culture of Listening in America, 1900–1933*. Cambridge MA: MIT Press, 2002.

Thompson, E. P. "Patrician Society, Plebian Culture." *Journal of Social History* 7, no. 4 (Summer 1974): 382–405.

Thomson, Guy P. C. "Bulwarks of Patriotic Liberalism: The National Guard, Philharmonic Corps and Patriotic Juntas in Mexico, 1847–1888." *Journal of Latin American Studies* 22, no. 1 (February 1990): 31–68.

———. "The Ceremonial and Political Roles of Village Bands, 1846–1974." In *Rituals of Rule, Rituals of Resistance: Public Celebrations and Popular Culture in Mexico*, edited by William H. Beezley and Cheryl English Martin, 307–342. Wilmington DE: Scholarly Resources, 1994.

Tweedie, Mrs. Alec. *Porfirio Diaz, Seven Times President of Mexico*. London: Hurst and Blackett, 1906.

Tyler, Marian. "Native Mexican Art," *New York Times*, February 1, 1931.

Vargas Hernández, Jorge, ed. *Oaxaca de la Colección de Imágenes de México de la Filmoteca de la UNAM*. DVD, Dirección General de Actividades

Cinematográficas de la UNAM. Mexico City: Universidad Autónoma de México, 2005.

Varner, John Grier, and Jeanette Johnson Varner. *Dogs of the Conquest*. Norman: University of Oklahoma Press, 1983.

Vasconcelos, José. *La raza cósmica, misión de la raza iberoamericana*. Mexico City: Espasa-Calpe Mexicana, 1966.

———. *Ulises Criollo*. Mexico City: Editorial Porrúa, 2001.

Vásquez, Genaro V. *Música popular y costumbres regionales del estado de Oaxaca*. Mexico City: n.p., 1924.

Vaughan, Mary Kay. *Cultural Politics in Revolution: Teachers, Peasants, and Schools in Mexico, 1930–1940*. Tucson: University of Arizona Press, 1997.

Vázquez de Knauth, Josefina Zoraida. *La intervención norteamericana 1846–1848*. Mexico City: Secretaría de Relaciones Exteriores, 1997.

———. *Nacionalismo y educación en México*. Mexico City: El Colegio de México, 1970.

Velasco Pérez, Carlos. *Oaxaca: Patrimonio Cultural de la Humanidad*. Oaxaca: Dirección de Educación, Cultura y Bienestar Social del Gobierno del Estado de Oaxaca, 1999.

Velázquez, María del Carmen. *El estado de guerra en Nueva España, 1760–1808*. Mexico City: El Colegio de México, 1950.

Vigil y Robles, Guillermo, comp. *Rectificaciones y aclaraciones a las memorias del Gral. Porfirio Díaz*. Mexico City: El Universal, 1922.

Wagner, Logan, Hal Box, and Susan Kline Morehead. *Ancient Origins of the Mexican Plaza: From Primordial Sea to Public Space*. Austin: University of Texas Press, 2013.

Wagner, Richard. *My Life*. 2 vols. Translator not identified. New York: Dodd, Mead, 1911.

Wagstaff, Grayson. "Processions for the Dead, the Senses, and Ritual Identity in Colonial Mexico." In *Music, Sensation, and Sensuality*, edited by Linda Phyllis Austern, 167–180. New York: Routledge, 2002.

Weckmann, Luis. *The Medieval Heritage of Mexico*. Translated by Frances M. López-Morillas. New York: Fordham University Press, 1992.

Weeks, Charles A. *The Juárez Myth in Mexico*. Tuscaloosa: University of Alabama Press, 2005.

Wright, Marie Robinson. *Picturesque Mexico*. Philadelphia: J. B. Lippincott, 1897.

Yeager, Gene. "Porfirian Commercial Propaganda: Mexico in the World Industrial Expositions." *The Americas* 34, no. 2 (October 1977): 230–243.

INDEX

Page numbers in *italics* indicate figures and maps.

Acevedo, Jesús, 77–78
Active Militia, 19
La Agrupación Musical
 Oaxaqueña de Charros, 90–91
Aguirre, Vicente, 16
Alameda (Oaxaca), 35, 37–38, 40
Alameda Central (Mexico City), 31, 73
Alameda de Léon, 168n54
albums, recorded, of BME, 127–28
Alcalá, Bernabé, 43, 147, 164n4
Alcalá, Bernardino, 35, 147
Alcalá, José, 44, 147
Alcalá, Macedonio, 116, 164n4
Alcázar, Adalberto G., 99–100
alcohol consumption, 106–7, 133, 190–91n55
Almadea de León, 168n54
Altamirano, Ignacio Manuel, 82–83
Andrade, Mario de, 180n31
Antequera, 51
archive, of BME, 115–16, 186n65

Article III of Mexican Constitution, 81, 84–85
artillery battalion, 57–58
artist, conflict between laborer and, 77, 108–9
Attali, Jacques, 11
audiciones extraordinarias, 104–6, 153–54
Auxiliares de Oaxaca, 45
Aztecs, 12, 119

Baltazar, Daniel: alleged rift between Acevedo and, 77–78; assists in Oaxaca's musical educatory project, 85–86; as BME director, 76, 147
Baltazar Velasco, Moisés, 103, 116
Banda de la República, 73
Banda de Música del Estado de Oaxaca (BME): archive of, 115–16, 186n65; budget and salaries of, 64; under Canseco, 61–64, 101–3; classification of members, 104; criticism of,

Banda de Música del Estado de Oaxaca (BME) (*continued*) 73–74; under Cruz, 134–35; dependencies, 151; directors of, 147–48; emergence of present-day form, 54–55; at end of nineteenth century, *63*; ethnicity of members, 158n5; extraordinary performances of, 104–6, 153–54; and *fiestas patrias*, 36–40; first directors of, 35–36; and governors during Porfiriato, 56–61; and Guelaguetza, 119–22; guest conducted by Leopold Stokowski, 109–10; under Innes, 113–17, 132–33; instability of, following Innes' departure, 130–32; institutionalization of, 41–43; instrumentation and repertoire of, 64–69, 78; kiosk as indispensable part of history and mission of, 47–51; as lens to examine Mexican history, 4–5; under Medina, 133–34; Mexican Constitution's effect on, 80–81; under municipal control, 103–10; name of, 191n64; in 1951, *115*; ca. 1947, *104*; during 1960s, 127–29; organization of, 137–38; pay raises given in, 77; performance of, at ecclesiastical events, 136; performs at 1923 Independence Day celebration, 98; performs at Il Festival Bandistico Internazionale Città di Besana, 138–39; performs at Teatro Macedonio Alcalá, 1–4; during Porfiriato, 43–47, 56; and post-Revolutionary educational project, 89–95; and present-day *fiesta patronal*, 139–45; recordings of, 127–28; recruitment from, 175n55; "religious" performance schedule of, 78–79; reorganization of, 111–13; reverts to state control, 110–11; before Revolution, 69–72; during Revolution, 74–77; role of, in state-sponsored cultural education, 85–86; roles of, 5; solidarity in, under Baltazar, 77–78; and tourism initiative of Oaxaca, 122–25; travels of, 72–74, 127; uniforms of, 63–64, 116–17, 131, 137; and Union de Filarmónicos de la Banda de Música Municipal, 108–9; and United Nations, 125–27

Banda Militar del Batallón de Zapadores, 61–62

Barragán Machuca, José, 16

Basilica de la Soledad, 136

La batalla de Tampico, Tamaulipas (Paris), 25, 26

Bautista Martínez, José, 130, 148

Becker, Marjorie, 167n51

"Benito Juárez Funeral March," 60, 61

Bermúdez, Francisco, 46–47

Bibiana, María, 121

Bourbon military reform, 14–16, 142

brass-band phenomenon, 161n10

Bremmer, Helmut, 68–69

Brena Torres, Rodolfo, 125, 127–28

Brill, George Martin, 73, 174–75n54
Brill, Mark, 168n54

Cabrera Carrasquedo, Manuel, 116–17
Calderón de la Barca, Frances Erskine, 20–21
Calles, Plutarco Elías, 106
Campos, Rubén M., 18, 85
Cañada, 139
"Canción Mixteca," 1–3, 4, 90
Canseco, Germán, 61–69, 74, 76–77, 101–3, 147
capitalism, 124
Cárdenas, Lázaro, 128
cargo system, 176n70
Carlos IV, coronation of, 15
Carmen Alto church, 119–20
Carranza, Venustiano, 75
Carrillo Trujillo, Julián, 109–10
Caso, Antonio, 12
Castro, Jesús Agustín, 75
Castro, José Domingo, 44
Castro, Miguel, 29
Castro Mantecón, Javier, 169n70
Catholic Church, 16–17
cavatina, 163n31
census of 1875, 41–42
Centros de Cultura Popular, 89
Charles V, 51, 171n18
Chassen-López, Francie, 69–70
Chávez, Carlos, 110
Chávez, Gregorio, 57
chotis, 173n31, 195
Cinco de Mayo, 27, 39–40, 43–44
citizens, role of music in formation of, 81–85

City of Besana International Wind Band Festival, 138–39
Civic Militia, 19–20
civil religion: celebrations of, 21–22; and history of Mexican education, 81–82; of Oaxaca, 8–9, 39–40
Civil War of the Reform (1855–1860), 27, 29–33
Clancy, Michael, 188n16
classification, of BME members, 104
colonization. *See* Spanish colonization
Concepción Pápalo, 139–41
Confederación Regional Obrera Mexicana, 108
conjunto music, 163n31
Conservatorio Nacional de Música, 61, 172n20
Constitution (1917), 80–81, 84–85
Constitutional Convention, 81
Constitution Day, 36–38, 43, 106
Convent of San José, 76
Convent of Santo Domingo, 115
Cortés, Hernán, 7
Cosio-Villegas, Emma, 31
Covarrubias, Miguel, 187–88n10
Cruz, Guillermo Cosme, 134–35, 137, 148, 191n64
Cruz, Josué de la, 91
Cuicatlán, 100
cultural patrimony, 125–27, 188n17
Cultural Sessions, 90–91, 93

Daniel, Oliver, 110
danzón, 78, 177n77, 195
Decree Four of 10 October 1872, 41
de la Cruz, Josué, 91

INDEX 211

Departmento de Cultura Indígena, 87
Department of Police and Public Security, BME placed under, 76
Department of State, reorganization of, 76
Día de la Bandera, 111
Día de la Expropriación Petrolera, 128–29
Día de la Marina, 109
Día de la Revolucíon, 106
Díaz, Félix, 32, 36, 52, 75
Díaz, Porfirio, 57; enlists in National Guard, 24–25; fights against French intervention, 27–28; and inauguration of Tehuantepec National Railroad, 72; mandates universal service in National Guard, 163n37; runs against Juárez in presidential election, 40; as state hero, 55; suspends military bands, 29, 30–31. *See also* Porfiriato
"Dios nunca muere" (Alcalá), 164n4
disciplinary action, 112–13
Discos Peerless, 189n34
Document No. 28, 64–65
Document No. 29, 65–66
Dominguez Castro, José, 147
drunkenness, 106–7, 133, 190–91n55

Echeverría, Luis, 126–27
education: BME's contribution to, 80–81; BME's role in state-sponsored cultural, 85–86; history of Mexican, 81–85; post-Revolutionary, 89–95; and Sociedad Filarmónica Mexicana, 171–72n20; and value of cultural *Mestizaje*, 86–89
1812 Overture (Tchaikovsky), 3, 110
escudo de distinción, 26
Esperón, José, 42, 166n33
European music: influence of, on Mexican music, 66–68; played by BME, 74
extraordinary performances, 104–6, 153–54
"Extraordinary" services, 112

Fernando Iturribarría, Jorge, 131
Il Festival Bandistico Internazionale Città di Besana, 138–39
Fiesta de la Raza Hispano Americana, 120, 176n73
fiestas: *fiesta patronal*, 139–45; *fiestas patrias*, 29, 36–40, 82, 83–84; urban versus traditional, 124
Fifty-second Cultural Session, 93
Flag Day, 111
flags, Mexican military, 128
Flores, José María, 16
El folklore y la música mexicana (Campos), 85
folkloric music, 159n17
foreign invasions: French Intervention of 1860, 27–29; influences of, on military music, 23, 29–33; war with United States, 24–27
fountains, 51, 169n65

foxtrot(s), 78, 177n75, 195
French Intervention (1860), 27–29, 32, 128, 170n1
funeral marches, 60–61

Gage, Thomas, 1
García Canclini, Nestor, 124, 125
García Moll, Roberto, 125
García Santos, Anastacio, 107, 109, 110–11, 147
Garrera, Domingo, 16
Garzón, Gabriel, 59–60, 147
Gaspar, Ysidro, 99
German music publishers, 67
Gomes, Antônio Carlos, 126, 189n27
Gómez Sandoval, Fernando, 123–24
González, Martín, 53
González, Próspero A., 103, 107–8, 109, 147
González Martínez, Agustín, 133, 191n57
Government Branch, BME budget included in, 75
Guardia Nacional, 24–25, 32, 42, 44–47, 160n6, 163n37
Guelaguetza, 117, 119–25, 140–41
Guelaguetza Oaxaqueña, 128
Guergué, Joaquín, 25

Hernández, Fidencio, 44, 166n33
Hernández Martínez, Lucas, 148
Hernández Toledo, Agustín, 103, 147
"Himno Socialista Regional," 91–93, 94
historical monuments, 125–27, 169n65

Homenaje Racial, 120, 121
Huaxyacac, 12
hymns, 161n14
"Hymn to the Meritorious General Antonio de León, The" (López Alavés), 26–27

independence: celebration of, 19; ignominies following, 23; military music following, 18
Independence Day, 29, 74, 98–100, 182n7
India Bonita, 120–21
indigenismo, 120
Innes Acevedo, Diego: as BME director, 113–17, 132–33, 148; decline of BME under, 131–32; experience of, 186n63; leaves BME, 130
inspections, 112
Inspectorate of Monuments, 125
Instituto Educativo Istmeño, 91
instrument inventory of BME, 64–65, 66, 103
Isthmian Educative Institute, 91
Iturribarría, Jorge Fernando, 70
Ixcatlán, 100

Jardín de la Constitución, 62, 168n54
jazz, 78
Jiménez, Mariano, 53, 56
Jiménez Luis, Abel, 148
Juárez, Benito, 27, 28, 29, 40–41, 70–71, 97. *See also* "Benito Juárez Funeral March"
Juchiteca, 121–22, 181n44
Junius Hart Music Company, 69
junta patriótica, 34–38

INDEX 213

Kaempfert, Bert, 135, 192n70
Kappey, J. A., 171n13
Kastner, Georges, 61
kiosk(s): celebrations at, 100; as indispensable part of BME's history and mission, 47–51; microphones and amplifiers installed in, 116; in Oaxaca, 51–55; repair and maintenance of, 102
Knight, Alan, 72–73

laborer, conflict between artist and, 77, 108–9
"La Guelaguetza, " 118
"La Marseillaise," 178n8
Lanson, Eugenio, 97
Lara, Agustín, 173n31
"La Sandunga," 121–22
late colonial period, 13–17
Leal, Fidel, 97
Lenten Friday performances, 78–79
León, Antonio de, 25–27
Lerdo, Sebastián, 40
Liga Filarmónica Socialista, 184n35
Loaesa, Gregorio, 97
López, Rick, 120
López Alavés, José, 26–27, 157n2
Lunes del Cerro, 119–20, 122, 123

Macunaíma (Andrade), 180n31
Madero, Francisco I., 72–73, 79, 177n84
march, 171n13
"Marcha fúnebre Benito Juárez," 60, 61
marimba, 111, 185n53

Martínez García, Eliseo, 1, 137, *138*, 144, 148, 175n55, 191n63
Martínez Hernández, Rogelio, 134, 135
Martínez Mota, Prisciliano, 107–8, 130
Martínez Vásquez, Leodegario, 131, 134, 148
Mason, Laura, 178n8
Mata, Eduardo, 185n41
Maximilian, archduke, 27, 29, 162n18
mazurka, 173n32, 195
Medina Tovar, Elipedio, 133–34, 148
Meixueiro, Francisco, 44–45, 47, 53–54, 166n33, 170n71
Menuhin, Yehudi, 136
mestizaje, value of cultural, 86–89
mestizo music, 159n17
mestizos, military service of, 14
Mexican Constitution (1917), 80–81, 84–85
Mexican Independence Day, 29, 74, 98–100, 182n7
Mexican military flags, 128
Mexican Philharmonic Society, 171n20
Meyer, Jean, 136
Meyer, Lorenzo, 106
Mier y Terán, Luis, 57–58
migration, 129–30, 190n43
Milicia Activa, 19
Milicia Cívica, 19–20
military bands: indigenous influences on, 36; perform at national festivities during Reform, 29; public performances of, 31; reform

and reorganization of, 35–36;
serenata and, 30; temporary
suspension of, 29, 30–31; and
U.S. invasion of Mexico, 25;
wind bands, 88
military flags, Mexican, 128
military music: foreign influences
on, 23, 29–33; influence of, on
Oaxaca, 17–21
military reform, Bourbon, 14–16,
142
military service: obligatory,
during war with U.S., 24; social
status through, 159n15
Mixe Indians, 99
Mixtecs, 6, 12, 119
Molière, 23
Molino del Rey, Battle of, 25–27
Mondragón Noriega, Samuel, 91,
181n43, 181n45
Monte Albán, historic
monuments in, 126–27
monuments, historical, 125–27,
169n65
Morales, Lorenzo, 16
Morelos, José María, 100
Morrow, Dwight, 90
municipal bands, precedents for
proliferation of, 96–101
municipalities: creation and
proliferation of, 96–97;
Independence Day celebrations
of, 98–100
municipal period, 76, 103–10
music: as didactic tool, 82–83, 90;
hybrid nature of, 141–42; as
means of maintaining
municipal loyalty, 97; as
political tool, 142–45; role of,

during Spanish invasion, 9;
role of, in state's educatory
project, 93–95; transition in,
16–17; types of Mexican, 159n17;
Vasconcelos and importance
of, in Mexican life, 86–87

Napoleon III, 27, 162n18
National Guard, 24–25, 32, 42,
44–47, 160n6, 163n37
nationalism, 9, 129
National Revolutionary Party, 106
"Nereidas" (Pérez), 130, 185n49
Neri, Leopold G., 76
New Orleans, Mexican bands in,
68–69
Newsom, Jon, 161n10
Niblock, James, 185n41
noise of violence, 11
norteño, 163n31
Nueva Antequera, 13
Nunó Roca, Jaime, 32

Oaxaca: achieving political unity
for, 11; Banda de Música del
Estado de Oaxaca as political
tool of, 5; Bourbon military
reform in, 14–16; civil religion,
nationalism, and political
culture of, 8–9; civil religion of,
21–22, 39–40; and Civil War of
the Reform, 29–33; Díaz as
governor of, 45; Esperón's
economic plan for, 42; ethnic
groups of, 6, 7; and French
Intervention of 1860, 28–29;
historic monuments in, 126–27;
history and demographics of,
5–8; languages of, 6, 7; during

Oaxaca (*continued*)
late colonial period, 13–17; migration from, 129–30, 190n43; military music in, 17–21; military units in, in 1846, 149; municipalities in, 96–97; national guard units in, in 1848, 149–50; plaza and kiosk in, 49, 51–55, 168n54; political culture of, 9; political unity for, 11; regions of, 6; religious, political, and musical transition in, 16–17; settlement of, 12–13; social and economic changes in, 84; Thomas Gage on, 1; tourism initiative of, 118–19, 122–25; unity for, 11; during war with United States, 24–27, 160n6
Oaxaca Junta Patriótica, 36–38
Obregón, Álvaro, 121, 122
O Guarani (Alencar), 189n27
O Guarani (Gomes), 126, 189n27
opera, 31–32
"Ordinary" services, 112
Orozco, Francisco de, 12
orquesta típica, 90, 178–79n14
Ortiz Rubio, Joaquín, 134
"outside work," 101, 176n70

Pacheco Gomes, Veronica, 186n57
padrón of 1875, 41–42
Paris, Carlos, *La batalla de Tampico, Tamaulipas*, 25, 26
Partido Nacional Revolucionario, 106
Paschedag, Theodore, 185n41
paso doble, 78, 173n30, 195
patria chica, 2–3, 121, 143

Peerless Records, 189n34
Peláez de Berrio, Juan, 13
Pérez Gasga, Alfonso, 96, 123
Pérez Torres, Amador: as BME director, 110–11, 130, 131–32, 148; compositions of, 126, 133, 185n49; leaves BME, 113
Petroleum Expropriation Day, 128–29
Pimentel, Emilio, 69–70, 71–72
Plan de la Noria, 40
Plaza de Armas, 52–54, 170n71. *See also* Jardín de la Constitución
plaza(s): BME performances in, 62–63; fountains and monuments in, 169n65; history and importance of, in Mexico, 48–51; in Oaxaca, 51–55; second, 167n51; vegetation in, 167n51
political music, transition in, 16–17
polka, 163n31, 195
Poole, Deborah, 120
popular music, 82–83, 159n17
Porfiriato: BME before Revolution, 69–72; BME during, 43–47, 56; Canseco as BME director during, 61–64; governors and BME during, 56–61; instrumentation and repertoire of BME during, 64–69; military wind bands during, 88; travels of BME during, 72–74
Portes-Gil, Emilio, 102
Preza, Velino M., 73
private bands, 100
Provincial Battalion of Oaxaca, 14

Puebla, Battle of, 27, 38
Purcell, Henry, 60

Racial Homage, 120, 121
Ramo de Gobernación, BME budget included in, 75
La raza cósmica, misión de la raza iberoamericana (Vasconcelos), 88
recordings of BME, 127–28
redowa, 163n31
"Reform of Military Orchestras" articles, 35–36
regional music, 83–84
"Regional Socialist Hymn," 91–93, 94
"Reglamento de Disciplina Interna de la Union de Filarmónicos des la Banda de Música Municipal," 107
Reglamento de la Banda de Música del Estado, 112–13
religion, civil: celebrations of, 21–22; and history of Mexican education, 81–82; of Oaxaca, 8–9, 39–40
religious music, transition in, 16–17
Revolution: BME before, 69–72; BME during, 74–77; post-Revolutionary educational project, 89–95; and value of cultural *Mestizaje*, 88–89
Riesgo, Vicente María, 35–36, 164n7
Rosalino, Simón, 16
Rosas, Juventino, 67, 68–69
Rosas Solaegui, Guillermo, 62, 73, 90–91, 121, 130–32, 172n22
Rotonda de las Azucenas, 123
Ruíz Torres, Rafael Antonio, 32

Sakar, Francisco, 35, 147, 163n35, 170n1
Saldívar, Gabriel, 68
Salon Rojo (Red Hall), 73
Sánchez, Carlos, 1–3
Sánchez, Policarpo T., 90
sanctions, 112–13
Sandoval, Gonzalo de, 12
San Mateo Riohondo, 99
Santa María Yucuhite, 100
Sappers Battalion Military Band, 61–62
schottische, 173n31, 195
Scott, Winfield, 25–26
Secretaría de Educación Pública, 85, 87–89
Semana del Oaxaqueño Ausente, 129–30
serenatas, 30, 32, 62
Sesiones Culturales, 90–91, 93
sheet music: dissemination of, 183n15; distribution and influence of, 66–67; inventory of BME, 65–66, 103, 115–16
Sierra, Justo, 81–82, 83
"Sobre las olas," 69
socialist education, 83–85
Socialist Philharmonic League, 184n35
Sociedad Filarmónica Mexicana, 171–72n20
Solis Félix, Zoilo, 132, 133, 148
"Solo Díos en el cielo" (Alcalá), 116
soundscapes, 34
sovereignty movement, 75
Spanish Army of the Americas, organizational chart of, 15

Spanish colonization: and establishment of Oaxaca's plaza and kiosk, 51; influence of, on Oaxaca, 6–7; late colonial period, 13–17; music and, 9, 141; and settlement of Oaxaca, 12–13
"Spanish Eyes" (Kaempfert), 135, 192n70
sports exhibitions, 106
Stephen, Lynn, 120
Stewart, Jack, 68
Stokowski, Leopold, 109–10

Taylor, William B., 191n55
Teatro Juárez, 184n35
Teatro Macedonio Alcalá, 1–4
Tehuantepec National Railroad, 72
Tello, Aurelio, 159n17
Thompson, Emily, 34
Thompson, E. P., 144
Thomson, Guy P. C., 32, 162n28
Thurmer bands, 162n26
tourism, 118–19, 122–25, 127
tours, of BME, 127
Tyler, Marian, 109

UNESCO, 126–27, 189n28
uniforms of BME, 63–64, 116–17, 131, 137
Union de Filarmónicos de la Banda de Música Municipal, 108–9
United Nations, 125–27
United States, war with (1846), 24–27, 160n6
unity, for Oaxaca, 11
urban fiesta, 124

Vargas, Alberto, 120
Vasconcelos, Eduardo, 110, 111, 113–14, 179n21
Vasconcelos, José, 86–89, 179n21
Vásquez, Genaro V.: adopts "Regional Socialist Hymn" as state hymn, 91; calls for creation of Centros de Cultura Popular, 89; and municipal bands, 101; politics of, 177n80; on popular music, 78; selects Convent of San José as rehearsal site, 76
Vásquez, Pablo, 35, 147
Vásquez Mellado, Alfonso, 80
Velasco, José María, 56, 59, 147
Vigil, Manuel García, 76
Villa Alta, 99–100
villages of evangelization, 48
Villa Segura de Frontera, 12–13
violence: alcohol consumption and, 191n55; among BME members, 107–8; noise of, 11

Wagner y Levien, 67, 98, 101
waltz, 67–69, 116, 195
Week of the Absent Oaxacan, 129–30
Week of the Migrant, 129–30
wind bands, 30, 88
work, outside, 101, 176n70

Yescas Vázquez, Bulmaro, *114*, 148

Zapotec language, 6
Zapotecs, 6, 12, 119
zarzuela, 173n32, 195
Zertuche, Albino, 58–59
Zócalo, 49, 52, 168nn54,55

In The Mexican Experience series

Seen and Heard in Mexico: Children and Revolutionary Cultural Nationalism
Elena Albarrán

Railroad Radicals in Cold War Mexico: Gender, Class, and Memory
Robert F. Alegre
Foreword by Elena Poniatowska

Mexicans in Revolution, 1910–1946: An Introduction
William H. Beezley and Colin M. MacLachlan

Celebrating Insurrection: The Commemoration and Representation of the Nineteenth-Century Mexican "Pronunciamiento"
Edited and with an introduction by Will Fowler

Forceful Negotiations: The Origins of the "Pronunciamiento" in Nineteenth-Century Mexico
Edited and with an introduction by Will Fowler

Malcontents, Rebels, and "Pronunciados": The Politics of Insurrection in Nineteenth-Century Mexico
Edited and with an introduction by Will Fowler

Working Women, Entrepreneurs, and the Mexican Revolution: The Coffee Culture of Córdoba, Veracruz
Heather Fowler-Salamini

The Heart in the Glass Jar: Love Letters, Bodies, and the Law in Mexico
William E. French

"Muy buenas noches": Mexico, Television, and the Cold War
Celeste González de Bustamante
Foreword by Richard Cole

The Plan de San Diego: Tejano Rebellion, Mexican Intrigue
Charles H. Harris III and Louis R. Sadler

The Inevitable Bandstand: The State Band of Oaxaca and the Politics of Sound
Charles V. Heath

Gender and the Negotiation of Daily Life in Mexico, 1750–1856
Sonya Lipsett-Rivera

Mexico's Crucial Century, 1810–1910: An Introduction
Colin M. MacLachlan and William H. Beezley

The Civilizing Machine: A Cultural History of Mexican Railroads, 1876–1910
Michael Matthews

The Lawyer of the Church: Bishop Clemente de Jesús Munguía and the Clerical Response to the Liberal Revolution in Mexico
Pablo Mijangos y González

¡México, la patria! Propaganda and Production during World War II
Monica A. Rankin

Murder and Counterrevolution in Mexico: The Eyewitness Account of German Ambassador Paul von Hintze, 1912–1914
Edited and with an introduction by Friedrich E. Schuler

Pistoleros and Popular Movements: The Politics of State Formation in Postrevolutionary Oaxaca
Benjamin T. Smith

Alcohol and Nationhood in Nineteenth-Century Mexico
Deborah Toner

To order or obtain more information on these or other University of Nebraska Press titles, visit nebraskapress.unl.edu.

www.ingramcontent.com/pod-product-compliance
Lightning Source LLC
Chambersburg PA
CBHW021840220426
43663CB00005B/329